# COSTLY DEMOCRACY

# COSTLY DEMOCRACY

Peacebuilding and
Democratization after War

Christoph Zürcher, Carrie
Manning, Kristie D. Evenson,
Rachel Hayman, Sarah Riese,
and Nora Roehner

Stanford University Press
Stanford, California

Stanford University Press
Stanford, California

Printed in the United States of America on acid-free, archival-quality paper

Library of Congress Cataloging-in-Publication Data

Zürcher, Christoph, author.
    Costly democracy : peacebuilding and democratization after war / Christoph Zürcher, Carrie Manning, Kristie D. Evenson, Rachel Hayman, Sarah Riese, and Nora Roehner.
        pages cm
    Includes bibliographical references and index.
    ISBN 978-0-8047-8197-8 (cloth : alk. paper)
    ISBN 978-0-8047-8198-5 (pbk. : alk. paper)
    1. Peace-building.  2. Democratization.  I. Manning, Carrie L., 1964–author.  II. Evenson, Kristie D., author.  III. Hayman, Rachel, author.  IV. Riese, Sarah, author.  V. Roehner, Nora, author.  VI. Title.
    JZ5538.Z87 2013
    327.1'72—dc23                                                   2012035994

Typeset by Thompson Type in 10/14 Minion

ISBN 978-0-8047-8467-2 (electronic)

# Contents

Preface                                                                    vii

1   Introduction                                                             1

2   Leverage, Adoption Costs, and the Peacebuilding Game                    20

3   The Legacy of War                                                       35

4   The Mission Footprint                                                   57

5   Aid                                                                     82

6   Neighborhood                                                           112

7   Conclusion: Explaining Postwar Democratic Transitions                  131

    Notes                                                                  155

    Bibliography                                                           163

    The Authors                                                            175

    Index                                                                  177

# Preface

PEACEBUILDERS EXPEND CONSIDERABLE RESOURCES AND EF-
fort on postconflict peacebuilding with democratization as a core objective. Why then do countries so rarely emerge from civil war as democracies?

Democratization has been formally enshrined in the postwar settlement
of nearly all civil wars ending after the Cold War. Scholars and practitioners
alike have promoted the use of democratic processes and institutions to transform armed conflict into peaceful political competition.

At the same time, the involvement of external actors like the United Nations and major bilateral donors in postconflict peacebuilding has grown
exponentially. External actors have taken on sweeping roles in helping to
monitor and implement peace processes, from overseeing the demobilization
of troops to helping administer elections. Often, extensive policy reform is
part of the peace process, including but not limited to the reform of political
institutions and processes.

Three decades after the advent of structural adjustment and aid conditionality, donors are well acquainted with the challenges associated with policy
reform. Conditioning aid on liberal economic policy has enjoyed only limited
success. Advocacy of political reform has proven still more challenging. Using
democratization as the cornerstone of peace, then, is an enterprise fraught
with peril.

All attempts to promote reform from the outside are plagued by the principal-
agent problem. The incentives of domestic actors who must implement reform

do not always align with the incentives of those advocating reform, a fact that is well established in the study of aid conditionality. But until very recently the importance of domestic political actors, particularly as *political actors*, has been neglected in both scholarly and policy studies. The latest OECD policy statements have only just begun to acknowledge the fragile politics of fragile states.[1]

This book focuses on domestic political actors and the incentive structures they face in contemplating the democratic postwar political settlement. That the outcomes of externally led peacebuilding missions are influenced by domestic political actors is obvious. Yet the question of when and how their preferences affect peacebuilding outcomes has not yet been systematically addressed in a comparative context. This book attempts to do so. We employ a qualitative comparative case analysis based on original field research on postwar democratic transition in nine countries: Afghanistan, Bosnia, East Timor, Haiti, Kosovo, Macedonia, Mozambique, Namibia, Rwanda, and Tajikistan.

Although the book has six authors, this is not an edited volume disguised as a monograph. The book is the product of an iterative process of research and discovery among a small group of scholars with wide-ranging regional expertise and a shared interest in understanding the linkages among external intervention, peace, and democracy in postconflict countries.

Collaboration began in Berlin in October 2008 with a workshop aimed at exploring the factors that might explain democratic outcomes in postconflict peacebuilding cases. The initial goals were modest: to examine the influence of external interventions on postconflict democratization efforts in a meaningful sample of countries. We were interested in interventions that included "boots on the ground" (such as UN peace operations), as well as the provision of financial resources. An international team of country experts was then commissioned to conduct nine structured case studies between October 2008 and December 2009.[2] These are available on the project website.[3] Our sample includes just under half of the available cases and includes variation in terms of outcome and relevant independent variables, including regional context, the character of the war and its resolution, aid amounts and modalities, and the size and scope of the UN peace mission (see Table 1.1, Chapter 1).

In the initial stages of research, the authors employed their country-specific expertise to gather empirical data using a consistent and detailed template for qualitative field research in nine cases. Given the geographic and temporal separation of these cases, it would have been difficult if not impossible for a single researcher to conduct primary research in all of them. Moreover, we were fortunate to have case study authors who had long studied these cases. All had already conducted fieldwork in these cases during the peacebuilding period.[4]

This first step allowed the authors to reexamine the empirical evidence through fresh fieldwork, using a different theoretical lens in countries they knew well. Once fieldwork was complete, the authors gathered at Free University Berlin for a second workshop. There we agreed to publish our findings with a focus on the distinctive circumstances and outcomes of each case. The eight case studies were published in a special issue of the *Taiwan Journal of Democracy*.[5]

Our most important finding was that whether a polity embraced democracy in the wake of war appeared to depend on demand for democracy among domestic political actors and how this demand shaped the interaction between peacebuilders and domestic political elites. While much of the literature has argued that democratic outcomes depend on capacity, our findings suggested that local demand is also important.

We set out to explore this insight more fully and to discover the implications for the theory and practice of postconflict peacebuilding. Together, seven of the nine case study authors drafted a set of four papers to be presented as a panel at the 2009 annual meeting of the American Political Science Association in Toronto. The papers examined the impact of four sets of variables on postconflict democratic outcomes in our cases: factors related to the war and its resolution, the size and scope of the international peace missions, the regional "neighborhood" in which each country was situated, and international aid.

This exercise convinced us none of these "usual suspects" typically used to explain the success or failure of peacebuilding missions had a clear, direct influence on the trajectory of democratization efforts. Though each of these sets of factors was important, it was clear that something was missing in the broader literature: a systematic analysis of the role of domestic political actors in peacebuilding outcomes. Out of this realization came the inspiration for this book.

In an effort to systematically capture the effects of domestic actors' preferences on peacebuilding outcomes, we have used the concept of adoption costs—the costs to domestic political actors of embracing democratic politics after civil war. Adoption costs are shaped by whether actors feel they stand to gain or lose physical, political, and economic security by playing the democratic game. These costs are obviously shaped by the particular contexts in which actors find themselves as well as by the large number of idiosyncratic factors that come into play. In this book we argue that adoption costs can be boiled down to threats to an actor's physical security and to his or her primary goals (be they economic or political). We can therefore employ the concept to analyze quite disparate cases comparatively, while remaining sensitive to empirical reality.

The theory that this book offers can be summarized as follows: We depict peacebuilding as an interactive process not only between former adversaries but also between peacebuilders and the victorious elites of a postwar society. We demonstrate that the preferences of domestic elites are to a great extent shaped by the costs they incur in adopting democracy, as well as the leverage that peacebuilders can muster to increase the costs of nonadoption. Implicit in this understanding of peacebuilding is the assumption that the preferences of peacebuilders and domestic elites are hardly ever aligned. Our approach thus parts with one of the most prominent yet underexamined assumptions of the peacebuilding literature (and presumably of peacebuilding practice): that the interests of domestic elites and peacebuilders coincide. As our sample cases demonstrate, this is rarely the case. Typically, domestic elites in postwar societies are keen to benefit from the resources—both material and symbolic—that peacebuilders can bring, but they are less eager to adopt democracy because they believe democratic reforms may endanger some or all of their substantive interests. Put differently, adopting democracy can be too costly a proposition for domestic elites, and the policies and resources of peacebuilders are rarely able to offset this cost. This book demonstrates the importance of understanding postwar democratic peacebuilding as an interactive bargaining process, which is shaped to a large extent by adoption costs. We hope that the book contributes to a better, more realistic understanding of postwar democratization and eventually to more effective policies.

We developed these arguments over several years. During this time, we were blessed with many sharp-eyed, thoughtful, and supportive friends and colleagues, who have contributed in various ways to the project. Christof Hartmann, Monica Malbrough, Anna Matveeva, Henri Myrttinen, Jens Narten, Hamish Nixon, Tome Sandevski, and Brendan Whitty generously shared their impressive knowledge of specific cases of peacebuilding with us. We benefited from the help of Amichai Magen when creating the research design. We gratefully acknowledge the support of Thomas Risse. Parts of this project were funded by the Max-Planck-Forschungspreis für Geistes- und Sozialwissenschaften, awarded to Thomas Risse (2003). We would also like to thank participants of workshops in Madrid, Stanford, and Berlin for valuable comments and suggestions. Finally, we thank Tim Brown, who provided invaluable research assistance and helped bring the final manuscript into shape.

COSTLY DEMOCRACY

# 1    Introduction

PEACEBUILDING MISSIONS CAN BRING PEACE TO WAR-TORN countries, but they seldom bring democracy. Why do countries so rarely emerge from civil wars as democracies? And what is the role of peace-builders in both failed and successful postwar democratic transitions? These questions lie at the heart of the collective research effort presented in this volume.

The evidence for successful postwar democratic transitions is not encouraging: Since 1989, the international community has launched nineteen major peacebuilding operations (see Table 1.1). These operations were reasonably successful in securing peace but much less successful in establishing democratic regimes. Five years after the operations began, only two countries were rated "free" by Freedom House[1] and qualified as "liberal democracy"; that is, as a regime that "extends freedom, fairness, transparency, accountability, and the rule of law from the electoral process into all other major aspects of governance and interest articulation, competition, and representation."[2] Also, no recent missions of significant size—including those in East Timor, Bosnia, Kosovo, and Afghanistan—have resulted in the establishment of a liberal democracy.

It is unrealistic, perhaps, to expect a *liberal* democracy to emerge from the ashes of war. But even when we apply a lower and less ambitious threshold for success, such as an *electoral* democracy (that is, according to Freedom House's definition, a regime that holds elections but provides less protection

**TABLE 1.1.** Major multinational peacebuilding missions after 1989: Democratic transition outcomes.

| | Year mission started | Freedom House score (five years after start) | Regime type (five years after start) |
|---|---|---|---|
| Namibia | 1989 | 2.5 | Liberal democracy |
| Cambodia | 1992 | 6.5 | Electoral authoritarian |
| Mozambique | 1992 | 3.5 | Electoral democracy |
| Rwanda | 1993 | 6.5 | Fully closed authoritarian |
| Haiti | 1994 | 5 | Electoral democracy |
| Angola | 1995 | 6 | Fully closed authoritarian |
| Bosnia | 1996 | 4.5 | Electoral authoritarian |
| Croatia | 1996 | 2 | Liberal democracy |
| Tajikistan | 1997 | 5.5 | Electoral authoritarian |
| Central African Republic | 1998 | 6 | Electoral authoritarian |
| Democratic Republic of the Congo | 2001 | 6 | Fully closed authoritarian |
| East Timor | 1999 | 3 | Electoral democracy |
| Kosovo | 1999 | 5.5 | Electoral authoritarian |
| Sierra Leone | 1999 | 3.5 | Electoral democracy |
| Macedonia | 2001 | 3 | Electoral democracy |
| Afghanistan | 2002 | 5 | Electoral authoritarian |
| Cote d'Ivoire | 2003 | 5.5 | Electoral authoritarian |
| Liberia | 2003 | 3.5 | Electoral democracy |
| Burundi | 2004 | 4.5 | Electoral democracy |

NOTES: We define a major mission as one mandated by the United Nations or another international organization that is aimed at both maintaining peace in a postconflict situation as well as at inducing social change, with the ultimate goal of creating a stable and democratic country. We include only missions deployed for six months or longer and that count at least 500 military personnel in the field. Only when these thresholds have been met do we code a mission start, even if the mission had an earlier start date but was smaller in character or scope. Multiple simultaneous missions are collapsed into a single observation. Subsequent missions in a single country not separated by more than twelve months are also collapsed into a single observation.

SOURCES: The coding for liberal and electoral democracy is taken from Freedom House (Freedom House 2005). Coding for electoral authoritarian and fully closed authoritarian is based on the World Bank's Database of Political Institutions (Beck et al., 2001). See also endnote 4.

for civil liberties than a liberal democracy), we still find that just nine out of the nineteen countries that hosted major peacebuilding missions qualify.[3] Among those governments that miss the mark, three are classified as fully authoritarian and four as electoral authoritarian—that is, ruled by autocrats who allow some form of multiparty elections that they almost certainly win by a comfortable margin.[4] Given the vast amount of resources and hopes that are invested in liberal peacebuilding, these are sobering results.

Scholars have offered several explanations as to why postwar democracy is so difficult to establish. To start with, some scholars argue that bringing democracy to a war-torn country is simply the impossible dream born of Western hubris; it is unreasonable, they say, to expect peacebuilders to socially engineer a society capable of producing and maintaining a liberal democratic regime in a matter of years, and they point to the fact that the emergence of social structures that enabled democracies to grow in Western Europe was a process that took centuries.[5]

Other scholars take a less radical stance but maintain that democratization after war is an extraordinarily rare event because most postwar societies lack the capacities to implement and sustain the complex and costly political institutions required for democratic and accountable governance. This echoes Seymour Martin Lipset's famous "social requisites of democracy" argument, which states that low economic development and a small middle class negatively affect democratization.[6]

A third explanation focuses on the geostrategic location of a country and states that the threat of violent spillovers from adjacent countries may discourage leaders from steering a more democratic course[7] or that support from an authoritarian leader in a neighboring country reduces the international pressure on elites for democratic reforms in a postwar country.[8]

Lastly, perhaps the most prominent strand in the peacebuilding literature centers on the cooperation problem between the warring parties and argues that the most obvious factor that hinders the emergence of democracy after war is war itself. Civil wars, especially when they are long, highly destructive, and fought between identity groups, can reduce a society's capacity for a stable and democratic peace because they create highly divided societies and elites who deeply mistrust one another.[9] Under such circumstances, actors may lack the capacities to overcome the cooperation problem and be unable to engage in a meaningful peace process or to accept the bounded uncertainty that comes with democratic rules. For all of these reasons, countries emerging out of war find it difficult to democratize.

And yet modern peacebuilding missions are designed precisely to address these challenges. They are launched to help domestic elites overcome the many difficulties presented by postwar democratic transitions. Peacebuilders bring tremendous resources to the table with budgets that frequently dwarf those of host governments, as we have seen in Afghanistan, Bosnia, Kosovo, and East Timor. They deploy civilian personnel who assume vital administrative functions and military personnel to guarantee security. Peacebuilders also bring economic aid, which frequently becomes the single most important source of government income. Aid is directed toward state institutions, election processes, and civil society. This assistance is usually committed over years rather than months, all of which has a tremendous impact on the economic, social, and cultural fabric of the intervened-upon society[10] but has, apparently, only a weak effect on postwar democratization, as Table 1.1 shows. What explains the limited impact of external actors and their resources on postwar democratization?

Beyond the aforementioned difficulties of democratic transitions, some scholars assume that poor implementation is also at the root of mission failure. Often, time and resource constraints are thought to doom democratization efforts. The assumption is that missions with a larger footprint in terms of financing, personnel, and mandate could perhaps achieve better outcomes. Lack of coordination between peacebuilders and an inability to learn from past mistakes are also cited as potential obstacles. Critics lament that peacebuilders rarely adapt strategies to specific contexts but tend to apply a cookie-cutter approach to their democratization efforts, which prioritizes political and economic liberalization over the construction of effective political and economic institutions.[11]

We do not discard any of these arguments, and we think that all of them encapsulate some of the aspects that explain why postwar democratic transitions rarely result in the liberal democracy that serves as the blueprint (at least in rhetoric) for all post–Cold War peacebuilding operations. However, we take issue with these existing approaches on two grounds.

First, we feel that these approaches, whether they refer to the general difficulties of postwar democratic transitions or to their faulty implementation, do not add up to a systematic explanation of the causes for success and failure of postwar democratic transitions. They may well explain success or failure in a specific case, but none of the previously mentioned arguments is systematically associated with success or failure across a substantial number of cases.

Applying the establishment of an electoral democracy as our threshold for success, we find, for example, that some peacebuilding operations were successful in poor countries lacking domestic capacity (such as Mozambique and East Timor), whereas others failed in richer countries with higher levels of development as well as viable administrative structures (such as Bosnia and Kosovo). Some robust and highly intrusive operations failed (Afghanistan, for example), and some succeeded (East Timor). The reverse is also true, with some relatively small, unintrusive peacebuilding operations meeting success (Namibia) and others ending in failure (Tajikistan and Rwanda). Some missions brought democracy despite a long and bloody war (Mozambique), while others did not, despite relatively brief periods of hostility (Kosovo). These few examples (the list goes on) underscore that none of the factors that are thought to explain failure or success are consistently and systematically associated with a particular outcome. It is quite apparent that we lack a consistent and parsimonious explanation of postwar democratic transition.

Related to this is our second concern: We think that existing approaches to postwar democratic transitions suffer from the fact that they ignore one of the most important and consequential aspects of contemporary peacebuilding, namely that peacebuilding is an interactive process not only between former adversaries but also between peacebuilders and the victorious elites of a postwar society, and that this interaction decisively shapes the process of peacebuilding and its outcomes. By ignoring the interactive quality of peacebuilding, much of the literature seems to implicitly assume that the interests of peacebuilders and of host country governments are typically aligned and therefore assumes that the peacebuilding process is a problem of capacity and coordination rather than one of cooperation.

We part with this assumption. We are convinced that one of the major determinants of peacebuilding is indeed the differing priorities of peacebuilders and domestic elites. Put simply, domestic elites may wish to benefit from the resources—both material and symbolic—that peacebuilders have to offer. However, for various reasons, they may resist some or all of the democratic policies that peacebuilders prescribe. They may perceive a democratic opening as being risky and as endangering their security. Or they may fear that democratization endangers their formal or informal grip on political power. Predatory elites in postwar countries may be reluctant to adopt democratic governance because this may endanger their rent-seeking strategies, and elites who rely on patronage may worry that democratic reforms may undermine their informal networks of power. In sum, domestic elites may think that adopting democracy could entail high personal and/or political costs. The higher they perceive these adoption costs to be, the less willing they will be to accept the peacebuilders' democratic prescriptions.

Peacebuilders, on the other hand, expect democratic reforms in exchange for the considerable resources they expend in a postwar country, and they may press domestic political actors to adopt these reforms. As a result, peacebuilders and domestic elites will engage in an informal bargaining process. The outcomes of peacebuilding, we argue, depend to a large extent on the outcome of the informal bargaining by which peacebuilders and domestic elites try to sort out their differences and agree (or fail to agree) on the kind of democratic peace they intend to build.

In this book, we argue that in important ways democratic peace depends on whether adopting democracy is in the interest of domestic elites. While this is likely also true for peace alone, it is even more essential to an understanding of democratic outcomes in peacebuilding cases. Democracy, unlike simple peace, requires the active cooperation and participation of domestic elites. Moreover, because democracy is a long-term process built around regular, periodic elections and the construction of self-sustaining, participatory institutions such as political parties and legislatures, it offers many opportunities for elites to go back on an initial commitment to democracy, to undermine democratic institutions, or to withdraw from the process.

Finally, democracy requires local actors to build trust in one another and the political institutions they are building. External guarantors may be important in the early years, but over the long term democracy cannot survive without at least an instrumental commitment to democratic rules of the game by domestic elites themselves. Depending on their circumstances at the time of peace, domestic elites stand to lose or gain in various ways by committing to democratic politics, and the stakes may be considerable. In addition, domestic elites have varying degrees of power and will to resist, ignore, or otherwise subvert the democratic peacebuilding agenda.

This book advances an understanding of the peacebuilding process that emphasizes the interests and preferences of both peacebuilders and domestic elites. Our focus on the interaction between peacebuilders and domestic elites is not intended to replace existing theories of postwar democratic transitions.

Rather, we increase the purchasing power of existing approaches by factoring in an understanding of peacebuilding as an intense interaction between domestic and external actors. This interaction, which can be depicted as an informal bargaining process, is contingent on other factors, some of which are structural, while others stem from policy choices. We examine four sets of factors. These are the following: the legacies of war, the footprint of the peacebuilding mission, the impact of aid, and the geostrategic location of the country. We investigate whether and how these factors shape the interaction between peacebuilders and domestic elites and to what extent they contribute to the outcome of postwar transitions.

The next chapter (Chapter 2) develops an illustrative model of peacebuilding that is informed by our guiding assumption that the preferences of peacebuilders and domestic elites are not necessarily aligned and that the higher the perceived adoption costs, the more reluctant domestic elites will be to adopt democracy. Peacebuilding then becomes an interactive process in which each side tries to protect its key interests by mustering its resources and capacities. We use this model as the analytical lens through which we capture the impact of other factors.

In Chapter 3 we take a closer look at the legacy of civil war. We argue that the calculation of adoption costs is to a large extent shaped by the war and how it ended. The literature has identified a number of war-related factors that are assumed to shape a country's transition from war to peace. Among them are the intensity and duration of conflict, the number of hostile factions, whether battles were fought along ethnic divides, whether the war ended in military victory for one side or in a negotiated agreement, and whether there were provisions for power sharing. Our empirical evidence suggests, perhaps surprisingly, that none of these factors is directly or consistently linked with a democratic or nondemocratic outcome. Instead, we find that the impact of these factors is mediated by their influence on local political actors as they weigh the perceived adoption costs of democracy. We are most likely to witness a democratic outcome where domestic political actors depend on external actors to support their goals (for example, sovereignty, domestic legitimacy, preservation of political power) *and* where embracing the democratic agenda is, in their eyes, unlikely to derail these goals. Conversely, a democratic outcome is less likely where domestic political actors think that democratization may endanger their security or otherwise threaten their primary objectives. Hence, we find that it is not war characteristics per se that influence democratic outcomes but rather how war changes domestic elites' calculation of the costs of adopting democracy. In other words, peacebuilding outcomes depend to a large extent, though not exclusively, on the incentives facing domestic political actors. These incentives are also shaped by war and its settlement but not in a mechanical and direct way, as much of the relevant literature assumes.

Incentive structures are not fixed, however. When external peacebuilders intervene in postconflict situations, their actions can change the calculations and decisions made by domestic political actors. In Chapter 4 we turn to the scope of peacebuilding operations. Peacebuilders bring resources, civilian experts, and soldiers to foster social change and establish peace and democracy. One of the few robust insights of existing peacebuilding scholarship is that well-resourced and well-staffed UN peacebuilding missions significantly increase the odds that a country remains at peace. In a groundbreaking study, Michael Doyle and Nicholas Sambanis showed that multidimensional peacekeeping operations (missions with extensive civilian functions, economic reconstruction, institutional reforms, and election oversight) are significantly and positively associated with securing peace.[12] Yet while robust peacebuilding can be successful at ending war, it is much less successful at bringing peace *and* democracy.

In this chapter, we systematically investigate the impact of peacebuilding operations on both war and democracy. One important question is whether "more is better": Do well-resourced, intrusive operations produce more democracy than smaller operations? To tackle this question, we first develop a framework that allows us to measure the footprint of the mission. Applying this measure to our empirical material, we find that the democratic outcome of peacebuilding missions is not consistently associated with the mission footprint. Hence, more intrusive, better-resourced, and longer missions do not lead to more democracy.

Rather, it is mission context that seems to matter. For example, local demand for a peacebuilding operation is consistently associated with more democratic outcomes. Demand, for its part, appears to be generated by security concerns and by the desire for increased autonomy and sovereignty. When there is a lack of demand, there appears to be an inverse relationship between intrusiveness and democracy: More intrusive missions seem to be associated with less democratic outcomes. Poor conditions, such as a highly destructive war or low levels of development, appear to accentuate this negative relationship.

Peacebuilders also bring vast amounts of aid money. Chapter 5 examines the impact of aid on democratic outcomes. Aid contributes to democratization in several ways: It can help build capacity for democratic governance and kick-start the democratization process. Examples may include funding for an electoral process or technical support to develop a new legislative framework. Aid can also give domestic political actors an incentive to democratize or signal a strong commitment on the part of peacebuilders to actors who uphold democratic values, which may in turn weaken antidemocratic opposition.

Further, we investigate whether general aid, as well as aid earmarked specifically for democratization, positively influences a democratic outcome. We find that aid can increase peacebuilders' leverage over domestic political actors but that this impact is mediated by the relationships between donors and between donors and domestic political actors. Aid impact is also mediated by its flexibility—the degree to which it is structured so as to allow donors to make timely interventions that lower the adoption costs of democracy. *Aid* per se is perhaps less important than *aid donors*, who structure the timing and the terms by which resources are deployed.

Finally, Chapter 6 looks at regional factors and investigates how the geostrategic position of a postwar country influences its propensity for democratic peace. "Neighborhood" indeed matters, but bad neighbors are more influential than good ones. Transnational security threats tend to aggravate the risks associated with democracy, and peacebuilders are rarely in a position to mitigate these threats because their mandate and resources tend to focus on national, rather than regional, issues. Moreover, when authoritarian regimes in neighboring countries lend support to a postwar regime, they can successfully undermine peacebuilders' demands for liberal peace. Conversely, and contrary to existing peacebuilding literature, we do not find that good neighbors significantly increase the likelihood for a democratic outcome. While the European Union and its economic and security promises provided some incentives that could have lowered the adoption costs of democracy for domestic elites in postwar regimes in the Balkans, these effects were to a large extent reduced by the highly intrusive nature of the peacebuilding operation in Bosnia and Kosovo, which strained the cooperative relation between peacebuilders and domestic elites. Only in Macedonia, where the mission was far less intrusive, did the prospect of EU membership provide domestic elites with positive incentives to comply with many peacebuilder demands.

## Definitions, Data, and Research Strategy

An inherent challenge in the empirical study of democratic peacebuilding lies in the fact that only a few major peacebuilding missions have been conducted since the Cold War. We define a major mission as one mandated by the United Nations or another international organization that is aimed both at maintaining peace in a postconflict situation and at inducing social change, with the ultimate goal of creating a stable and democratic country. To omit minor missions that cannot be expected to have a meaningful impact on a host society, we include only missions deployed for six months or longer and count at least 500 military personnel in the field. Only when these thresholds have been met do we code a mission start, even if the mission had an earlier start date but was smaller in character or scope. Multiple simultaneous missions were collapsed into a single observation. Subsequent missions in a single country not separated by more than twelve months were also collapsed into a single observation. According to this definition we count nineteen major peacebuilding missions (see Table 1.1). Such a sample is too small to be explored in meaningful ways by statistical analysis. We have therefore chosen to examine these cases through qualitative comparative analysis.

We make full use of the nineteen cases to identify major trends in peacebuilding missions and to search for meaningful patterns. (Table 1.2 provides a descriptive statistic of the main characteristics of the nineteen cases in our sample.) But, as previously reported, we do not find a stable and consistent association between the outcome and commonly cited explanatory variables such as local capacities (typically measured by gross domestic product, or GDP), material support (measured by aid per capita), and a mission's footprint (which depends both on the numbers of military and civilian personnel as well as on the scope of the peacebuilders' mandate). This leads us to develop an alternative explanation: We assume that the outcome of postwar democratic transitions is not predominantly determined by these structural factors but by the strategic interaction between peacebuilders and domestic elites. This interaction is structured by the preference and the bargaining power of the actors. To better understand this process, we rely on empirically rich case studies. Case studies allow for process tracing, which is indispensable for discovering causal mechanisms;[13] case studies also allow researchers to treat each case as a whole, which facilitates the identification of multiple causation.[14] Finally, case studies can be arranged into different sets of structured comparisons to study one specific aspect of the problem under investigation. For all of these reasons, case study approaches offer tremendous heuristic power, but they also require an intimate knowledge of the cases.

We opted to select a subsample of cases to be studied in greater detail. Our subsample consists of nine cases—roughly half of all available cases—and includes Rwanda, Macedonia, Bosnia and Herzegovina, Kosovo, Mozambique, Namibia, Afghanistan, Tajikistan, and East Timor. Our case selection ensured that the cases show variance both on the dependent variable (success or failure of postwar democratic transition) and on a number of important explanatory variables, such as war characteristics, external aid, neighborhood, and, most important, the footprint of the peacebuilding mission, which is assessed here in terms of the scope of the mandate, number of personnel deployed, and the duration and cost of the mission (see Chapter 4 for details). Because the cases in the sample show variation on the outcome and on important explanatory factors, we can construct different sets of comparisons. While we present neither these comparisons nor the cases themselves in a detailed and formalized way, the analysis presented in the following chapters is nevertheless based on the wealth of data we have gathered.

Before we turn to a more detailed description of the nine cases in our subsample on which the fine-grained data of our analysis rests, we need to briefly justify our definition of "democratic success or failure." As previously mentioned, we speak of a democratic success if, five years after the start of a peacebuilding mission, a country clears the threshold of an *electoral* democracy (as defined by Freedom House). Given this definition, we treat Mozambique, Namibia, Macedonia, and Timor-Leste as successes, and Afghanistan, Tajikistan, Rwanda, Bosnia and Herzegovina, and Kosovo as failures.

There are, of course, other possible definitions of "success." We could apply the relatively high standards of a *liberal* democracy. But, while this fits the rhetoric of many international organizations, we feel it is unreasonable to expect a liberal democracy to emerge within five years of war.

Another alternative might be to define success as the progress a country makes over time rather than to insist on an absolute threshold. There is a certain appeal to this approach because building postwar stability *and* democracy is immensely challenging and rarely occurs overnight. The flip side of

**TABLE 1.2.** Key characteristics of the nineteen cases of major peacebuilding operations after 1989 (five years after mission start).

| | Croatia | Namibia | East Timor | Macedonia | Liberia | Mozambique | Sierra Leone | Burundi | Bosnia | Afghanistan |
|---|---|---|---|---|---|---|---|---|---|---|
| Time period—five years after intervention start | 1996–2000 | 1989–1993 | 1999–2003 | 2001–2005 | 2003–2007 | 1992–1996 | 1999–2003 | 2004–2008 | 1996–2000 | 2002–2006 |
| Democratic quality | Liberal democracy | Liberal democracy | Electoral democracy | Electoral democracy | Electoral democracy | Electoral democracy | Electoral democracy | Electoral democracy | Electoral authoritarian | Electoral authoritarian |
| Level of violence during first five years of operation | No violence; stable | No violence; stable | No violence; stable | No violence except first year; relatively stable | No violence except first year; relatively stable | No violence except first year; relatively stable | Repeated incidents of violence | Continuous armed conflict | No violence except first year; relatively stable | Relapse into war |
| Freedom in the world score | 2 | 2.5 | 3 | 3 | 3.5 | 3.5 | 3.5 | 4.5 | 4.5 | 5 |
| Polity IV score | 8 | 6 | 6 | 9 | 6 | 6 | 5 | 6 | –66 | –66 |
| Real GDP per capita, year of intervention start | 6,438 | 2,959 | 403 | 1,939 | 141 | 201 | 286 | 137 | 1,071 | 213 |
| Peacekeeping troops, peak strength | 4,849 | 4,493 | 6,399 | 3,500 | 15,021 | 6,939 | 17,368 | 5,357 | 54,000 | 28,700 |
| Peacekeeping troops per 1,000 inhabitants | 1.4 | 3 | 7.2 | 1.7 | 3.2 | 0.5 | 4.3 | 0.7 | 15.5 | 1.4 |
| Aid per capita | 18 | 131 | 258 | 122 | 92 | 104 | 67 | 57 | 311 | 79 |

NOTES: Real GDP per capita (in constant 2000 US$) and aid (offical development aid) from World Development Indicators (WDI) from World Development Indicators (WDI) of the World Bank. Number of peacekeeping troops provided by the United Nations (www.un.org/en/peacekeeping/). The coding for liberal and electoral democracy is taken from Freedom House (Freedom House 2005). Coding for electoral authoritarian and fully closed authoritarian is based on the World Bank's Database of Political Institutions (Beck et al. 2001). See also Chapter 1, endnote 4.

We coded levels of violence during the first five years of the peacebuilding operation based on Uppsala Conflict Data Program (UCDP) data and the Political Terror Scale (PTS) data. With respect to UCDP data sets, we relied on the Armed Conflict Dataset, v.4-2011 (Gleditsch et al. 2002), the UCDP Non-State Conflict Dataset, v.2.3-2011 (Eck, Kreutz, and Sundberg 2010), and the One-Sided Violence Dataset, v.1.3-2011 (Eck and Hultman 2007). All UCDP data sets are available online at www.pcr.uu.se/research/ucdp/datasets/; for PTS, see http://politicalterrorscale.org/download.php.

| | Haiti | Cote d'Ivoire | Kosovo | Tajikistan | Angola | Central African Republic | Democratic Republic of the Congo | Cambodia | Rwanda | Bosnia |
|---|---|---|---|---|---|---|---|---|---|---|
| Time period—five years after intervention start | 1994–1998 | 2003–2007 | 1999–2003 | 1997–2001 | 1995–1999 | 1998–2002 | 2001–2005 | 1992–1996 | 1993–1997 | 2002–2006 |
| Democratic quality | Electoral democracy | Electoral authoritarian | Electoral authoritarian | Electoral authoritarian | Fully closed authoritarian | Electoral authoritarian | Fully closed authoritarian | Electoral authoritarian | Fully closed authoritarian | Electoral authoritarian |
| Levels of violence during first five years of operation | No violence except first year; relatively stable | Continuous armed conflict | No violence except first year; relatively stable | No violence; stable | Relapse into war | Repeated incidents of violence | Relapse into war | Repeated incidents of violence | Relapse into war | Relapse into war |
| Freedom in the world score | 5 | 5.5 | 5 | 6 | 6 | 6 | 6 | 6.5 | 6.5 | 5 |
| Polity IV score | −7 | −88 | no data | −1 | −3 | 5 | −88 | 1 | −6 | −66 |
| Real GDP per capita, year of intervention start | 363 | 815 | 893 | 195 | 526 | 334 | 136 | 274 | 462 | 213 |
| Peacekeeping troops, peak strength | 24,278 | 11,837 | 50,000 | 28,000 | 7,062 | 1,350 | 15,775 | 15,991 | 5,590 | 28,700 |
| Peacekeeping troops per 1,000 inhabitants | 3.1 | 0.6 | 21.1 | 4 | 0.5 | 0.4 | 0.2 | 0.1 | 0.9 | 1.4 |
| Aid (ODA) per capita | 79 | 11 | 0 | 26 | 39 | 29 | 29 | 44 | 113 | 79 |

NOTES (continued): We coded as "no violence; stable" those countries where no armed violence beyond a threshold of twenty-five deaths (battle-related deaths in the Armed Conflict Dataset, death related to one-sided violence or nonstate conflict with respect to the other two data sets) occurred in any of the second to fifth years of intervention and that did not have a PTS score below 3 in the first five years after the start of intervention.

We coded as "no violence except first year; relatively stable" when the same applied with respect to UCDP data sets, but PTS scores were below 3 in any given year within the first five years after the start of intervention.

We coded "repeated incidents of violence" when violence above a threshold of twenty-five deaths occurred in up to three among the first five years after conflict and "continuous armed conflict" when this threshold was crossed in three years or more. When violence occurred beyond a threshold of 1,000 deaths in any year except the first year of intervention, we coded this as "relapse into war."

such an approach that prioritizes progress over an absolute threshold is that a slight improvement within an authoritarian regime would also be coded as a success. We are, however, interested in *democratic* outcomes, and we think that a transition from autocracy to democracy implies a qualitative change in the relationship between a state and its citizens and, with it, novel strategic risks for domestic politicians.

Finally, it is also possible to anchor a discussion of postwar democratic "success" or "failure" on an entirely qualitative assessment, informed by deep case-by-case knowledge. Such an approach respects the fact that, as practitioners of peacebuilding remind us, every case is unique and poses its own challenges that peacebuilders and domestic elites must overcome. These peculiarities can be missed by even the most sophisticated data sets. For example, many experts continue to argue that Rwanda is moving in the right direction and has, given its horrifying past experiences, made positive steps toward good (enough) governance.[15] According to this perspective, an accurate assessment of democracy in a given regime must be based not on generalized snapshots, which data sets such as Polity IV provide, but on a comprehensive account of a country's challenges and on prospects for future democratic development.

Each of the preceding definitions of success reflects different facets of the complex phenomenon of democratic transition, and we remain mindful of the various ways one might plausibly define "success." For the sake of consistency, however, we generally equate a postwar democratic success with an "electoral democracy."

## Preparing the Case Studies

On selecting our cases, an international team of country experts prepared nine comprehensive case studies between October 2007 and November 2009.[16] These structured case studies were based on a research template consisting of 101 questions. When preparing these questions, we followed an agnostic research strategy. We scrutinized the literature for existing hypotheses that attempt to explain democratic outcomes in the context of peacebuilding operations and then translated these hypotheses into questions. Country experts then addressed these questions, generating a tremendous amount of data, which we used for comparative analysis.[17]

The first section of the template is devoted to a description of the outcome with regard to security, democracy, and state capacities. The objective of this section was to produce a detailed and precise description of the political regime and the achieved level of stability and security five years after intervention start.

We then turned to long-term factors. We asked about economic development, about previous experiences with democracy, and about neighborhood factors. Another section was devoted to factors such as the duration and type of war, numbers of factions, level of war-related destruction, and how the war was terminated. Next, we inquired about the scope and characteristics of the external intervention, focusing on both military and nonmilitary aspects. We also asked whether and how diplomacy, normative pressure, and/or persuasion contributed to the democratization process. Another set of questions explored the interaction between domestic elites and the interveners, their respective preferences, and constraints. These questions let us reconstruct the strategic interaction and bargaining process, which we assume contributed to the outcome. The final section of the template covered development aid. It collected data on the aid flows and inquired about the most important donors and the prevailing modalities of delivery. We asked case study authors to collect disaggregated aid data on sectors such as elections, the rule of law, human rights, administration capacity, civil society, civil–military relations, and others. Based on these data, we were able to map the flow of democracy aid to our sample cases.

Various drafts of the case studies were then discussed during several author meetings, and the discussions were used to further fine-tune the template.

Once the final case studies were produced, we mined them for causal mechanisms that could explain a democratic outcome; hypotheses were developed, tested against our data, and ultimately refined or rejected. Over the course of intensive discussions, we concluded that none of the variables that scholars typically associate with mission success or failure is consistently linked to a particular outcome across all cases. For example, we could not find a clear relationship between war characteristics and a mission's democratic outcome. Similarly, our data did not support the notion that democratic outcomes are determined by structural factors such as GDP or demography. Nor did they support the popularly held belief that a mission's footprint (its personnel, resources, or duration) or aid flow is consistently associated with a given outcome.

On the other hand, it seemed counterintuitive to discard all of these factors as insignificant. We began to critically reassess much of the conventional wisdom on peacebuilding. Our collaborative research effort then developed into a dialogue between commonly accepted knowledge and our empirical observations, driven by what we increasingly perceived as a mismatch between the two. The more we mined our cases for causal mechanisms, the clearer it became that the outcomes of postwar democratic transitions are contingent events, shaped not only by structural factors but to a large extent by the interaction between peacebuilders and domestic political actors. On this painstaking, structured exchange between ideas and data stands this book.

## The Cases

In this book, we are primarily concerned with the causal mechanisms that explain the democratic outcomes of major peacebuilding missions. The next chapters present the findings we derived from a close analysis of a sample of major peacebuilding operations. We do not present the full case studies in our book, but we will briefly highlight some important features.

As reported before, we treat Namibia, Macedonia, East Timor, and Mozambique as cases of successful democratic postwar transitions, and Afghanistan, Bosnia, Kosovo, Rwanda, and Tajikistan as failures. This is a somewhat crude distinction, and we are aware of the many and meaningful differences among these postwar regimes. With regard to democratic outcomes, Namibia leads the pack. It is a stable electoral democracy with sound institutions and the only case in the sample that is rated a liberal democracy by Freedom House. Macedonia, East Timor, and Mozambique are electoral democracies. Tajikistan, Kosovo, Afghanistan, and Rwanda are all authoritarian regimes, with Rwanda being the most authoritarian of all.

There are also major differences with regard to the intrusiveness of the mission (for a full account, see Chapter 4). Kosovo, Bosnia, East Timor, and Afghanistan all had highly intrusive peace missions, whereas Namibia, Tajikistan, Rwanda, and Macedonia all experienced a lighter peacebuilding footprint. The most intrusive missions also attracted the highest amounts of aid per capita. Afghanistan, Kosovo, and Bosnia received the most, while Mozambique, Rwanda, and Tajikistan received the least.

There are further and important differences among the cases with regard to the origins of the war and the nature of the peacebuilding mission: *Namibia's* civil war (1966–1989) was also a war of independence, and it ended in an internationally brokered transition to democracy in 1989. SWAPO (South

West Africa People's Organization), the armed liberation movement, had employed universal suffrage as a rallying cry throughout its struggle against South African apartheid. Democratization was thus intrinsic to SWAPO's victory and legitimacy. The UN mission (UNTAG, the United Nations Transition Assistance Group) had transitional administrative authority and was decisive in securing positive peacebuilding outcomes. Unlike in Mozambique, however, aid was of little consequence. Instead, the regional context was critical, as Namibia's peace deal was tightly linked to peace negotiations in neighboring Angola and could not have been achieved without the fall of the apartheid regime in South Africa.[18]

*Mozambique*'s sixteen-year war (1977–1992) was also heavily influenced by its regional context. Exclusionary regimes in Rhodesia and South Africa fueled an enduring internal conflict sustained by the government's heavy-handed socialist agenda, economic collapse, and ethnoregional grievances. The end of apartheid shifted regional circumstances to favor peace. The war was ended with the help of a sizable UN intervention force (UNOMOZ, or United Nations Operation in Mozambique) with a robust mandate, a strong leader, and adequate resources bolstered by an engaged and informed group of donors who worked with the government to address the drought and humanitarian emergency that followed in the wake of war. Five years after the war the country boasted a growing economy, capable leaders, and a viable political opposition.[19]

Between 1990 and 1994, *Rwanda* was embroiled in a civil war rooted in economic and political crises but fought along ethnic lines. The war began when the overwhelmingly Tutsi Rwandan Patriotic Front (RPF) invaded from neighboring Uganda, hoping to overthrow the Hutu-led government. In 1993 international efforts to institute peace and democracy through a UN peace mission (UNAMIR, or United Nations Assistance Mission in Rwanda) collapsed with the assassination of Rwanda's president, which sparked the 1994 genocide. Rwanda's war is the only case that ended in military victory; the RPF assumed political power and control of Kigali in July 1994. Unlike other cases, Rwanda did not hold elections in the immediate wake of the conflict. Instead, the RPF formed a broad-based government emphasizing national unity and ethnic inclusion. Postwar national elections were first held in 2003. Thus, at the end of the five-year period following intervention (1993–1998), Rwanda was not democratic and had only just reached a relatively nonviolent status. Official development assistance has played a critical role in Rwanda's peacebuilding outcome, which like Mozambique is heavily aid dependent.[20]

*Bosnia*'s war was relatively brief (1992–1996) and was fought along ethno-nationalist cleavages. The international peacebuilding intervention was in this case large and intrusive; international authorities were authorized to remove politicians and enact (or veto) legislation—all in the name of the internationally brokered Dayton Peace Agreement. Here the regional context was important, both in fomenting conflict and in bringing international attention and support to the fore. Five years after peacebuilders entered the country, Bosnia could be described as relatively stable but not fully democratic.[21]

Like Bosnia, *Kosovo*'s conflict and peacebuilding outcomes were heavily influenced by both regional and international factors. Following its brief armed conflict (1998–1999), Kosovo found itself on the end of a massive intervention that gave international authorities almost unlimited executive, legislative, and judicial power. Five years after the mission's establishment, Kosovo's sovereignty was still in question and its government institutions subject to international powers. Kosovo was classified as relatively stable and democratic, though, as Narten points out, this outcome was and remains heavily dependent on outside actors.[22]

*Macedonia*'s conflict was shortest of all, beginning in February 2001 and ending in August of the same year. As elsewhere in the Balkans, the battle lines followed ethnonationalist divides, and external actors played a decisive role in the peacebuilding process and outcome. In 1999, in the wake of the North Atlantic Treaty Organization's (NATO's) intervention in Kosovo, Albanian nationalists in Macedonia took an opportunity to advance their own goals through insurgency. Together NATO, the OSCE (Organization for Security and Co-operation in Europe), the United Nations, and the European Union established structures and processes that effectively created incentives for peace and democratization. After five years, Macedonia was both relatively stable and democratic.

In *East Timor*, a twenty-three-year struggle for independence from Indonesia (1975–1998) ended in a referendum. Virtually every aspect of state building was supervised and funded by international actors under the aegis of a highly intrusive UN mission (United Nations Transitional Administration in East Timor, or UNTAET). Five years after the 1999 referendum that established the basis for an independent East Timor, the country was considered among "the most successful cases" of external democracy promotion.[23] Although a national crisis dampened expectations in 2006, East Timor remains a success story in the annals of democratic peacebuilding.

*Tajikistan* emerged from its brief civil war (1992–1997) stable but far from democratic. The war ended in a power-sharing agreement in which competing factions exchanged peace for access to state resources.[24] Russian military and political support for a stable, yet autocratic, outcome effectively undercut peacebuilders' will and capacity to impose the usual menu of democratic measures.

The war in *Afghanistan* (1996–2001) ended ambiguously in almost every respect. Formally democratic institutions compete with informal sources of authority and ongoing challenges from armed groups such as the Taliban and Al Qaeda. In addition, the activities of neighboring Pakistan have complicated this massive and highly intrusive mission. Afghanistan was not democratic five years after the intervention began and had relapsed into war.

# 2   Leverage, Adoption Costs, and the Peacebuilding Game

CENTRAL TO MODERN PEACEBUILDING IS THE AIM TO BRING peace *and* democracy to host countries. Fortna argues with regard to peacebuilding missions that, "second only to stable peace, democratization is a core goal of the international community."[1] Many other scholars have made similar claims.[2]

In the wake of the Cold War it is no longer good enough to bring about a truce or ceasefire. Instead, peacebuilders seek to build fully developed, democratic, and economically viable states on the ruins of war. This bears witness both to how ambitious and all-encompassing the peacebuilding agenda has become and also to how deeply international organizations involved in peacebuilding believe in their ability to socially engineer postwar societies. Contemporary peacebuilding is, in short, state building aimed at "constructing or reconstructing institutions of governance capable of providing citizens with physical and economic security. This includes quasi-governmental activities such as electoral assistance, human rights and rule of law technical assistance, security sector reform, and certain forms of development assistance."[3] Much effort, then, is invested in imbuing the state with the capacity to deliver services and public goods that will enhance the welfare of society. But, importantly, peacebuilders are also interested in producing a particular kind of state—a liberal, democratic state organized around markets, the rule of law, and democracy.

When peacebuilders deploy, they are met by a local political elite who may share some aspects of the peacebuilders' vision but not others. Superficially, peacebuilders and domestic political actors have a common objective—building peace—but this objective is defined loosely enough to allow a constant bargaining over the exact form of the peace: that is, who will control the peacebuilding process, peacebuilding priorities, resource allocation, and, most importantly, who will determine political reform policies. What is at stake is not only how the peace will be built but also the kind of state that will emerge from this process.

Even for UN missions conducted under a Chapter VII mandate that does not require host government consent, the experience of peacebuilders, from high-level executives to field officers, is a constant bargaining with domestic political actors. Indeed, peacebuilders are expected to negotiate and cooperate with their hosts to ensure local "ownership." As in any bargaining process, the outcome is determined by what the parties want and the resources and determination they can mobilize to achieve their goals.

Peacebuilders, for their part, want to implement reforms that lead to a liberal peace: They want to deliver services and assistance that will create new institutions that (re)distribute political and economic power in a transparent, accountable, and democratic way. However, peacebuilders typically operate under serious constraints; they operate with limited time and resources because voters at home will not support an expensive peacebuilding mission indefinitely.[4] Most importantly, peacebuilders need to minimize casualties; otherwise their governments will lose the support of the electorate. Consequently, peacebuilders may prioritize stability over the kinds of structural reforms necessary to achieve the liberal democracy they desire. In addition, peacebuilders are highly dependent on their domestic counterparts because cooperation is often essential for the effective, smooth, and stable implementation of various projects. Without local consent and support, peacebuilding programs will not gain traction, and security for international personnel may be compromised. This creates a strong incentive to collaborate with domestic political actors, even when these same actors are skeptical of democracy. This is not to say that local leaders generally harbor ill will or false motives but that they often lack the incentive to pursue genuine democratic reform.

Leonard Wantchekon has tabled a powerful theoretical argument that frames the conditions under which a democratic transition may be in the interest of elites.[5] He argues that predatory warring factions will engage in an alliance with the citizenry and choose democracy over autocratic rule (1) when their economic interests depend on productive investment by the citizens; (2) when citizens' political preferences are such that power will be more equally distributed under democracy than autocracy; (3) when there is an external agency (for example, the United Nations) that presides over the peacebuilding process; (4) when the conflict has reached a stalemate in which the probability of victory by either side has become very low; and (5) when the country is devoid of natural resources and the factions do not receive foreign aid.

Under such circumstances, liberal peace offers relief from a hurting stalemate, leaving both parties better off. The paradox of "warlord democracy" can thus be explained, according to Wantchekon, by a combination of the economic constraints of the warring elites, economic preferences of the citizens, and the presence of a mediating external agency. In such a situation "the degree of economic dependence of the factions on citizens' investments"[6] begins to work toward democratization since democracy is considered to ensure a win-win situation: Warring factions maintain their expropriation interests through high citizen investment levels and taxes, while citizens' security interests are also preserved.[7]

This is a powerful theoretic argument, and it proves the theoretical possibility of a democracy emerging out of warlordism. But the main contribution of this argument to the empirical study of postwar democratization is that it helps explain why successful democratic transitions so rarely occur. The conditions he sets for a successful postwar transition to democracy are, first, a hurting stalemate; second, a reasonably prosperous citizenry upon whose productivity elites rely; and third, a peacebuilding mission that is strong enough to redistribute military and human resources. These conditions are hardly ever met. Civil wars only rarely lead to a military stalemate. Also, most postwar countries are very poor, and elites are hardly ever dependant on taxes from the citizenry. The median income of postwar countries in real GDP is only $911 (the mean is $1,540). Revenues in poor, postwar countries typically stem from natural resources, formal and illicit import and export duties, state licenses on telecommunication, or from outright illegal economic activities. Finally, UN peacebuilding missions are seldom deployed. Since 1945, in only 12 percent of all wars was a robust peacekeeping operation deployed, and in just 3 percent a peace enforcement mission. A large majority of civil wars (71 percent) received no UN mission at all.[8] Given these observations, it is easy to see that elites in postwar societies will typically be exposed to an incentive structure that is not conducive to democracy.

So what do domestic elites want? We start with the rather uncontroversial assumption that domestic political actors want to preserve their political power and to ensure that the peacebuilding process either enhances or preserves their security, political, and economic interests. It is possible that domestic political actors perceive full cooperation with peacebuilders to be in their best interests, as we have seen in Namibia. However, it is more likely that the priorities of domestic elites will differ from those of peacebuilders. Domestic political actors may welcome peace but not democracy, for several reasons. First, local elites may believe that democratic rules threaten their security interests. In some postwar countries, democratization has been followed by mass mobilization, riots, and finally civil wars. For example, democratic openings paved the way for civil war in Rwanda, Tajikistan, and Bosnia. Such experiences do not inspire enthusiasm for democratization.

Moreover, peacebuilding experts reinforce what many elites intuitively assume: Democratization can increase the risks of violence in a postwar country.[9] This is because democratization opens up the "political space in the area of political competition (elections), and freedom of expression (media), as well as reforms of the security sector that are crucial to democratization. However, in the transitional period, these institutions are flawed or ineffective, providing opportunities for substantial maneuvering for elites who are willing to take advantage of the situation to fan violence."[10] It is also true that, once a regime has survived this transition and enjoys a consolidated democracy, prospects for future violence are reduced. However, initial steps towards democracy are dangerous,[11] especially when the country is poor.[12] Because poverty is a defining characteristic of most postwar countries, it is not surprising that their leaders associate democratization with security risks.

A second reason elites may be reluctant to embrace democracy is that the norms surrounding "good governance" restrict a leader's ability to reign arbitrarily and to extort and expropriate state resources at will. Unfortunately, many an elite in postwar countries has built his or her empire on illegal economic activities.[13] These activities may include trafficking and smuggling commodities and goods such as drugs, petroleum products, arms, and ammunition but also racketeering and illicit taxation. Often the entrepreneurs who best exploit the war economy become leading political elites in peacetime or at least maintain friendships in high places once the war has reached its conclusion.

Thirdly, a democratic election may weaken or even rescind a leader's grip on power. Elites who emerged victorious from civil war may reasonably fear that they will lose at the ballot box what they won on the battlefield. This is not to say that elites will categorically oppose democracy; today the penalty for such behavior is exceedingly high in terms of international reputation, legitimacy, and access to aid and support. But rather than work to win public favor, elites may choose the simpler and less costly investment in patron–client networks, which can also yield a popular vote. As a result, clientelism is strengthened, while larger parts of the population are excluded from meaningful political participation.

This brings us to a fourth reason that elites may be reluctant to embrace democratization. Democratic procedures and good governance can threaten the very foundation on which the authority (and very survival) of many a regime in postconflict states is built: the patron–client network. Clientelism forms the basis of support in many nondemocratic systems, where an ambitious elite cultivates ties with a subset of society to make an implicit bargain—political support in exchange for state jobs or targeted public goods.[14] Clientelistic networks are an endemic feature of weak states; arguably they are the most basic form of governance practiced in countries where infrastructural power is weak. Christopher Clapham writes that clientelism is "the most salient type (of authority) organization in the Third World because it corresponds to the normal forms of social organization in precolonial societies."[15] Bratton and van de Walle elaborate that, in neopatrimonial regimes, the right to rule is ascribed to a person rather than an office and that relationships of loyalty and dependence pervade the formal political and administrative system.[16] Positions in the state administration are exploited to acquire personal wealth and status, and the distinction between private and public interests is intentionally blurred. For leaders who cannot rely on a solid governance infrastructure based on a professional and loyal bureaucracy, clientelism is a primary source of authority. This is especially true in volatile postwar countries where political endurance may depend on an ability to co-opt potential rivals into a patron–client relationship.

A transition to democratic standards endangers these mechanisms, and it is only natural that elites buttressed by clientelistic networks oppose reforms that complicate patronage and make co-option more difficult. A case in point is President Hamid Karzai's reluctance to relinquish his patronage network in Afghanistan. After meeting with Karzai in July 2007, a clearly irritated U.S. ambassador Karl W. Eikenberry cabled home that "we must also convince Karzai to put his backing behind democratic institutions and (that) professionalized security forces are better equipped to lead Afghanistan into the future, rather than Karzai's preference for *tribal structures and informal power networks*" (italics mine).[17] In fact, Karzai's "preference for tribal structures and informal power networks" might make perfect sense, given that these informal power networks account for what little central authority exists in many postwar countries.

It is important to note that elites in postwar countries often rely on patronage networks because they lack alternative sources of power. This is especially true in places where traditional social structures such as tribe, clan, village community, big men, or religious leaders continue to play an important role in the everyday life of the population. In such situations, central authority may be extended to the peripheries only by co-opting these structures.[18] Thus, Karzai's alleged preference for informal power networks may be less a personal inclination than a pragmatic accommodation of the existing power structure.

Karzai's example also highlights the fact that, in most postwar societies, the government is not the only power broker with a stake in the peacebuilding process. Other elites may have considerable political influence. Militias or warlords may challenge the central government, entrenched provincial elites may defend their autonomy vis-à-vis the central state, an ethnic minority may agitate for increased representation, or tribal leaders may defend their fiefdoms. Often such groups enjoy a high degree of de facto autonomy from the central state, and they are distrustful of the central state's attempts to increase its reach. Because peacebuilders are typically statist in their preferences—supporting central oversight, good governance, and accountability—such groups logically oppose the peacebuilding agenda. Depending on their relative strength, the government may need to accommodate their demands. As a result, the government may become less responsive to peacebuilders' prescriptions.

This is not to say that democracy is impossible in countries with well-entrenched systems of patronage. But it is unlikely that the regime will be a liberal democracy because the prevailing patronage system will likely constrain the type of democracy that will develop.[19] Where patronage systems are entrenched, politicians can win elections by directing resources to patrons who control voting subpopulations. Under such circumstances, democracy will not yield its full benefits because patronage invalidates the supposed social contract based on mutual obligations between political elites and the voting public. Local patrons will continue to act as gatekeepers, separating the population from elected officials, and mediating this interaction.[20]

To sum up, political actors in a postwar country often have good reason to fear that a transition to a more democratic regime will endanger their access to political power and resources, as well as their way of ruling via patronage. In a volatile postwar situation where opposing political fractions typically retain their capacity for organized violence, security concerns may be foremost in leaders' minds. Moreover, elites who lose political power may also lose their lives. For all these reasons, the transition to a liberal and democratic state can impose considerable adoption costs on postwar elites. Thus, a push for democratization may, in the eyes of domestic political actors, be perceived as a problem rather than solution. They may therefore strategize by weighing the opportunities that peacebuilders offer against the threats that democratization poses to their survival. They will therefore attempt to steer international peacebuilders in a direction that furthers their interests: attracting as many resources—material and symbolic—as they can, while implementing the fewest reforms possible in areas that might threaten their security or undermine their ability to rule and extract resources.

What follows from this discussion is that, unless the interests of the domestic political actors and peacebuilders are perfectly aligned, the peacebuilding trajectory will be determined by how peacebuilders and domestic political actors negotiate their differences with regard to their primary objectives. Peacebuilding can thus be depicted as a bargain between peacebuilders and postwar elites. As in any negotiation, the outcome will reflect their respective bargaining power.

## Peacebuilding as Interaction: An Illustrative Model

For illustrative purposes, we can now describe the interaction between peacebuilders and domestic political actors as a simple bargaining model over the contents of "the peace." In reality, peacebuilders and domestic political actors will negotiate reforms in many different policy fields, such as security provisions, power sharing, human rights, regulatory policies, minority rights, economic policies, and so on. Hence, the bargaining that we have in mind is best conceived as a set of negotiations between myriad peacebuilders and their domestic counterparts. These negotiations typically drag on over months and years and are, as every practitioner will confirm, the daily business of peacebuilders on the ground, be they high-level UN representatives or NGO (nongovernmental organization) personnel. It is the aggregate outcome of these negotiations that in the end determines the kind of state that will be built. We are also aware of the fact that not all policy fields are equally contested and that these contests will vary according to mission.

For the sake of argument, we simplify this complex reality and make the following assumption: Peacebuilders and domestic political actors are both unitary actors who bargain over both the reforms they will implement to create liberal peace as well as control over mission resources. We assume that peacebuilders make the first move and offer domestic political actors a package that combines a certain amount of resources with a bundle of reform policies aimed at creating a liberal and democratic postwar regime. If domestic political actors accept, the bargaining game is over, and peacebuilding proceeds cooperatively, with a shared vision of a liberal democratic end state.

But domestic political actors might reject the peacebuilders' offer, proposing instead a revised package, which includes more resources for the elites and less reform. If peacebuilders accept, the bargaining game ends, and peacebuilders and domestic political actors engage in a peacebuilding process that results in a less democratic outcome than peacebuilders originally hoped for. But peacebuilders can also reject this counteroffer: They can either withdraw from the peacebuilding process altogether, or they can try to push domestic political actors to accept their original proposal. Neither option is particularly attractive for peacebuilders, however; if they withdraw, war may resume, and peacebuilders would lose credibility. Confrontation, on the other hand, may force peacebuilders to assume the unwelcome mantle of colonial administrator instead of neutral peacebuilder.

Let us now relax the oversimplifying assumption that local elites are a unitary actor. In many postwar societies, there are several relevant players. A rebel group or entrenched provincial elites may challenge domestic political actors, wary of losing their autonomy vis-à-vis the central state. Now assume that a bargaining process takes place between domestic political actors, peacebuilders, and this secondary elite, this time with the structure of a two-level game.[21]

As in the first game, peacebuilders make the first move and offer domestic political actors a package that includes resources and reform policies designed to create a liberal and democratic postwar regime. Before domestic political actors can accept this package, they must negotiate its acceptability with secondary elites. It is possible that secondary elites fully embrace a move toward a more democratic and liberal system. However, it is also possible (and actually more plausible), that secondary elites will oppose such a move because liberal reforms necessarily strengthen the central administration, thereby reducing the autonomy of secondary elites. In the unlikely event that both secondary elites and domestic political actors do accept, then the game is over and peacebuilders, domestic political actors, and secondary elites engage in cooperative peacebuilding. If secondary elites reject the offer, however, then domestic political actors face a choice: Either they can renegotiate the package with peacebuilders (which will lead to a less liberal and therefore compromised peacebuilding effort), or they can try to force secondary elites to accept peacebuilders' original offer, risking a new round of violence—an option palatable to neither peacebuilders nor domestic political actors.

Evidently the peacebuilding game is complicated by the existence of secondary elites. These groups also reinforce what has been described as the "paradox of weakness": If domestic political actors can credibly argue that their scope of action is constrained by strong internal opposition—that is, that they are simply unable to push certain democratic reforms without risking renewed violence—then their bargaining position relative to peacebuilders is actually strengthened. Peacebuilders may soften their demands for stringent reform out of fear that this will provoke secondary elites and put their partners at risk.

The crucial insight that this simple model offers is that the trajectory of a peacebuilding process (and thus a democratic outcome) is determined by the interaction of domestic political actors and peacebuilders. This interaction, in turn, is shaped by player preferences as well as the resources and capacities that each player brings to the table. A cooperative peacebuilding process leading to democracy is most likely when peacebuilders exert a high degree of leverage over domestic political actors and when domestic political actors perceive the costs of prescribed reforms to be low. On the other hand, when peacebuilders exert less leverage over domestic political actors, and when the perceived adoption costs for reforms are higher, it is more likely that the democratic vision will be compromised.

Our conceptualization of peacebuilding as social interaction urges us to think about the costs domestic political actors must incur when adopting a given peacebuilding package and about the ways peacebuilders can exert leverage to offset these costs. In the next section, we discuss possible sources of adoption costs and leverage.

## Adoption Costs and Leverage

We define adoption costs as the perceived costs to domestic political actors of adopting democracy as part of a peacebuilding process. Depending on their situation at the time of peace, domestic political actors stand either to lose or to gain by committing to democratic politics, and the stakes may be considerable. Democracy, in the words of Valerie Bunce, is a system which "features *certain* political procedures, but *uncertain* political results."[22] For democracy to succeed, domestic political actors must be willing to accept uncertain outcomes in exchange for definite political procedures. Domestic political actors will consider how embracing democratic politics affects their own agendas, as well as their security. They will embrace postwar democratization when, on balance, they judge the benefits to outweigh the costs. Otherwise, they will resist it. Where domestic political actors prefer resistance, the outcome depends on the relative strength of their position, which in turn depends on the ability of external guarantors either to reward compliance or to punish noncompliance.

The preceding cost-benefit analysis is contingent on many factors, some of which may be highly idiosyncratic. But we would argue that, in general, domestic political actors calculate adoption costs based on the degree to which the terms of the peace settlement and the content of the peacebuilding package will affect their physical *security* and the achievement of their *primary political objectives*.

For example, domestic political actors may consider democracy to be a security threat when they believe that a liberal political regime will strengthen a hostile opposition group capable of waging war, or when they fear that democratization will weaken the central government's grip on power. They may also perceive a threat when their power is rooted in patronage and informal, predatory resource extraction, as in Afghanistan.

Democracy can also threaten the prime political objective of elites. In Bosnia, all ethnic parties were anxious to maintain political dominance over their respective fiefdoms—an objective that was incompatible with democratic standards. On the other hand, elites in Namibia embraced democracy because it was seen as the fastest route to independent statehood: a primary objective of both politicians and the population at large. (In Chapter 3 we will explore how the war and its conclusion shape both adoption costs and the ability of external actors to influence these perceived costs through rewards and sanctions.)

In sum, domestic political actors assess the implications of democratization to their security and their primary political objectives. If transition to a democratic peace promises high adoption costs, then domestic political actors will try to renegotiate or subvert the offending policies or will demand that peacebuilders offset some of these costs by transferring more resources or by providing a credible security guarantee. The latter point is especially important. When domestic political actors feel that their security depends on external peacebuilders, the credibility of this protection becomes a decisive factor. If the trust gap between peacebuilders and domestic political actors is too big, there is little room for a cooperative peacebuilding process. Such is the case in Afghanistan. The Afghan political elite under Hamid Karzai's leadership is highly dependent on international forces. Yet, because the Afghan elite does not feel it can depend on steadfast international support—and not without reason, given the clear inclination of most Western political leaders to pull out as soon as possible—it has hedged its bet, keeping international backers at arm's length to keep backchannels open with elements of the insurgency. Thus President Karzai said publicly in April 2010 that Afghans were increasingly coming to see only "a thin curtain" between international involvement and "invasion,"[23] considerably straining his relationship with peacebuilders. Cooperative peacebuilding thus gives way to an unhappy marriage of convenience. Democratic peace does not blossom under such circumstances.

But the calculations of domestic political actors are not only informed by the costs of adopting democracy; they are also informed by the costs of *not* adopting democracy. When local elites think they may need external support to achieve a primary objective or fear they will incur sanctions for spurning democratic norms, they may be willing to adopt peacebuilders' prescriptions. In other words, peacebuilders can sometimes use their clout to impose their will. Perhaps their most important source of leverage is the degree to which their presence guarantees peace. Another source of leverage is the degree to which domestic elites depend on peacebuilders and other international actors present, such as bilateral donors, to achieve a prime political objective. For example, elites in Namibia and East Timor depended on external support to win their independence.

Leverage can also stem from domestic political actors' dependence on foreign assets. Peacebuilders usually arrive with considerable financial resources. They provide aid for immediate humanitarian relief and capacity building; set up trust funds for certain sectors; fund state budgets; and offer loans. A government that depends on such funding for reconstruction, macroeconomic stability, security provision, or the daily running costs of government might be more inclined to cooperate with peacebuilders than a government that receives relatively little support.

Peacebuilders' leverage may also increase if they are perceived to be legitimate.[24] In a peacebuilding setting, the degree of legitimacy hinges on "popular assent" to the peacebuilding process.[25] Peacebuilders must work to legitimize their new social order (that is, establish its intrinsic "rightness"), or risk its collapse.[26] Without a modicum of legitimacy, any peacebuilding policy lacks credibility and sustainability on the ground. To earn this legitimacy, it is rarely enough that the peacebuilders are backed by a UN mandate. Legitimacy also depends on outputs (are peacebuilders improving the situation on the ground?) and on how well domestic political actors and society at large buy into the peacebuilders' vision. Foreigners may compensate for their lack of democratic legitimacy by establishing local consultative organs, as they did in Timor in 2002 and in Kosovo 2004. They also may try to compensate by, for example, increasing humanitarian aid, providing security, or supporting basic human needs—because, when peacebuilders enjoy a high degree of legitimacy within a postwar society, they may be able to pressure domestic political actors into accepting reforms. Perhaps because of this, peacebuilders often find their legitimacy challenged by local voices. Domestic political actors may accuse peacebuilders of imposing policies that lack local support or ownership. They may critically assess the record of peacebuilding achievements. They may also accuse peacebuilders of establishing foreign (quasi-colonial) rule over the postwar society. In so doing they hope to reduce peacebuilders' leverage by establishing the superiority of their own legitimacy.

To sum up, domestic political actors calculate adoption costs by assessing the impact that democratization will have on their security situation and on their ability to achieve a prime political objective. They may also take into account the costs of not adopting democracy (that is, of alienating peacebuilders). These costs are higher when domestic political actors depend on peacebuilders and when peacebuilders exert a high degree of leverage over their local counterparts.

Table 2.1 summarizes democratic adoption costs for the major domestic political actors in our nine cases. It focuses on the security threat, if any, posed to local political actors in adopting democracy, the threat to these actors' substantive goal posed by democracy, and the costs and benefits that

**TABLE 2.1.** Selected initial adoption costs of democracy.

| Case country | Domestic political actors | Perceived physical security threat to LE posed by democracy | Goal | Threat to domestic elites' main goal posed by democracy | Domestic elites' need for international legitimation/PB support to achieve major goal | Domestic elites' fear of direct sanctions for resisting democratization | Overall assessment of adoption cost at beginning of mission |
|---|---|---|---|---|---|---|---|
| Namibia | SWAPO | Low | Independence | None | High | High | Low |
| East Timor | FRETILIN | Low | Independence | None | High | Low | Low |
| Mozambique | Renamo | Low | Domestic and international legitimacy | None | High | High | Low |
|  | Frelimo | Low | Retain power | None | Low | High |  |
| Macedonia | Albanian opposition | Low | Equality | None | High | High | Low |
|  | Government | Low | EU inclusion | None | High | High |  |
| Kosovo | Kosovo Albanian elite | Medium | Autonomy/independence | None | High | Low | Low |
|  | Serb minority | High |  |  |  |  |  |
| Bosnia | Serbs | Medium | Preserve RS | Medium | High | Low | Medium |
|  | Croats | Medium | Maximize ethnic autonomy | Medium | High | Low |  |
|  | Bosniaks | Medium | Preserve BiH | Low | High | Low |  |
| Tajikistan | UTO | Low | Gain a share in power | Low | None | None | High |
|  | Government | Low | Retain power | Low | None | None |  |
| Rwanda (pre-1994) | FAR (Habyarimana) | High | Retain power | High | Medium | Medium | High |
|  | RPF | Medium | Take power | High | High | Medium |  |
| Rwanda (post-1994) | RPF | Medium | Retain power | High | High | Low | High |
|  | Ex-FAR | High | Regain power | High | n/a | Low |  |
| Afghanistan | Government | High | Retain power | Medium | High | Low | High |

external actors could impose in exchange for compliance or defection from the democratic political settlement. As we detail in later chapters, peacebuilder leverage does not necessarily remain constant over the life of an intervention but often fluctuates in response to regional events, changes in aid levels and modalities, and the like.

Out of our nine cases, we find that Macedonia, Namibia, Mozambique, Kosovo, and East Timor had lower levels of initial adoption costs. In other words, domestic political actors stood to gain overall by embracing peacebuilders' policy prescriptions: The terms of settlement did not threaten their security or their primary goals. In the early 1990s, Mozambique and Namibia—both aid dependent—had every reason to believe that scarce aid resources would be reserved for countries like their own that had adopted donors' democratic agenda.

Moreover, in neither country did warring parties depend on lucrative natural resources or other forms of predation (such as cigarette smuggling or other informal trade made profitable under a wartime monopoly). Furthermore, elites assumed they could retain their political power through a democratic transition. In Mozambique, the ruling party was in a strong position given Renamo's lack of political experience and resources, while in Kosovo, Namibia, and East Timor, prewar elites had already been removed from the political equation through either the war or its settlement. In either case, the "losers" of the postwar dispensation were not in a position to protest.[27] Warring parties who laid down arms had little reason to fear for their physical security because peace missions in these countries were robust, fully resourced, and clearly committed.

We find that Afghanistan, Tajikistan, Rwanda, and Bosnia had higher levels of initial adoption costs. Elites in these countries had little to gain by accepting democratic reforms. In Afghanistan, Tajikistan, and Bosnia, a shift toward democracy would have endangered rulers' privileged access to political power, which, ironically, elites in Afghanistan and in the political entities of Bosnia-Herzegovina were granted in the first place by the international community. Hamid Karzai was made president of post-Taliban Afghanistan at the Bonn conference in 2001; likewise, Bosniaks, Serbs, and Croats were given political supremacy in their respective fiefdoms at the Dayton conference in 1995. In Tajikistan and Afghanistan, democratization would have also curtailed elite's privileged access to lucrative informal predation and patron–client networks.[28]

In Rwanda, absolute military victory gave the Rwandan Patriotic Front (RPF) little incentive to compromise its monopoly on political power or to open rent-generating opportunities to former adversaries. Moreover, the genocide, and the lingering presence of Hutu militias in the neighboring Democratic Republic of Congo, gave credence to the government's claims that democracy and the demilitarization of politics would constitute an unacceptable threat to the nation's security, as well as to that of the RPF.[29]

It is clear that adoption costs are associated with democratic outcomes. Leaders in Namibia and East Timor enjoyed atypically low costs, and both countries were high performers with regard to their democratic outcomes. In contrast, Rwanda, Afghanistan, and Tajikistan had high adoption costs and were low performers. But to understand the peacebuilding process, it is not enough to note the relationship between adoption cost and outcome. Rather, it is important to understand *to what extent adoption costs matter and whether peacebuilders can offset some of these costs through their policies.* Peacebuilders can bring security guarantees; they can grant autonomy or even sovereignty; they may be able to coerce domestic political actors into adopting reforms; and they bring resources to sweeten the deal for domestic political actors. To what extent can these policies offset the burden of democracy on domestic political actors? Can international actors truly compensate for primarily domestic impediments to liberal peace? Can peacebuilders create enough leverage through positive and negative incentives to shift the political calculus of local decision makers? If so, they may be able to foster a transition to liberal peace. If not, then the informal "contract" between peacebuilders and domestic political actors will be renegotiated, and the sides will practically—if not formally—agree to build a peace that is less than liberal.

In the following chapters we describe the origins and sources of adoption costs for the nine cases in our sample and explore in more detail when, how, and to what extent peacebuilders can offset these costs. Our research suggests that adoption costs matter greatly but not in a deterministic way. Rather than serving as an intervening variable that consistently translates the impact of other factors such as particular war characteristics, mission characteristics, and the like into fixed outcomes, adoption costs are part of a process characterized by multiple, conjunctural causation.[30] Thus in different cases the same set of factors may combine in different ways to produce similar cost-benefit calculations by domestic political actors. We develop this idea more fully in the next chapter where we discuss how wars and their conclusions affect adoption costs.

# 3   The Legacy of War

## Overview

Does the nature of a civil war, or the terms on which the war was ended, affect the chances of successful postwar democratization? A sizeable literature explores the impact of various war characteristics and war settlement provisions on the duration of peace. However, we know little about whether or how such characteristics might affect the chances for postconflict democratization.

This chapter begins with a brief review of the largely quantitative literature on war-related factors believed to influence the success of peace-building efforts. The intensity, duration, and central cleavage of the conflict, as well as the number of hostile factions and whether the war ended in victory or stalemate, have each been found to influence the duration of peace after civil war. The creation of institutions for power sharing is also considered important. We ask whether these same factors might also explain the success or failure of postwar democratization, and we test them against the nine cases within our subsample: Afghanistan, Bosnia, East Timor, Kosovo, Macedonia, Mozambique, Namibia, Rwanda, and Tajikistan.

We find that the war-related variables that dominate the quantitative literature on peace duration have little direct, systematic impact on the success of postwar democratization, with the important caveat that stability is a necessary but not sufficient condition for democratization. Countries that relapsed into war during the first five years of the peacebuilding operation were, as a rule, not democratic after five years. On the other hand, Kosovo, Bosnia, and Tajikistan avoided violence, yet did not even clear the threshold of an electoral democracy (look back again at Table 1.2).

However, successful cases of postwar democratization vary considerably on most of the war characteristics usually deemed relevant, including the intensity, duration, and root causes of the conflict. Similarly, both successful and unsuccessful cases in our sample include wars that ended in negotiated settlement, that had postconflict power-sharing provisions, and that had external guarantors—all factors generally associated with longer-lasting peace.

To explain these results, we rely on the concept of adoption costs introduced in Chapter 2: the assessment by domestic political elites of the costs and benefits of embracing democratic politics. Simply put, we argue that postwar democratization succeeds when domestic political elites calculate that the benefits of adopting democracy outweigh its costs. Theoretically, postwar democratization could also succeed where domestic political elites prefer not to embrace democracy, but external peacebuilders possess sufficient leverage to impose it.

In our formulation, war characteristics matter because they influence the calculations of domestic political elites as well as the leverage that external peacebuilders can exert. To understand how, when, and why the war matters for peacebuilding outcomes, we must consider not only the characteristics themselves but how these characteristics affect the perceptions and preferences of domestic political elites and the ability and willingness of external actors to act decisively and effectively.

Numerous considerations factor into these calculations, and adoption costs are an assessment of net costs. No single factor is able to account for the variation across cases. Cases that differ starkly on many dimensions—including key war-related variables—may have the same outcome depending on the relative weights of these factors. Recasting peace-building outcomes as functions of the calculations and interactions of political actors (local and external) provides a dynamic causal mechanism that has been missing in much of the peace-building literature. The next section provides a brief review of the literature linking war characteristics to prospects for peace.

## War Variables and Peace

There is a sizable literature on a wide range of war-related variables and their effects on the duration of peace, including the war itself as well as its conclusion. Features of the war include the intensity and duration of the war, the number of hostile factions, and whether the war was based on identity issues. Relevant characteristics of war termination include whether the war ended through military victory or negotiations, the degree of power-sharing envisaged in the peace settlement, and whether a credible third-party guarantor is available to oversee the peace. While there is by no means uniform agreement, there is broad consensus on a few key issues.

### War Characteristics

First, there is considerable evidence that higher-intensity wars—those that cause high numbers of deaths and large scale displacement—are less likely to be followed by lasting peace.[1] Indeed, Doyle and Sambanis argue that *intensity* is a more powerful factor than the *type* of war. They write that "war type is overwhelmed by the hostile effects of human misery, whatever their source."[2]

There is less agreement in the literature on the effect of a war's duration, primarily because it is closely related to other factors such as intensity and the degree of polarization between warring factions. On one hand, many authors find that longer wars tend to end in more durable peace settlements, providing support for the "war weariness" theory.[3]

Other scholars suggest that countries that have experienced longer wars are more likely to return to war.[4] Longer wars result in greater mistrust between opposing sides, and warring parties face significant sunk costs in warfare, as well as high risks if they surrender their arms. More effective security guarantees are thus required to secure a lasting peace after long wars. However, on balance, the literature suggests that, all else being equal, longer wars should tend to facilitate the construction of lasting peace. We return to the question of power sharing and its effects on peace later on.

Wars that center on ethnic or other identity differences are widely believed to last longer and to be less likely to lead to durable peace. Doyle and Sambanis observe that "wars with an ethnic or religious overtone are less likely to be resolved."[5] Regan and Aydin find that "religious and ethnic conflicts have a longer expected duration than ideological conflicts . . ."[6] Hartzell and her coauthors argue that a return to war is four times more likely in cases of ethnic war.[7] Fortna, on the other hand, finds the evidence that identity wars are harder to end definitively inconclusive, as do Mattes and Savun.[8]

The number of rebel factions involved in a war might also affect the chances of peace. Doyle and Sambanis argue that a larger number of hostile factions significantly reduces the chances of both sovereign peace (absence of conflict) and participatory peace (peace plus minimal democracy).[9] Fortunately, conflicts involving more than one rebel group constitute a minority of civil wars, varying between 12 and 30 percent between 2002 and 2006.[10]

In summary, there is substantial support in the quantitative literature for the claim that wars of higher intensity, wars with more than one rebel faction, and wars that center on ethnic or other identity conflict are less likely to be followed by durable peace.

### War Settlement Characteristics

The literature on postconflict peacebuilding also suggests that the way a war ends may have important implications for the duration of peace. Here the most relevant variables are military victory versus negotiated peace, power-sharing versus majoritarian-based government, and the presence or absence of third-party guarantors of the peace.

Military victory for one side is more common than any other definitive outcome in civil wars. The most recent data set compiled by the Uppsala Conflict Data Project (UCDP) finds that more than a third of civil wars between 1945 and 2006 ended in military victory, compared to just 13.5 percent settled through negotiated agreement. A number of studies have found that peace produced by military victory appears to be more durable than negotiated peace, though Fortna argues that this result is less robust for conflicts ending after the Cold War.[11]

There are several explanations for the finding that military victory reduces the chances of conflict recurrence. The durability of peace after military victory might be explained by the fact that the defeated side lacks the capacity to mount continued or renewed resistance, having been incapacitated by the victor.[12] Toft argues that military victory increases the threat of harm to violators of the agreement.[13] Another possibility is that an outright win or loss on the battlefield is an undeniable source of information for belligerents: "Civil wars where neither side achieves an outright victory, where essentially stalemate leads to negotiated agreement, may not have resulted in enough information revelation to satisfy both sides that victory is not still possible."[14]

Though a large proportion of civil wars do end in military victory, an even larger share (40 percent) simply peter out, with neither a victory nor a peace treaty to mark the end of conflict.[15] In fact, this indeterminate outcome is the most common ending to civil war. Scholarly conclusions regarding the implications of this finding remain elusive. If wars sputter out because one or both sides have exhausted the resources needed to fight, the threat of recurrence

may be lower. However, in the absence of an explicit agreement to stop fighting we might expect that, should new or additional resources become available, fighting could easily resume. Certainly the preponderance of the literature finds that explicit peace agreements support durable peace.

Another key variable linking war settlement characteristics and peacebuilding is the presence of institutions for power sharing. There is a sizeable
literature on the relationship between power sharing and peacebuilding outcomes. The solution proposed by the power-sharing approach is to contain
the uncertainty of democratic elections and the security concerns of parties
recently involved in violent conflict by granting each party a share of central
power, a certain amount of group autonomy, or both. Bearing in mind the
security dilemma belligerents face in laying down their weapons, Walter and
others argue that institutional provisions for power sharing and third party
guarantors are the critical factors in securing peace.[16]

This approach has in fact become part of the standard repertoire of international interventions, as recent experiments in ethnically divided Bosnia
and Herzegovina, Burundi, and Afghanistan illustrate.[17] Yet the empirical evidence on the outcome of power-sharing arrangements is mixed. In many African conflicts, power sharing failed as peace agreements lacked political support from the outset,[18] while in Lebanon some studies find that power-sharing
arrangements are frequently superseded by regional turmoil.[19] Conversely,
among large-$N$ studies of power sharing, Walter as well as Hartzell and Hoddie find that power sharing, combined with external guarantees, indeed
contributes to peace.[20] Derouen finds that power-sharing agreements have a
stronger positive effect when a war ends in military victory. But he suggests
that political power sharing reduces the durability of peace in cases where the
war was about control of government rather than control of territory.[21]

Different authors define power sharing differently, and this complicates
the search for definitive answers. For some, power sharing means guaranteed
representation for all key groups, while for others it requires only the existence of checks and balances within government. For still others, power sharing refers to provisions for territorial autonomy.

Like the rest of the literature on war characteristics, the scholarship on
power-sharing agreements is predominantly concerned with the effects power
sharing has on peace, rather than on democracy. Authors who focus specifically on postwar democratization have argued that while power sharing
might be helpful and often necessary in the immediate aftermath of conflict,

it can pose problems for both peace and democracy in the consolidation phase because it provides ethnic leaders with both the incentives and the means to escalate conflict.[22] This is because it accentuates precisely those divides that initially fuelled conflict and provides leaders who want to exploit these divides with political power and resources.

In one of the few studies that deals specifically with the impact of postwar power sharing on democracy (rather than peace), Riese (2008) finds that power sharing only rarely has been conducive to postconflict democracy and only when the obstacles to peace building were atypically low. Other cases of power sharing led to prolonged phases of peace but not to more democracy. In these cases power sharing was largely imposed by powerful outside actors who acted not so much as guarantors of an agreement but as parties to the conflict. In the majority of cases power sharing either failed completely or was a mere interim step to an authoritarian consolidation of power. Riese concludes that power-sharing success might very well be a result rather than a cause of cooperation between the parties to the conflict.[23]

Finally, the presence of a credible third-party guarantor has been cited as important for durable peace. Hartzell and Hoddie find that having a third-party enforcer reduces the chance of peace settlement failure by fully 87 percent.[24] With Walter, they argue that the presence of a third party to enforce the terms of the peace builds confidence and alleviates the "security dilemma" that combatant groups face on laying down arms.[25] To some degree, as previously noted, power-sharing arrangements and external guarantors have been seen as interchangeable, or at least as serving a common purpose; that is, mitigating the fears of formerly warring parties regarding the threats to their physical, political, or economic security that come with surrendering arms.

In sum then, the literature finds that chances for lasting peace are diminished in the wake of wars of high intensity, wars where there are more than two warring factions, and wars where conflict is organized around ethnic or other communal identities. And most scholars argue that, all else being equal, the longer the war, the greater the likelihood of peace.

As for war settlements, the literature finds that wars ending in military victory result in more durable peace than those ending in negotiated settlements and that credible external guarantors improve the chances of lasting peace. Investigations into the impact of power sharing have yielded mixed results.

These are helpful signposts. But the literature provides no guidance on the relative weights of these factors, so that it becomes difficult to assess their importance when these factors occur in various combinations. Are high-intensity ethnic wars with multiple warring factions that end with a power-sharing agreement more or less likely to be followed by durable peace than low-intensity wars over territory with no power sharing and an external guarantor?

This problem can be illustrated by summing up the factors discussed in the previous paragraphs for our nine cases (Table 3.1). Because each country had an external peace mission, the presence of a third party guarantor is not included in the table. For most variables, we assign a 0 if the value of this variable in a conflict should, based on the literature, have a negative impact on peace. We assign a 1 if the effect should be positive. The variables are scored in terms of their expected impact on peace (stability), but the last row also reports on the political outcome (democratic or undemocratic).

Namibia and East Timor received the highest aggregate scores, with a 6 and a 5 respectively. Based on what we might expect from the literature, these cases exhibit the highest number of favorable conditions for peace. Mozambique and Kosovo both received scores of 4. All four of these cases were stable and non-violent after five years, and Mozambique, East Timor, and Namibia qualified as democracies (with a Polity IV rating of 6 or higher). Kosovo did not.

The remaining five cases scored no higher than a 2, indicating that, on the basis of the conventional wisdom, they would have poor chances of a durable peace. Of these five cases, three were in fact stable (Bosnia, Macedonia, and Tajikistan), and two unstable (Afghanistan and Rwanda). Nevertheless, Rwanda, Macedonia, and Bosnia all earned a 2, while Afghanistan earned a score of 1 and Tajikistan received a 0. Of these four cases, all but Macedonia failed to achieve the requisite Polity IV score to qualify as a democracy by our definition.

These results highlight the ambiguity surrounding the correlations found in the quantitative literature between war characteristics and the chances of peace. It is easiest to see this by describing the disparate "positives" that added up to a score of 2 in our exercise. In Afghanistan, relatively low intensity (deaths per capita over duration) and low intensity provided some optimism for a more durable peace (look again at Table 3.1 for intensity scores). In Bosnia, it was the fact that the war was over territory and that there was some measure of territorial autonomy provided for in the peace settlement. In Macedonia, low intensity and a single rebel faction provided positives, and in Rwanda, the advantageous war variables were military victory and a single

**TABLE 3.1.** Peace index (higher score indicates a greater probability of durable peace).

| Conflict | Afghanistan 1996–2001 | Bosnia 1992–1995 | East Timor 1975–1999 | Kosovo 1998–1999 | Macedonia 1999 | Mozambique 1976–1992 | Namibia 1966–1989 | Rwanda 1990–1994 | Tajikistan 1992–1997 |
|---|---|---|---|---|---|---|---|---|---|
| Identity conflict | 0 | 0 | 0 | 0 | 0 | 1 | 1 | 0 | 0 |
| Duration | 0 | 0 | 1 | 0 | 0 | 1 | 1 | 0 | 0 |
| Territory or government? | 0 | 1 | 1 | 1 | 0 | 0 | 1 | 0 | 0 |
| Intensity | 1* | 0 | 1 | 1 | 1** | 1 | 1 | 0* | 0 |
| Number of rebel factions | 0 | 0 | 1 | 1 | 1 | 1 | 1 | 1 | 0 |
| War termination | 0 | 0 | 0 | 0 | 0 | 0 | 0 | 1 | 0 |
| Territorial power sharing or autonomy | 0 | 1 | 1 | 1 | 0 | 0 | 1 | 0 | 0 |
| Totals | 1 | 2 | 5 | 4 | 2 | 4 | 6 | 2 | 0 |
| Outcomes | Unstable Undemocratic | Stable Undemocratic | Stable Democratic | Stable Undemocratic | Stable Democratic | Stable Democratic | Stable Democratic | Unstable Undemocratic | Stable Undemocratic |

**Type:** identity conflict = 0, nonidentity conflict = 1

**Duration:** shorter than sample mean = 0, longer than sample mean = 1

**Territory or government:** conflict over control of government = 0, conflict over control of a certain territory = 1

**Intensity:** defined as total battle deaths per capita during conflict, divided by years of conflict. Higher than sample mean coded 0; lower than sample mean coded 1.

**Number of rebel factions:** more than one faction = 0, one faction = 1

**War termination:** negotiated settlement = 0, military victory = 1, other outcome = −1

**Territorial power-sharing or autonomy provisions:** no = 0, yes = 1

**Democratic:** electoral democracy according to Freedom House

**Stable:** no armed violence beyond a threshold of 25 deaths per year

SOURCES: Prio Battle Deaths data set for battle deaths, unless otherwise noted. Data for all other variables from Uppsala Conflict Data Project War Termination dataset.

*Data on battle deaths for these cases are from Doyle and Sambanis 2006.

**Data on battle deaths from Sandevski 2009.

rebel faction. Tajikistan had no such advantages, yet emerged, five years after war's end, stable, if not democratic.

The literature is better at predicting success than failure. East Timor, Mozambique, Namibia, and Kosovo all earned scores at the high end of the spectrum (4 or higher). All were stable five years after the war's end. But it is interesting to note that the four cases with scores of 4 or better had little in common. Neither Mozambique nor Namibia was an identity conflict, but both East Timor and Kosovo were. Mozambique, Namibia, and East Timor were long-lasting, low-intensity conflicts; Kosovo was short. Kosovo, East Timor, and Namibia were wars over territory; Mozambique was not. Settlements in Namibia, East Timor, and Kosovo included territorial autonomy provisions, while the settlement in Mozambique did not. Moreover, no factor or set of factors systematically distinguishes the cases with scores of 4 or better from those with lower scores. Lacking a clear understanding of the causal mechanisms behind the correlations offered in the quantitative literature, we still know little about the circumstances under which external peacebuilding interventions are likely to lead to durable peace and even less about the propensity for successful democratization.

## War-Related Variables and Democratization Outcomes

The literature we have just discussed focuses almost exclusively on peace as the outcome. Can we reasonably expect that factors that are conducive to peace will similarly affect democratic outcomes?

As we noted earlier, peace is a necessary but insufficient condition for postwar democratization. But democracy is more demanding than peace. Unlike simple peace, which can be imposed by incapacitating belligerents, democratization requires active, sustained participation by domestic political elites. And democratization is arguably more demanding in terms of confidence building than simple peace, defined as the absence of violent conflict. The interposition of a superior force can stop two sides from fighting; democracy, meanwhile, requires a leap of faith by actors who must tolerate a degree of mutual dependence on their erstwhile enemy.

Moreover, democratization is an iterative process. Democratic politics provides political actors with many opportunities to reinforce or undermine the foundations of the system. At least for the first few electoral cycles (fifteen to twenty years), successful democratization demands that political actors regularly renew their commitment to democracy at innumerable choice points both during and between election periods. After the first election, this will typically have to happen without the aid of a significant external presence.

Because local actors have so many opportunities to renege on their commitment to democratic politics, confidence building, enforcement, and predictability become even more important than they are for building peace. A sizeable military imbalance at the end of the war—with the extreme case being military victory—is likely to undermine the weaker side's confidence in its opponent and diminish chances for democracy. On the other hand, written peace agreements, power-sharing institutions, a credible external guarantor, and fewer hostile factions might all contribute to boosting local actors' confidence in one another and in the likelihood that cooperation will pay off and that breaking the rules will be punished.

In the rest of this section we examine the intuition linking each of the variables from Table 3.1 to postconflict democratic outcomes. Taking the variables from Table 3.1 in turn, we assume that high-intensity war, a larger number of factions, and identity conflict are all likely to reduce mutual confidence between former adversaries and cause them to demand more in terms of security guarantees from external guarantors.

We might expect that high-intensity conflicts would increase the confidence gap and require stronger guarantees from an external power. The same might be expected in identity wars. If conflict is organized along identity lines, democratic politics may follow suit, producing rigid cleavage lines rather than the shifting alliances that are believed to underlie successful durable democracy. Wars in which there are numerous rebel factions present problems of coordination and cooperation between factions and may require more skillful intervention from a well-trusted or powerful external guarantor.

However, our evidence shows that, contrary to expectations, these war variables do not have a systematic, direct effect on democratic outcomes. Table 3.1 shows that, in the cases that rated best in terms of democracy (Namibia, Mozambique, East Timor, and Macedonia), these war-related variables produce no consistent impact. Two of the democratic cases were identity-based conflicts; three lasted more than two decades; and one lasted less than a year. Only two ranked in the top four in terms of intensity measured either in terms of deaths or displacements. (Look again at Table 3.1.)

The fourth war-related variable from Table 3.1, war duration, could have either positive or negative effects on the chances for successful democratization. A longer war might lead to entrenched mistrust, or a protracted war might produce conflict fatigue, lowering each side's resistance to compromise. In our sample, all three cases whose conflict duration was above the sample mean of 9.9 years—East Timor, Mozambique, and Namibia—succeeded in building postwar democracies. However, so did Macedonia, whose conflict lasted less than one year.

Table 3.1 also includes two variables dealing with war settlement provisions: whether the war ended in military victory and whether there are provisions for power sharing. According to the literature, wars ending in military victory are more likely to produce stable settlements. However, there is reason to believe that wars ending in military victory will be less likely to proceed toward democratization. Victors have few incentives to share power with the opposition, and opposition trust in their domestic counterparts will be very weak. "Victor's justice" is more likely than genuine efforts at tolerance or reconciliation. The confidence gap, in other words, will be considerable. Though military victory might increase the chances of durable peace, it seems unlikely to be a democratic peace.

We have one case ending in clear military victory: Rwanda. Here the results seem to support our expectation of a nondemocratic outcome. However, results are mixed in the other cases, all of which ended in negotiated settlements. None of our stable, democratic cases ended in military victory. This wide range of outcomes highlights the complex relationships between factors affecting the success of postwar democratization efforts. Given the infrequency of negotiated settlements of civil wars over the last 100 years and their near ubiquity since 1990, it may be that the way a war is settled is primarily due to the preferences of external actors and/or global trends and may be a less meaningful predictor of postwar political outcomes.[26]

The literature also produces an expectation of greater stability in cases that end in territorial division. Territorial power sharing would be expected to alleviate threats to domestic political elites' physical security and political and economic power, at least for the rebel side. Four of our cases resulted in some degree of territorial autonomy for one of the warring sides: Bosnia, East Timor, Kosovo, and Namibia. Two of these cases, Namibia and East Timor, were stable and democratic five years after war's end. Bosnia and Kosovo were both stable but undemocratic. This suggests that power sharing alone does not guarantee successful democratization.

In short, we find no systematic linkage between the characteristics of war—as measured by intensity, number of hostile factions, and the underlying cleavage—and democratic outcomes. Nor do we find evidence to support

**TABLE 3.2.** Initial adoption costs of democracy.

| Case country | Domestic political actors | Perceived physical security threat to domestic elites posed by democracy | Goal | Threat to domestic elites' main goal posed by democracy | Domestic elites' need for international legitimation or support by peacebuilders to achieve major goal | Domestic elites' fear of direct sanctions for resisting democratization | Overall assessment of adoption cost at beginning of mission |
|---|---|---|---|---|---|---|---|
| Namibia | SWAPO | Low | Independence | None | High | High | Low |
| East Timor | FRETILIN | Low | Independence | None | High | Low | Low |
| Mozambique | Renamo | Low | Domestic and international legitimacy | None | High | High | Low |
| | Frelimo | Low | Retain power | None | Low | High | |
| Macedonia | Albanian opposition | Low | Equality | None | High | High | Low |
| | Government | Low | EU inclusion | None | High | High | |
| Kosovo | Kosovo Albanian elite | Medium | Autonomy/ independence | None | High | Low | Low |
| | Serb minority | High | | | | | |
| Bosnia | Serbs | Medium | Preserve RS | Medium | High | Low | Medium |
| | Croats | Medium | Max. ethnic autonomy | Medium | High | Low | |
| | Bosniaks | Medium | Preserve BiH | Low | High | Low | |
| Tajikistan | UTO | Low | Gain a share in power | Low | None | None | High |
| | Government | Low | Retain power | Low | None | None | |
| Rwanda (pre-1994) | FAR | High | Retain power | High | Medium | Medium | High |
| | RPF | High | Take power | Low | High | Medium | |
| Rwanda (post-1994) | RPF | Medium | Retain power | High | High | Low | High |
| | Ex-FAR | High | Regain power | High | n/a | Low | |
| Afghanistan | Government | High | Retain power | Medium | High | Low | High |

the idea that power sharing promotes democracy. It seems that any of these factors may be associated with democratic outcomes or with undemocratic ones. This leads us to our central hypothesis: that war characteristics matter to democratic outcomes because they influence domestic political elites' calculations regarding the costs and benefits of adopting democracy. Table 3.2 summarizes adoption costs in our cases.

## War Variables, Adoption Costs, and Democratic Outcomes

### Lowest adoption costs

War characteristics affect primarily the first two considerations in Table 2.1: threats to the physical security of domestic political elites and threats to the achievement of their primary goal. The third consideration, which is a measure of peacebuilder leverage at the outset of the intervention, is influenced more heavily by the factors discussed in the next three chapters, namely aid, mission footprint, and region.

Domestic political actors' low adoption costs in Namibia, East Timor, Macedonia, Mozambique, and Kosovo reflect the fact that elites in each case had little to fear from embracing democracy. These cases varied widely in terms of the causes, duration, and intensity of their conflicts. The terms of war termination also varied across cases. In some cases, there were provisions for power sharing or diffusion, through decentralization in Macedonia and territorial division in Kosovo and East Timor. There were no such provisions in Namibia or Mozambique, however. Similarly, the set includes identity conflicts as well as conflicts over territory, all of which suggest that these factors by themselves had little to do with the positive democratic outcome. The single war-related variable that was common across all five cases was that in each conflict there was but a single important armed opposition faction.

What accounts for the fact that democracy posed little risk to domestic political actors in each of these five cases? First, the characteristics of the war and the way it ended contributed to low democracy adoption costs in each case, despite variation in war characteristics and settlement terms. Most importantly, the security threat to domestic political elites at the end of the war was minimized, though for different reasons in each case. In Namibia and East Timor, the wars were essentially wars for independence, and once domestic political elites emerged victorious, they no longer faced a political opposition, as the ancien régime had collapsed. In Kosovo and Macedonia, the massive presence of peacebuilders provided ample security guarantees. And, in each case, there was only a single armed opposition faction to deal with, which simplified commitment problems. All of these conflicts ended through negotiation rather than victory. By war's end, both sides had some experience in bargaining with one another, and neither side was strong enough to impose its will on the other. Based on the official roles provided for external peacebuilders and on domestic political elites' previous experience with these actors, external actors offered reasonably credible commitments to enforce the rules of the game in each of these cases.

Second, in none of these cases did democracy threaten the primary objectives of domestic political elites. On the contrary, democratization was a necessary step toward the achievement of these goals. All of these countries were highly dependent on international support to achieve their primary political objective, which included independence or autonomy for Namibia, East Timor, and Kosovo; eventual EU membership and greater political inclusion at home for domestic political elites in Macedonia; and political recognition for Renamo and continued donor support for Frelimo in Mozambique. In each of these cases, external guarantors played a critical and positive role, and in each case external guarantors conditioned their support on a democratic political settlement.

In Namibia, international acceptance and support for SWAPO as the legitimate representative of the Namibian people was essential to ending South African rule there. The transition depended on intensive diplomatic involvement by Western governments and the United Nations, who justified their intervention as bringing democratic self-rule to the region. As Reno points out, "Central to SWAPO strategy was securing and then increasing international diplomatic support for its position as the sole legitimate majority rule rebel organization in Namibia; this strategy eventually led to a UN-supervised election in November 1989 and independence in March 1990."[27] Power for SWAPO was "a prize that they won in the voting booth rather than on the battlefield."[28]

In Kosovo the primary objective of domestic political elites was territorial autonomy and protection from interference by former Yugoslavia, and in both Kosovo and Macedonia it was the promise of eventual inclusion in the European Union. In each of these cases, success rested on the goodwill of external guarantors who made democratization an explicit and central condition for their support. Heavily aid-dependent Mozambique, as well as Kosovo and East Timor, required the active and long-term financial backing of donor countries who were heavily invested in the peace process.[29]

Thus domestic political elites in three of these countries—Namibia, Mozambique, and Macedonia—had reason to fear sanctions from the international community if they resisted democratization. In Namibia, independence was tied to democratization, as was peace in heavily aid-dependent Mozambique. Domestic political actors in these countries had good reason to believe peacebuilder threats to condition aid and international support on democracy. This threat was no longer credible by the time East Timor and Kosovo began their peacebuilding processes. However, domestic elites in these cases saw other factors weighing in favor of democracy. Notable among these was their expectation of electoral success.

In East Timor as in Namibia, the main opposition was rendered irrelevant by the peace settlement. The dominant parties that remained saw elections as central to their legitimation and an easy victory. Moreover, in both cases the countries' postindependence leaders had been engaged in liberation struggles that championed democratic processes. In Kosovo the situation was similar. The small Serbian minority for the most part boycotted the first elections in 2000 and 2001, and the main contest was between Kosovar Albanian parties, for whom elections provided legitimacy and a likely share of political power.

In Macedonia and Mozambique, too, the major domestic political actors on both sides claimed to be more democratic than their rivals. To be seen as supporting democracy was a key part of their international and domestic legitimation. In Mozambique, both Renamo and the ruling Frelimo party sought to cast themselves as the true champions of democratization. Macedonia had been democratic for nearly a decade prior to the outbreak of conflict in 2001. And provisions for local self-governance and the redrawing of municipal boundaries to favor greater self-governance in minority-dominated regions gave ethnic Albanian politicians incentive to compete effectively in electoral politics. Thus, in each case, domestic political actors who were in a position to act as spoilers believed they had a high chance of electoral success.

### Highest Adoption Costs

Rwanda, Tajikistan, and Afghanistan were at the high end of the range of adoption costs. In Tajikistan and Afghanistan, the war left multiple warring factions in a position to threaten domestic political elites who had laid down arms. In Rwanda, the RPF associated political competition with the outbreak of genocidal conflict. Moreover, these leaders still faced threats from hostile armed groups just across the border.

As in the five cases with low adoption costs, here again the intensity of these conflicts varied. In terms of other war characteristics, they were similar, however. All three conflicts were relatively short, though in Afghanistan and Rwanda the conflicts can be viewed as the most recent episode in a string of violent conflicts extending back several decades. All three wars revolved to some extent around communal identity. Perhaps most pertinent is the fact that, in each of these conflicts, the war's conclusion left belligerent factions in a position from which to threaten domestic political elites. In the case of Rwanda, genocidaires sought refuge in neighboring Zaire, from which they launched attacks on Rwandan territory.

Moreover, unlike the cases with low adoption costs, the primary goals of key domestic actors did not depend on compliance with democracy. Nor was significant financial support conditioned on domestic actors' embrace of democratic ideals. Instead, what distinguishes these cases with high adoption costs is that external guarantors did not have the requisite incentives on hand (positive or negative) to induce domestic political elites to accept the costs of the postwar democratic settlement. In addition, in two of these cases (Tajikistan and Afghanistan), multiple hostile factions made it more difficult to coordinate implementation of various agreements on disarmament, reintegration, and the distribution of economic resources and political positions, thus raising the costs of compliance for these factions.[30]

Finally, these cases were marked by the absence of consistent, credible external guarantors. While international involvement in Afghanistan's peace process was intense, external actors failed to send a consistent and clear signal that democratization was a high priority, notwithstanding their initial organization of elections. External actors failed to punish local actors who did not comply with democratization or other key aspects of the agreement. This is hardly surprising, given peacebuilders' proliferating goals and soaring ambitions for Afghanistan. Indeed, in the words of Nixon and Whitty, "Afghanistan became the proving ground of a multifaceted effort that encapsulated regime change, stabilization, counter-terrorism, reconstruction and humanitarian relief, counter-narcotics, statebuilding and democratization all at once."[31]

Tajikistan's postwar political settlement was designed for stability rather than democracy. As Matveeva points out, "The agreement reduced open political competition, weakened the accountability of elites, and led to an increased informal rivalry for intergroup resource allocation, but also provided a mechanism to reach intergroup consensus behind the scenes, as long as elites groups retained bargaining power."[32] The involvement of Western powers and Russia in postconflict peace operations weakened the leverage of prodemocracy external actors. Western powers involved in peacebuilding simply ended up deferring to Russia, which "was mostly interested in stability rather than in democracy or justice," as Matveeva points out.[33] Thus, in Tajikistan as in Afghanistan, domestic political elites had the least to gain and most to lose if they chose to play by the rules because they had little confidence that, if they did so, others would not take advantage of their good faith.

Rather than negative enforcement power, Rwanda's external guarantor had only positive incentives to offer, which only came into play gradually. Military victory gave the RPF little incentive to compromise its monopoly on political power or to expand patronage networks to include an enemy that had perpetrated genocide on the ethnic group the RPF represented. Moreover, the genocide and the lingering presence of Hutu militias in the neighboring Democratic Republic of Congo gave credence to the government's claims that democracy and the demilitarization of politics would constitute an unacceptable threat to the nation's security, as well as to that of the RPF.[34]

Virtually the only leverage available to external peacebuilders was Rwanda's dependency on aid for economic survival. Although donors did not make aid strictly conditional on democratization, aid dependency ultimately did (after the genocide) constrain the Rwandan government's ability to blatantly violate the postwar political dispensation. However, in the first stage of the conflict (1991–1993), poor understanding of the real political dynamics in Rwanda and the weak international peacekeeping mission led to the collapse of the peace process and the genocide.[35]

## Bosnia: Variation in Adoption Costs over Time and across Issue Areas

Bosnia is an intermediary and particularly interesting case for our model. The most important legacy of the war was the fact that the settlement depended on the inclusion of three highly mistrustful ethnic factions in a complex web of power-sharing arrangements. At roughly four years, Bosnia's was a relatively short war, and in terms of intensity falls just above the sample mean (look again at Table 3.1). It was an identity conflict that ended in territorial division. External guarantors were given unprecedented powers to enforce the settlement.

However, the war left in place three highly mistrustful ethnonational factions—formerly warring parties—each of whom demanded a share of political power as a condition to end the war. The delicate balance created by a highly complex constitutional arrangement to guarantee power sharing, combined with a contrasting message that called on parties to downplay ethnic differences in elections, left the three primary domestic actors feeling that a full commitment to democracy posed potential threats both to their own security and to the achievement of their respective primary goals (an ethnic homeland in the case of the Croats and Serbs and the preservation of Bosnia's territorial integrity for the Bosniaks).

In Bosnia, the relative leverage enjoyed by domestic political elites and external peacebuilders shifted over time and across issue areas. In addition, the fact that sovereignty was formally shared between domestic political elites and external peacebuilders created considerable ambiguity. Officially, the Republic of Bosnia was a sovereign nation, but after 1997 an external actor, the Office of the High Representative, was empowered to overrule the decisions of Bosnia's governing institutions, pass legislation it deemed necessary to implement the Dayton Peace Accord, and remove elected officials from office. Shared sovereignty made it difficult for domestic political elites to assess and predict adoption costs across time and issue areas.[36]

So too did the erratic priorities of external peacebuilders, whose focus shifted between breaking the political monopoly of the ethnically based dominant parties, dismantling the patronage networks and economic monopolies established during the war, and empowering and protecting minorities. At times, refusing to embrace democratic politics constituted a threat to the political power monopoly of Bosnian Serbs or Croats, while at others it bolstered their political power. As long as the ethnic nationalist parties could command sufficient loyalty, fear, or patronage to win elections, compliance with democracy did not threaten their political power monopoly. So long as they maintained the ability to win elections, they could also maintain habits of lucrative informal predation, at least until international authorities began to focus on privatization and anticorruption measures. But when the international authorities began to remove politicians from party lists or political office for making statements that contradicted the Dayton Peace Agreement, they threatened elite access to political power and, indirectly, to economic power because winning office meant controlling state resources that could be channeled to individual or party coffers.

Moreover, Bosnia's complex constitutional arrangements created different incentive structures for local actors in the Federation of Bosnia and Herzegovina and in the Serb Republic. Bosnian Serb politicians professed fears for the security of their co-ethnics should the Serb Republic lose its status as a separate entity under the Republic of Bosnia. They depended on the support of the international community (and its adherence to the Dayton Peace Agreement) to uphold the status of the Serb Republic and to keep it from being dismantled. While the Dayton Agreement guaranteed the republic's existence, it also required its democratization, putting Serbian politicians in a bind. Bosnian Croat politicians from HDZ (the Croatian Democratic Union) and other ethnic nationalist parties, on the other hand, felt they had little to lose by resisting the democratization agenda in protest at their treatment as a "minority" without an entity of their own.[37]

## Conclusion

This chapter has demonstrated that the characteristics of civil wars do not directly or systematically affect the likelihood of postwar democracy. The same is true for settlement characteristics, such as whether the war ended in military victory for one side or whether there were territorial power-sharing provisions.

Instead, the impact of these characteristics is mediated by domestic political elites' calculations of adoption costs—the price exacted by democratic politics. Democratization has been an intrinsic part of peacebuilding efforts since the end of the Cold War, and domestic elites' rejection of the democratization agenda could put material support or legitimation by the international community in jeopardy. Depending on their goals for the postconflict period and on their perceptions of their security risks, domestic political elites were more or less motivated to embrace democracy.

The evidence from our cases suggests that democratic outcomes were more likely where domestic political elites did not see democratization as a threat to their security or to the achievement of their substantive goals. War characteristics contributed to these calculations in several ways. Most important were the circumstances under which the war ended. Where armed groups still posed a security threat, as in Rwanda, or where neighboring countries offered support for factions whose commitment to the democratic peace agreement was in question (as in Bosnia, Kosovo, and Afghanistan), the perceived cost of democracy was high.

Where local actors were highly dependent on international support or legitimation to achieve their postconflict goals, they were more likely to accept democratization, particularly if they had reason to believe that this support would be withdrawn if local actors strayed from the democratic agenda. Domestic political elites were highly dependent on international actors for support in wars for independence or secession. Here the nature of the war clearly mattered.

These conditions combined to produce low adoption costs in Mozambique, Namibia, and Macedonia. In Mozambique, for example, both of the former belligerents were dependent on external actors for financial support and domestic legitimation; they had reason to believe that donors would withdraw support if democracy were rejected. Namibia and East Timor relied on international intervention to broker transitions to independence, and in Macedonia domestic elites sought something only the international community could offer: security for both parties and EU inclusion for the state. In Kosovo, too, domestic elites were dependent on external peacebuilders to achieve the postwar goal of autonomy and ultimately independence from the former Yugoslavia.

In Bosnia, Rwanda, and Afghanistan, domestic elites likewise depended on the support and involvement of international actors to achieve their goals. However, democracy itself posed a threat to goal achievement as well as to the security of domestic political elites. In each of these cases, ruling elites faced security threats that external actors had not been willing or able to address. Democratic politics also posed potential threats to elites' primary postwar goals. In each of these cases, local elites' ability to retain political power (Afghanistan) or vindicate wartime objectives (autonomy for ethnic Serbs and Croats in Bosnia, security for Tutsis in Rwanda) was undermined by democracy. In Tajikistan, domestic political elites were primarily dependent on external actors (the Russian-dominated peace force) who were not interested in democracy promotion.

Our research suggests the need to reexamine two critical assumptions that run through much of the literature on postconflict peacebuilding. The first concerns how and why war characteristics are likely to affect the chances of peace and democracy after a conflict has ended. The second concerns how and to what degree external actors can affect postconflict state-building outcomes.

First, we have found that war characteristics such as intensity, duration, and whether the conflict is identity based do not have a direct impact on the outcomes in our cases. Neither do they appear to factor significantly in domestic political elites' cost-benefit analysis of adopting democracy after the war. The single common denominator across successful (stable, democratic) cases is the number of hostile factions. This makes sense because fewer factions may lower coordination costs and make confidence building easier.

Second, although the role of external actors is indeed critical, the importance of this factor is harder to estimate than previously imagined. The civil war literature has identified the credibility of external guarantors as important to peacebuilding outcomes. Recasting peacebuilding outcomes as a function of adoption costs (which are in turn affected by interaction with peacebuilders at the bargaining table), we find support for this assertion. But as we discuss in detail in the chapters on aid and mission footprint, assessing whether a third-party guarantor is credible is both more complex than the literature suggests and unlikely to be decisive itself in determining whether local actors embrace democracy. Credibility in an external guarantor is a contingent concept. It depends not only on the force, money, or mandate of a peace mission but also on the relationships established between the external guarantor (and/or its component members) and various local actors before, during, and after the conflict. Moreover, credibility may vary both across time and across issue areas.

Lastly, we cannot safely assume that the presence of an external power that is willing and able to enforce democratic rules will be likely to improve the chances that local actors will embrace those rules. Indeed, local actors may in some cases embrace the rules only if they believe they will not actually be forced to abide by them (that is, if they believe they will be able to manipulate the rules in practice to ensure outcomes favorable to themselves.) But a given actor benefits in this scenario only if that actor is uniquely exempted from the rules while others are made to follow them. Therefore, we assume that adoption costs are raised if actors initially believe, or come to find, that an external guarantor cannot or will not enforce the rules evenly across the board.

The concept of multiple conjunctural causation frames our findings. This chapter has focused on the impact of war characteristics on postconflict democratization. War characteristics factored into domestic political elites' assessments of the costs and benefits of embracing democracy, but in each case it was the interaction of these factors with one another and with other forces that determined domestic political elites' reactions.

What mattered most was whether domestic political elites needed international support to guarantee their own security or to achieve their primary goals. War characteristics influenced this calculation. Somewhat surprisingly, however, the most commonly examined characteristics did not appear to factor highly in this regard. These include, most importantly, the intensity and duration of the war and whether it revolved around identity cleavages. Among the conventional war characteristics, only the number of hostile factions appeared to be somewhat important.[38] More decisive was whether the balance of power between belligerents or the existence of potential spoilers at the end of the war left domestic political elites feeling vulnerable and whether achieving one's war aims required the cooperation of the international community.

According to this perspective, democratization is primarily a goal of external actors that may also be of instrumental value to domestic political elites. As such, democracy triumphs only when it serves the ends of domestic political elites or when peacebuilders can offset adoption costs with leverage. The constellations of factors that contribute to peacebuilder leverage are the subject of the next three chapters.

# 4    The Mission Footprint

## Is More Better?

Does the "footprint" of a peace mission have an impact on its democratic outcome? Do factors such as the number of troops and civilian staff, resource expenditures, mission duration, and the range of competencies that external actors adopt increase the probability of a successful postwar democratic transition? In other words, is more better?

It is tempting to assume that it is. According to our understanding of peacebuilding as an interaction between peacebuilders and domestic elites, peacebuilder leverage is an important determinant of the final outcome. The higher this leverage or the stronger the incentives peacebuilders are able to provide, the more likely it is that domestic elites will adopt democratic policies. Hence it seems reasonable that a more intrusive mission should result in a more democratic regime. It is not surprising that the public discourse and many practitioners attribute the modest democratic outcomes of many recent peacebuilding operations to a lack of commitment, scarce resources, and short time horizons.

The scholarly literature, however, is more cautious. Case studies on highly intrusive missions in Bosnia, Afghanistan, Kosovo, and East Timor provide little evidence that their massive footprint led to a democratic outcome.[1] This is also true of comparative studies that examine the impact of peacebuilding.[2]

To the contrary, some authors have even argued that intrusive missions can undermine democracy, creating a situation in which means vitiate the ends.[3] For example, the United Nations has been criticized for its attempt to establish peace, security, and ultimately democracy in East Timor and Kosovo by means of "colonialism in a new guise."[4]

In this chapter we empirically investigate the association between mission footprint and outcome with regard to democracy. We find that a larger footprint does not necessarily bring more democracy; it typically brings less. We identify two causal mechanisms that account for this. First, where the adoption cost of democracy is atypically high, even well-resourced missions struggle to offset these costs and shift the political regime toward democracy. Second, we find that highly intrusive missions can actually negate the democratization project. This is because greater mission intrusiveness and external tutelage per se generate domestic resistance against the peacebuilders.

We proceed as follows. To delineate the concept of "mission footprint," we first discuss measurements for the various dimensions of a peacebuilding mission. We argue that important characteristics of a mission include its duration, operation and management costs (both civilian and military), and the number of military and civilian personnel on the ground. These are straightforward dimensions of a mission that can be readily measured. We use these measurements to describe a mission's *scale*.

The footprint of a mission depends not only on its scale but to an even greater extent on its content. While it is important to know the number of people who work in a country for a given cost and a certain length of time, we also need to account for their ambition and mandate to restructure the political and social order of the host country. In other words, we also need a measurement for the mission's *scope*. We describe one such measurement based on the policy fields in which a mission is engaged. By combining the measurements for scale and scope, we can then construct a composite measure of mission *footprint*. Equipped with these measurements, we are able to present some descriptive statistics.

We then address the most salient question: Do missions with a heavier footprint lead to better results than missions with a lighter footprint? This question has immense policy implications and is therefore hotly debated. Our data allow us to infuse the debate with a dose of objectivity. Using the composite measure for "footprint," we fail to find a clear relationship between the footprint of a mission and its democratic outcome. A heavier footprint appears to have little bearing on democracy.

In the final section of the chapter, we closely examine our subsample of cases to identify causal mechanisms that might explain this finding.

## Measuring the Footprint
## of Peacebuilding Operations

An important dimension of a peacebuilding mission is its deployed resources. These consist of management and operation costs, the number of personnel, and finally the duration of the mission. We construct a measure of the scale of the mission by combining the data on expenditures, personnel, and duration. The *scale* of a peace mission is calculated as the product of its duration, personnel, and resources, divided by the size of the host population. Table 4.1 summarizes the scale of recent peacebuilding missions.

But the scale of a mission describes only one aspect of its footprint. Another is peacebuilder authority to make political decisions across various policy fields. This we call the *scope* of the mission. Because this is a difficult concept to measure, most quantitative studies either ignore this aspect or use the type of the UN mandate as a proxy. Because our approach is based on a small-*n* comparative framework, we construct a more sophisticated measure of scope based on empirical observation. We look at eight important policy fields and assess peacebuilders involvement. The coding is binary. We code a 1 when the peacebuilders are decisively involved and a 0 when they are not. The more policy fields are decisively shaped by the peacebuilders, the greater the mission scope and the greater their potential leverage to initiate democratic reform. We briefly describe these policy fields below: Table 4.2 gives on overview of the scope of recent peacebuilding missions.

1. *Did external actors enforce peace with military power?* Peace missions with a robust Chapter VII mandate are authorized to use force in self-defense but also to protect civilians and to achieve the objectives of their mandate. We code peace enforcement as present when there is a Chapter VII mandate, a sufficient number of adequately armed troops, and a general readiness to use force to achieve mission objectives.

2. *Did external actors participate in executive policing?* Executive policing refers to the maintenance of public order and security by international police as well as judiciary police, strategic and criminal intelligence, and administrative police. It is a short-term effort to provide law enforcement where there would otherwise be a serious gap in domestic security. Without law enforcement, spoilers could easily destabilize the fragile democratization process. We code executive policing as present when the mission is mandated to police and genuinely

**TABLE 4.1.** Scale of peacebuilding missions, all nineteen cases.

| Peace mission | Duration | Duration (months) | Resources in thousands USD (first five years) | Maximum total personnel: civilian and military | Population | Scale |
|---|---|---|---|---|---|---|
| Central African Republic | April 1998– Feb 2000 | 23 | 120,970 | 1,612 | 3,631,000 | 1.24 |
| Croatia | Jan 1996– Jan 1998 | 25 | 197,625 | 5,349 | 1,386,5000 | 1.91 |
| Macedonia | Aug 2001– June 2006 | 59 | 66,500 | 3,500 | 2,027,000 | 6.77 |
| Tajikistan | Nov 1997– July 2007 | 117 | 57,000 | 28,320 | 6,280,000 | 30.07 |
| Angola | May 1995– June 1997 | 26 | 481,080 | 7,302 | 12,450,000 | 7.34 |
| Mozambique | Oct 1992– Dec 1994 | 27 | 492,600 | 7,213 | 14,861,000 | 6.46 |
| Rwanda | Mar 1993– Mar 1996 | 37 | 453,900 | 5,645 | 5,752,000 | 16.48 |
| Burundi | June 2004– Dec 2006 | 31 | 700,180 | 5,755 | 7,255,000 | 17.22 |
| Namibia | April 1989– March 1990 | 12 | 416,200 | 8,493 | 1,388,000 | 30.56 |
| Haiti | Sept 1994– June 1996 | 22 | 1,369,975 | 24,943 | 7,878,000 | 95.43 |
| Cambodia | March 1992– Nov 1993 | 21 | 2,299,073 | 22,000 | 10,372,000 | 102.41 |
| Democratic Republic of Congo | May 2001– ongoing | 110 | 3,773,112 | 17,389 | 58,326,000 | 123.74 |
| Cote d'Ivoire | July 2003– ongoing | 84 | 2,794,520 | 13,191 | 18,532,000 | 167.09 |
| Sierra Leone | July 1999– Dec 2005 | 78 | 2,720,000 | 18,329 | 4,545,000 | 855.60 |
| Liberia | Sep 2003– ongoing | 82 | 2,990,374 | 16,664 | 3,449,000 | 1184.75 |
| Afghanistan | Oct 2001– ongoing | 105 | 8,000,000 | 28,905 | 27,770,000 | 874.33 |
| East Timor | June 1999– ongoing | 133 | 2,000,000 | 10,169 | 976,000 | 2,771.47 |
| Bosnia | Dec 1995– ongoing | 175 | 1,940,000 | 56,047 | 3,657,000 | 5,203.16 |
| Kosovo | June 1999– ongoing | 133 | 2,000,000 | 61,020 | 1,764,000 | 9,201.43 |

SOURCES: Resources: UN documents, case study authors, authors' own research.
Maximum total personnel: Case study authors, UN documents, SIPRI Multilateral Peace Missions Database, authors' own research.
Population: UN World Population Prospects, 2010 edition, retrieved on August 3, 2012, from http://esa.un.org/wpp/unpp/panel_population.htm.

**TABLE 4.2.** Scope of peace missions.

| Peace mission | Peace enforcement | Executive policing | Security sector reform | Executive powers | Legislative powers | Constitution | Judicial powers | Economic policies | Scope factor |
|---|---|---|---|---|---|---|---|---|---|
| Tajikistan | 0 | 0 | 0 | 0 | 0 | 0 | 0 | 0 | 0 |
| Central African Republic | 0 | 0 | 0 | 0 | 0 | 0 | 0 | 0 | 0 |
| Angola | 0 | 0 | 0 | 0 | 0 | 0 | 0 | 1 | 0.125 |
| Macedonia | 0 | 0 | 0 | 0 | 0 | 1 | 0 | 0 | 0.125 |
| Mozambique | 0 | 0 | 0 | 0 | 0 | 0 | 0 | 1 | 0.125 |
| Rwanda | 0 | 0 | 0 | 0 | 0 | 0 | 0 | 1 | 0.125 |
| Cote d'Ivoire | 1 | 0 | 1 | 0 | 0 | 0 | 0 | 0 | 0.25 |
| Haiti | 1 | 0 | 0 | 0 | 0 | 1 | 0 | 0 | 0.25 |
| Liberia | 1 | 0 | 1 | 0 | 0 | 0 | 0 | 0 | 0.25 |
| Namibia | 0 | 0 | 0 | 1 | 0 | 1 | 0 | 0 | 0.25 |
| Sierra Leone | 1 | 0 | 1 | 0 | 0 | 0 | 0 | 0 | 0.25 |
| Burundi | 1 | 0 | 1 | 0 | 0 | 1 | 0 | 0 | 0.375 |
| Democratic Republic of Congo | 1 | 0 | 1 | 0 | 0 | 1 | 0 | 0 | 0.375 |
| Afghanistan | 1 | 0 | 1 | 0 | 1 | 1 | 0 | 1 | 0.625 |
| Cambodia | 0 | 0 | 0 | 1 | 1 | 1 | 1 | 1 | 0.625 |
| Croatia | 1 | 0 | 0 | 1 | 1 | 1 | 1 | 0 | 0.625 |
| Bosnia | 1 | 0 | 1 | 1 | 1 | 1 | 1 | 1 | 0.875 |
| East Timor | 1 | 1 | 1 | 1 | 1 | 0 | 1 | 1 | 0.875 |
| Kosovo | 1 | 1 | 1 | 1 | 1 | 1 | 1 | 1 | 1 |

engages in this function for at least six months. Only East Timor and Kosovo meet these requirements.

3. *Did external actors engage in Security Sector Reform (SSR)?* We understand SSR in its narrow sense as the restructuring, reform, and training of security forces, primarily the military and/or the police. The objective of SSR is to establish national institutions capable of maintaining order and providing long-term security for the population—a vital aspect of democracy. We code SSR as present when peacebuilders are committed to security sector reforms and allocate resources to it.

4. *Did external actors take on executive powers?* In some missions, peacebuilders take on executive powers and day-to-day responsibilities in areas such as labor and social welfare, trade and industry, education and science, health, agriculture and rural development, environment, transport, spatial development, communications, and culture, youth, and sports. When peace missions assume executive functions, their ability to introduce democratic institutions and practices is—in theory—immense. We code executive powers as present when peacebuilders have a mandate to assume executive powers and execute it, as they do in Cambodia, Croatia, East Timor, Bosnia, and Kosovo.

5. *Did external actors take on legislative powers?* Legislative power signifies the authority to make, amend, and repeal laws or to declare which national laws are applicable in the postconflict state. When external actors assume legislative powers as part of an international interim administration, they frequently do so in the absence of a national legislature. The impact of their powers is significant in the long run because much of this legislation remains in place once they leave. External actors assumed legislative powers in Cambodia, Croatia, Afghanistan, Kosovo, Bosnia, and East Timor.

6. *Did external actors shape the new constitution?* The constitution defines state–society relations, including the powers and limitations of the state and human and civil rights. When external actors help draft the constitution of a state that is emerging from war, they will have an enduring influence on its legal and institutional foundation. External actors primarily want to ensure that the constitution protects basic human rights and international norms. But their involvement also allows them to incorporate standards of democracy and market economics into the document. These may or may not clash with the

cultural tradition of the host country. Peacebuilders decisively shaped the new constitution in Macedonia, Haiti, Namibia, Afghanistan, Burundi, Cote d'Ivoire, the Democratic Republic of Congo, Cambodia, Croatia, Bosnia, East Timor, and Kosovo.

7. *Did external actors take on judicial powers?* External actors assume judicial powers such as the administration of the law, the appointment of international judges who interpret and apply the law, and executive authority to institute legal and judicial reform. Peacebuilders assumed judicial powers in the same countries where they assumed legislative powers: Cambodia, Croatia, Afghanistan, Kosovo, Bosnia, and East Timor.

8. *Did external actors decisively shape economic policies?* Economic and fiscal policies shaped by external decision making include budget formulation, customs and taxation, currency reforms, and, more generally, the initiation of economic liberalization processes. These measures may or may not be linked to the postconflict peacebuilding portfolio. The immense influx of donor money into postconflict states is in itself an intrusion into the economies of these states. Aid dependency and the conditionalities that donors can impose in terms of governance, democracy, and/or market liberalization give external actors an informal but powerful role in policy development and implementation. This factor is coded present if external actors decisively shaped the economy by providing external aid and technical assistance and if they made aid contingent on the government's adoption of economic policies and reforms. This was the case in Angola, Mozambique, Rwanda, Cambodia, Afghanistan, Kosovo, Bosnia, and East Timor.

## Footprint

We now combine our measures of scale and scope into a single indictor for the overall intrusiveness, or "footprint" of the peacebuilding mission:

Footprint = log[scale + (scale * scope)]

Because the distribution of the product of scale and scope is highly skewed, the natural log is used to center the distribution on the median. The raw score of scale is added to the product of scale and scope to avoid missing values in cases where no governmental functions were temporarily executed by external actors and the product of scale and scope is therefore 0 (for example, in Tajikistan.) These footprint scores are to be interpreted as an ordinal measure rather than in absolute terms. Figure 4.1 depicts the footprint of recent peace-building missions.

It can be seen that the missions in Kosovo, Bosnia, East Timor, Afghanistan, and Liberia have had the largest footprint. The missions with the smallest footprint were launched in the Central African Republic, Croatia, Macedonia, and Angola.

The data also show that missions became, by and large, more expensive over time (see Figure 4.2). Earlier missions such as Namibia, Mozambique, Rwanda, and Angola cost much less than later missions. Among the most costly mission are Sierra Leone (1999), the Democratic Republic of Congo (2001), Afghanistan (2002), Cote d'Ivoire (2003), and Liberia (2003). However, the trend is not absolute. Cambodia is an example of a costly early mission, and Macedonia and Burundi are recent examples of relatively cheap missions. The figures reveal a simple truth: Ambitious mandates are costly. For example, the combined costs of the military and civilian components for the missions in Kosovo and Bosnia amounted to roughly US$20 billion over the first five years, primarily attributable to military expenses. East Timor was less costly at about US$2 billion for the first five years, but its budget was still large compared to previous missions in Mozambique, Rwanda, and Namibia, which are estimated to have totaled US$400 to 500 million.

A similar picture can be observed with regard to the duration of the missions (see Figure 4.3). Again, the earlier missions (Namibia, Mozambique,

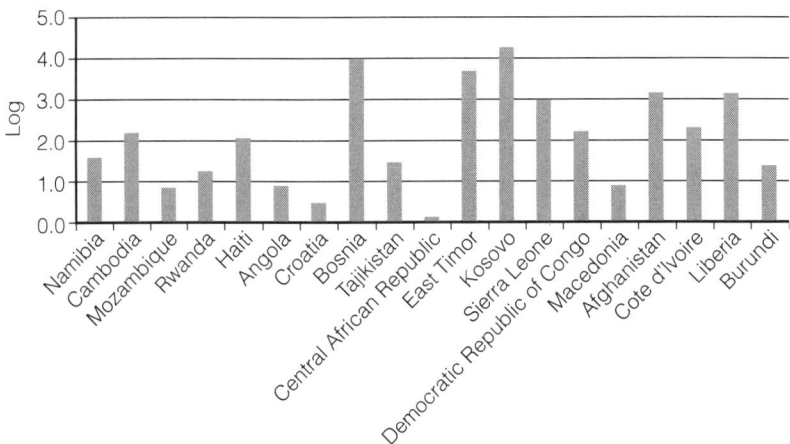

FIGURE 4.1. Mission footprint.

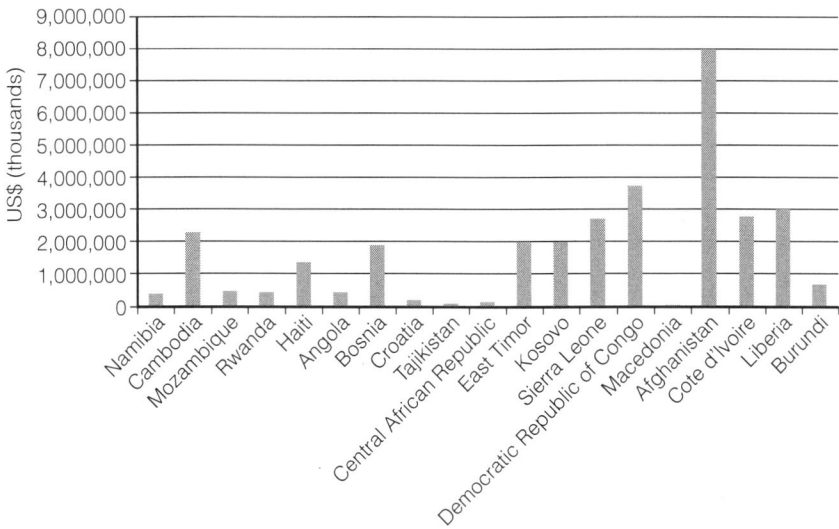

**FIGURE 4.2.** Mission cost.

Rwanda, Haiti, and Angola,) were relatively short. Bosnia was the first of the longer missions. It is ongoing, as are the missions in East Timor, Kosovo, the Democratic Republic of Congo, Afghanistan, Cote d'Ivoire, and Liberia. Again the trend is somewhat ambiguous, as there are also recent missions that have been shorter, such as the Central African Republic, Macedonia, and Burundi. Yet it is clear that, starting with Bosnia, the international community became engaged in an increasing number of very long, intensive missions that have tended to drag on without a clear exit strategy.

Equipped with a reliable and valid measure of the mission footprint, we can now take a look at possible relationships between footprint and democratic outcomes. A correlation test reveals a correlation coefficient of 0.081; hence, the two measures are not correlated. Figure 4.4 shows the position of the countries with regard to democracy and intrusiveness. The chart suggests that, contrary to conventional policy assumptions and practitioner demands for higher commitment and intrusiveness, democratic outcomes do not improve with intrusiveness.

*Why Does a Heavy Footprint Not Always Lead to Democracy?*
Why do more intrusive missions with larger footprints fail to achieve democratic outcomes, and why is it that in some cases a smaller, lighter mission can achieve democracy? To explore these questions, we now turn to a close

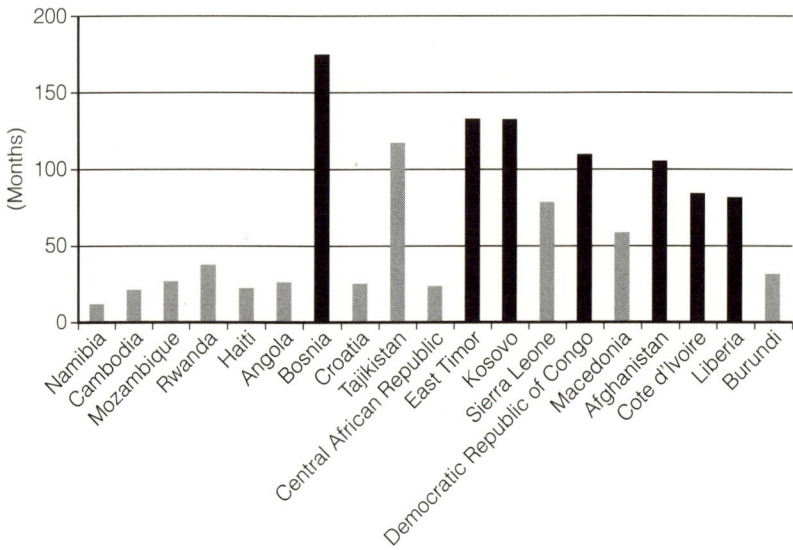

**FIGURE 4.3.** Mission duration.

Black bars represent ongoing missions. Gray bars represent completed missions.

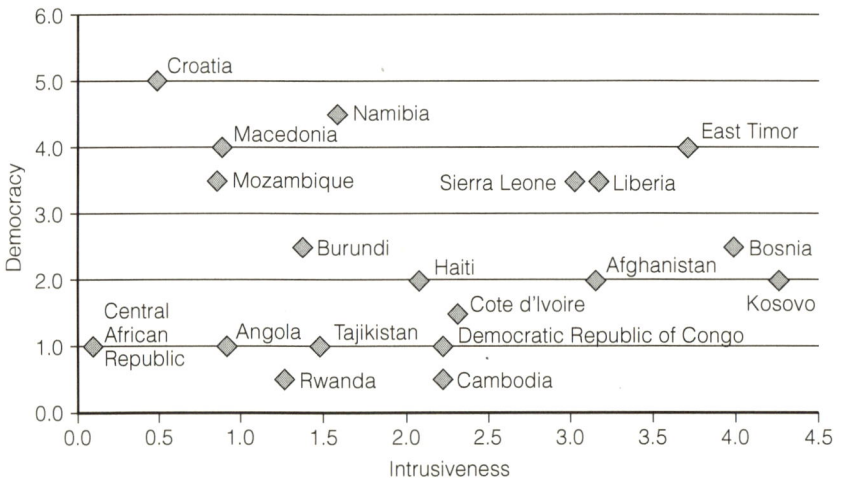

**FIGURE 4.4.** Mission footprint and democracy.

Democracy: Freedom in the world score (reversed, with 6 indicating most democratic and 0 least democratic regime).

|  | Light footprint | Heavy footprint |
|---|---|---|
| **Democratic** (= Electoral democracy) | Macedonia* Namibia* Mozambique* | East Timor* |
| **Nondemocratic** | Rwanda Tajikistan | Afghanistan Kosovo* Bosnia |

Light footprint    Heavy footprint
(= score of 3 or more)

\* cases with low adoption costs

**FIGURE 4.5.** Mission footprint and democracy.

reading of the nine cases in our subsample. Figure 4.5 shows our nine cases, the size of their mission, and the outcome. Relevant to our purpose is the upper left cell, which contains cases that achieved democracy with a small and unintrusive mission, as well as the lower right cell, which contains cases that failed to achieve democracy despite a large and intrusive mission.

The asterisk marks cases for which adoption costs were low (see our discussion in Chapter 3, Table 3.2, pp. 46). As we predicted, all cases in the upper (democratic) cells have low adoption costs. The nondemocratic cases have medium to high adoption costs. Kosovo is an outlier case—it is nondemocratic but has low adoption costs.

These observations suggest that, when adoption costs are high, even a heavy footprint does not lead to democracy. When adoption costs are low, a lighter footprint may be sufficient to foster a democratic outcome. In the next section, we examine our cases to find causal mechanisms that help explain these findings.

## Low Adoption Costs and Sufficient Footprint: East Timor, Macedonia, Mozambique

We begin our discussion by taking a closer look at examples where adoption costs were low and outcomes were democratic. East Timor is a clear case in point; the domestic elite did not associate democratization with a threat to security, popular demand for democracy was high, and the main objective of the domestic elite, independence, could only be achieved with peacebuilder support. Furthermore, the UN interim administration provided ample resources and expertise and acted as a credible guarantor and supporter of the locally inspired democracy. Hence, in East Timor, adoption costs were low, the footprint was large, and peacebuilder leverage was high.

In Namibia, Macedonia, and Mozambique, adoption costs were equally low. In none of these cases did domestic elites perceive democratization to be a security threat, and in each case their prime objective—independence for Namibia, security guarantees, and an end to the hurting stalemate for Mozambique, and EU membership for Macedonia—could only be achieved with peacebuilder support. In contrast to the mission in East Timor, peacebuilders in these three cases brought limited resources. Yet the military component in each case constituted a credible security guarantee in the eyes of domestic elites. Even when missions did not have a robust mandate under Chapter VII of the UN Charter (Namibia and Macedonia), elites thought that the mere presence of military observers would shield them from security threats. The light footprint of these missions proved an adequate support for the preexisting demand for democratization.

## Adoption Costs Outweigh Mission Footprint: Tajikistan and Rwanda

A democratic outcome becomes less likely when adoption costs outweigh the leverage that peacebuilders can muster. Rwanda and Tajikistan exemplify this scenario. In both cases adoption costs were high and the "footprint" of the mission was relatively small. Unsurprisingly, peacebuilder leverage was low, and the status quo prevailed.

In Tajikistan, the appeal of democracy among the Tajik elites and society was limited, mainly because the horrors of civil war in the early 1990s were attributed to failed democratic experiments. While the population craved security and stability, politicians suspected that democracy was a new ideological front and a trigger of new regional separatism. Also, neighboring Russia provided a compelling example of a functioning alternative to democracy. The 25,000 Russian soldiers in Tajikistan provided military muscle for peacekeeping but did not use their considerable leverage to pressure for more democracy. As a result, Tajikistan remains an authoritarian state.

In Rwanda, the political system under Habyarimana in 1990 and the subsequent emergence of extremist forces that led to genocide created in Rwandan society a deep mistrust of democracy, which was viewed as a catalyst of ethnic violence. Popular demand for democratization after the war was therefore low; people instead craved security and reconciliation. Domestic elites feared that democracy could empower an irredentist opposition. The footprint of the international mission was small to medium. One could argue that the peacebuilders possessed substantial potential leverage due to their massive outlays in foreign aid (which did not figure in our definition). Yet, overall, the international community was in a weak bargaining position relative to the new postwar government. In failing to halt the genocide, external actors had lost much of their leverage and were therefore unable to push through democratic reforms against local resistance.

## High Adoption Costs Meet Heavy Footprint: Bosnia, Afghanistan

So far we have discussed cases where the mission footprint generated enough leverage to offset low adoption costs (East Timor, Macedonia, and Mozambique) and cases where adoption costs were high and the footprint of the mission was relatively small, resulting in low peacebuilder leverage (Rwanda and Tajikistan). The outcome—democracy in the former case, perpetuation of the status quo in the latter—is not surprising. We now turn to more complex cases, namely Bosnia and Afghanistan, in which large-footprint missions are confronted with high adoption costs. In many respects, the outcome of these cases differ: Bosnia is a relatively stable state that is de facto governed by international administrators and remains highly dependent on external actors for its economic and political survival. Afghanistan today looks back on a decade of insurgent warfare, defying hopes that the Bonn agreement of 2001 could bring peace and a new political beginning to a war-torn country. What these cases have in common are high adoption costs, a heavy mission footprint, and a lack of democracy. Five years after mission start, both countries were rated "not free" by Freedom House and belong to the underachievers within our sample, with a Freedom House score of 4.5 in Bosnia and 5 in Afghanistan. Why is it that these heavily resourced and highly intrusive missions proved unable to offset adoption costs?

*Bosnia*

The internationally brokered Dayton Accords brought an end to the murderous civil war in Bosnia Herzegovina. The peace treaty covered the cessation of hostilities and foresaw implementation of the agreement through the Office of the High Representative (OHR), a civilian agency granted authority to execute the political blueprint for the building of the state of Bosnia and Herzegovina. The Dayton Accords guaranteed that new state institutions and electoral procedures would reflect the importance of Bosnia's three ethnic constituencies. The agreement thus consolidated the ethnification of politics, determining the interaction between domestic elites and peacebuilders for years to come.

The Dayton Accords were also backed up by the deployment of a massive multinational force. Peacebuilders initially deployed to tiny Bosnia numbered 54,000 soldiers under NATO command.[5] The Stabilization Force (SFOR) took over in 1997 and gradually reduced its numbers. Bosnia also attracted the highest aid flows ever for a peacebuilding mission: According to a study by Open Society, between 1995 and 2000, aid totaled $7–8 billion in humanitarian aid; $10–12 billion in reconstruction, economic, and recovery assistance (including the initial $5.1 billion); and $5–6 billion in other assistance (democratization, media, civil society, and the like) for a grand total of $22–24 billion.[6] The Bosnia mission also had a very strong mandate. The OHR established in 1998 has had such far-reaching plenipotentiary powers that it has often been portrayed as a modern form of colonial rule. For all these reasons, we consider the Bosnian mission to be the second most intrusive mission.

Security fears were to some extent mitigated by the massive peacekeeping force, although hatred, mistrust, and reluctance to cooperate continued to dominate relations between the three major ethnic groups. But what kept adoption costs especially high was the fact that the three ethnic parties to the Dayton Accords used the agreement to legitimate their power within their respective ethnic territories and constituencies. Their main interest lay in safeguarding their power and in maintaining security for their ethnic kin. They were interested neither in transparent democratic structures, nor in ceding power to the central government.[7] This position was at odds with the vision of peacebuilders. For them, the agreement was a means to end civil war in Bosnia and to build a sustainable democratic, federal, and multiethnic state. Because of these mutually exclusive visions, the history of post-Dayton Bosnia is above all one of constant bargaining between ethnic political leaders and the international community, represented most prominently by the OHR. Because the Dayton Accords were vague on many issues, external and internal actors have been in constant negotiation to jointly interpret and implement their criteria.

Due to the very heavy footprint of this mission, peacebuilders were able to use large carrots and large sticks. They contributed huge amounts of development assistance and pointed out that a multiethnic democratic state could eventually become an EU member. On the other hand, peacebuilders could fire public officials, freeze financial assets, or impose travel restrictions. But while the most flagrant obstructions of the Dayton Accords were sanctioned, the Bosnian leadership was by and large quite able to secure and strengthen its political power and to subvert many peacebuilder attempts to institute transparent democratic procedures.

The Bosnian domestic elites did not have to express their resistance through violence: The Implementation Force (IFOR) and SFOR troops had experienced severe direct attacks during the war and were determined not to provoke renewed violence during the peace process. For fear of public uprisings they initially even declined to detain indicted war criminals. This stance later changed when peacebuilders realized that their fear of violence against mission troops and among different ethnic groups was not justified. Thus they have more assertively implemented their mandate and have self-confidently used the Bonn Powers (which included the right to draw up legislation for institution building) to annul legislation drafted by parliament and to dismiss obstructive domestic officials.

In our sample, Bosnia is the only case where peacebuilders actually used some of their leverage, even though they were careful to avoid strained relations with domestic elites. Yet at no time were external funds completely cut off, nor did local parties believe that the international community would leave. Ethnic parties were confident that so long as they did not too obviously work against "the spirit of Dayton," the international community would continue to supply resources for state building while making the unpopular decisions that state elites would rather avoid. In essence, Bosnia and Herzegovina became a protectorate of the international community, whose native institutions worked only if promoted by the political institutions of the protectorate. Peacebuilders were successful in their effort to prevent a recurrence of war, but they were much less successful in implementing their political agenda— despite a willingness to expend vast resources and to deploy a strong military force. Ironically, the Dayton Accords helped establish Bosnia as an association of ethnic fiefdoms. The central government is weak, and political leaders are largely unaccountable for their actions. Bosnia has proved immune to further democratization beyond the level it had achieved shortly after Dayton.

### Afghanistan

The Bonn agreement of 2001 was supposed to end the war in Afghanistan and to pave the way to its peaceful and democratic future. The agreement's explicit goal was to produce a state that would be committed to democracy, social justice, market-led growth, and Islamic values. Hamid Karzai was chosen to partner with the West in this endeavor. In 2002 he became first chairman of a transitional administration and was elected president in 2004.

There is little reason to doubt that Karzai and his team of primarily Western-trained reformers were initially committed to the democratic and liberal vision that the peacebuilders outlined in Bonn. But, as quickly became clear, the cost of adopting democracy was quite high. Afghanistan is a highly fragmented country, and no central government in its modern history has effectively governed the provinces. Rather, state authority has always been based on shifting alliances and patronage networks.[8] Karzai soon realized that he faced a deeply entrenched provincial elite that was apprehensive about liberal peacebuilding. The vision of a democratic, centralized state did not resonate well with power holders in the provinces: tribal leaders, first- and second-tier warlords, and regional strongmen saw the peacebuilders' vision as a threat to their autonomy and fiefdoms.

What is more, many of the regional strongmen and warlords received substantial support from the United States. Warlords who cooperated with the U.S. war on terror received rents, resources, and recognition that strengthened their political power.[9] As one former British diplomat recalled, "After a while, I realized that while I was running around encouraging and cajoling politicians to engage in the Loya Jirga process, the purpose of which was in part to take power back from the warlords, others were running around doling out bribes to buy the loyalty amongst those very same warlords."[10] In addition, because Afghanistan is a very rural country with a volatile security situation, peacebuilders were extraordinarily dependent on provincial elites to help them implement their programs. NGOs rented offices, buildings, and storage facilities from warlords and their relatives, typically at prices far above local standards. They invited local strongmen to visit NGO headquarters, thus conferring on them greater legitimacy. In return, rural elites provided NGOs with protection and allowed them to work in relative safety. International peacebuilders, moreover, possessed little knowledge of the local context and had few opportunities to study it. "Afghanistan lurked behind the high walls that protected us from the 'outside,'" recalled the same former diplomat. Making few trips into rural areas to meet with local leaders, the "thick screen or 'armor plating' and bodyguards . . . separated us from reality."[11]

The result of this dependence was that it gave a heterogeneous group of regional strongmen the capacity to veto many aspects of the peace process. They were strong enough to resist the weak president, and they exploited their strategic position to frustrate peacebuilder plans as well. Most regional elites were status-quo oriented and hijacked various liberal reform efforts, most notably the judiciary, and contrived to outwit an array of poorly coordinated international donors by provoking competition between agencies, thus maximizing their benefits while hindering implementation of real reforms.[12] State ministries routinely and ritualistically mimicked the discourse of Western developmentalism (conditionalities, financial constraint, fiduciary planning, and so on) but demonstrated little follow-through.

As the weakness of the central government vis-à-vis secondary elites became apparent, Karzai relied increasingly on patronage, clientelistic co-optation, and ad hoc alliances to gain influence in the provinces. Karzai found himself caught between peacebuilders, who were demanding liberal reforms, and a powerful secondary elite, who were inclined to defend their autonomy and who could threaten Karzai's political (and likely physical) survival. As Karzai understood the high adoption costs of democracy, he increasingly abandoned his commitment to reforms and progressively relied on clientelistic networks as a means to govern.

Peacebuilders pushed for a more open democratic process, urged Karzai to live up to his commitments, and encouraged him to implement decisive measures against corruption, the opium economy, patronage, and clientelism. Although Karzai and his team now only paid lip service to reformist agendas, peacebuilders continued to back their chosen president, lending him political support and supplying him with generous amounts of aid money. Overall, donors pledged US$46 billion in Tokyo (2002), Berlin (2004), London (2006), and Paris (2008), never actually applying conditionality.[13] Donors pointed to the constraining power of secondary elites to justify support for the derailed democratic peacebuilding process, suggesting that Karzai could only cautiously and gradually implement reforms. They also insisted that abandoning Afghanistan would seriously jeopardize global security.

Five years after the Bonn agreement, however, it was clear that the interaction between peacebuilders and the Karzai government was strained and that the unraveling peace process was not at all democratic. The large, powerful, and highly diverse secondary elite clearly had little interest in the peacebuilding process and continued to defend their autonomy from the central government. President Karzai increasingly distanced himself from peacebuilders, staking his governing power on networks of patronage, co-optation, and corruption. Peacebuilders, while critical of these developments, essentially accepted that Karzai had forsaken democracy and nevertheless continued to support his government with massive financial aid and an ever-increasing troop presence.

After the fraudulent presidential election in 2009, relations between peacebuilders and the government grew even more strained. Karzai further distanced himself from his international backers in April 2010, saying that coalition troops risked being seen as invaders rather than saviors of Afghanistan.[14] The political elite in Kabul routinely instrumentalized widespread anti-Western feelings, sending a message that pressuring the local elite to implement more reforms could lead at anytime to a dangerous anti-Western and anti-U.S. backlash, which would jeopardize the peacebuilding mission and harm Western security interests.

At the same time, international engagement in Afghanistan had now clearly shifted toward counterinsurgency. The war against the Taliban had become central, whereas state building diminished in importance. Ten years after the Bonn agreement, which was supposed to launch a democratic peace- and state-building operation, the West found itself fighting a war in Afghanistan. In the shadow of this war, it is far from clear whether the informal contract between the government and peacebuilders will hold for much longer. But, as long as it does, the government will continue to profit from massive resource transfers and military support, while conceding little in terms of liberal reforms.

## An Outlier Case: Kosovo

The case of Kosovo poses a challenge to our theoretical framework. At first glance, adoption costs appear to be relatively modest. The Kosovar elite had little reason to fear that ongoing democratization would pose a threat to their security. NATO's war against Serbia in March 1999 signaled a clear commitment to protect Kosovo against Serbian aggression, and KFOR's (the Kosovo Force's) initial occupation of the territory of Kosovo, conducted by more than 40,000 troops, was an overwhelming show of force. Furthermore, the prime objective of the Kosovar elite, gaining independence, required peacebuilder support and was thus a strong incentive to embrace their policy prescriptions. The new elite was relatively unified in their aspirations and enjoyed the popular support of most Kosovars. Moreover, Kosovo is, according to our measurement, the most intrusive of all recent peacebuilding missions, with massive civilian and military deployment, a broad mandate, and huge flows of aid money. According to our model, these are conditions that are conducive to democracy after war, and we would therefore expect Kosovo to be one of the most democratic postwar countries. However, according to Freedom House, Kosovo was at the same low level of democracy as Tajikistan five years after its mission start and only slightly ahead of Rwanda. It trailed all other countries in our sample, including Afghanistan. Clearly, Kosovo is an outlier case. As such, it not only requires explanation but also maps the limits of our model's explanatory power. We believe that Kosovo's transition from war to a hybrid regime with limited democracy is due to a backlash against democratization, caused by an overly intrusive mission that was further fueled by a number of highly idiosyncratic factors.

In the immediate aftermath of the intervention, the UN mission in Kosovo (UNMIK), which was widely perceived as the security guarantor against an aggressive Serbia, enjoyed a high level of legitimacy among Kosovars and easily managed to gain authority within Kosovo. The influence of the Kosovo Liberation Army (KLA) on the political process was significantly curbed, and relations between the new domestic elite and the peacebuilders were cooperative. The peacebuilders' objectives were to end the hostilities between Serbian forces and the KLA. Once this was achieved, UNMIK sought to establish an efficient Kosovar administration that operated according to democratic principles. They also wanted a multiethnic Kosovo where Serbs and other minorities could live securely and freely participate in politics. Finally, both KFOR and UNMIK were opposed to the idea of an independent Kosovo and hoped to reach an agreement with regard to the degree of autonomy of Kosovo within a Yugoslav or Serbian state.

Initially, the Kosovar elite agreed to postpone their demand for Kosovo independence, and the relationship between the peacebuilders and the domestic elite appeared to be highly cooperative. UNMIK rewarded this cooperation by transferring executive powers to Kosovo government structures after parliamentary elections in autumn 2001 and the subsequent establishment of the Provisional Institutions of Self-Government (PISG) in early 2002. The cooperative relationship soured, however, and gave way to conflictive interaction when domestic elite expectations of a quick transfer of authority were not fulfilled. In an attempt to block demands for greater autonomy, UNMIK introduced the standards-before-status policy, which initiated a new phase in the bargaining process among peacebuilders, domestic elites, and the local population. In March 2004, widespread riots seriously strained relations between Kosovars and peacebuilders. Ethnic violence was directed mainly against the Serb-speaking community (Serbs and Roma) in Kosovo's enclaves. The riots left nineteen people dead, more than 900 injured, and thousands of Serbian houses and religious buildings destroyed. They led to the renewed displacement of about 4,000 Kosovo-Serbs and Roma to Serbia proper, as KFOR and international police looked on. The aggressors were primarily youth and radical spoiler groups associated with the Kosovo-Albanian majority. But some local democracy advocates also adopted temporary spoiler positions to challenge the international interim administration in Kosovo and gain political profit. The peacebuilders responded to the riots with a temporary troop increase. Although a drawdown process had already been underway, the contingent was reinforced to control the situation. Subsequently, peacebuilders felt compelled to open up Kosovo's unresolved status question, to initiate the Vienna status talks in 2006, and eventually to accept Kosovo's unilaterally declared independence from Serbia in 2008. This political compromise between Western international actors and the domestic elite marked a significant revision of the original peacebuilding agenda for multiethnic democracy in Kosovo. Peacebuilders' willingness to commence status talks in 2006 demonstrated an important power shift from external to local actors. As civil society movements and paramilitary groups continued their push for independence, Western powers capitulated. This development was sustained by Serbia's stubborn refusal to cooperate with peacebuilders, which derailed all attempts at a negotiated solution. The clear winners were the Kosovars, who had finally secured international support for their maximalist position.

In nine years, the Kosovar elite had successfully renegotiated an informal contract with peacebuilders, which promised security guarantees and development aid in exchange for high democratic standards within an autonomous (but not independent) polity. They ultimately managed to enlist peacebuilder support for the sovereignty movement. Peacebuilders revised this contract when the security situation deteriorated; they perceived that granting independence and greater authority to Kosovar elites was the only way to avert crisis. In so doing they ceded much of their leverage. Kosovo was stabilized as a hybrid regime unaccountable to democratic standards with an excluded minority and poor governance structures. The lofty aims of the peacebuilders who pushed for "standards before status" were forgotten. Kosovo is today a de facto monoethnic polity without a strong civil society or independent media. Furthermore, Kosovo is widely regarded as one of the most corrupt political regimes in Europe, where political elites and organized crime walk hand in hand.[15] In December 2010 an inquiry prepared for the Council of Europe named the prime minister, Hashim Thaci, as a crime boss whose network exerted control over numerous rackets including the heroin trade.[16] Part of this development can be attributed to peacebuilders' negligence. Under the international police presence, drug smuggling, human trafficking, and the illicit arms trade were hardly ever restricted. Peacebuilders did not use their enforcement and veto power to end these criminal activities, in large part because they felt constrained by their objective to foster national ownership and accountability. When peacebuilders surrendered their leverage by agreeing to Kosovo independence, the democratic trajectory of the country became tied to the political preferences of domestic elites and to the pervasive informal institutions already in place, neither of which proved conducive to democracy.

It is instructive to compare the mission in Kosovo with East Timor. As in Kosovo, the mission in East Timor was highly intrusive. Adoption costs were low: Domestic elites were not threatened by democracy, did not face political competition, and were highly dependent on peacebuilders to achieve their primary political objective. At the outset the preferences of domestic elites and peacebuilders were aligned, and both parties were eager to establish a sovereign and democratic state. This initially cooperative relationship changed when key East Timorese politicians expressed frustration over the slow transfer of power within the East Timor Transitional Administration (ETTA) framework. In fact, many East Timorese people felt disempowered by international actors who apparently took decisions on their behalf. On winning independence in May 2002, domestic elites openly defied their onetime "mentors." The violent protests that erupted in December 2002, in which several international supermarkets were burned to the ground, similarly demonstrated popular UN resentment.[17] Although the riots were relatively small in scale, they had an immense impact on the small country.

But, unlike in Kosovo, the fact that domestic elites assumed more power did not lead to an antidemocratic backlash. Five years after the mission's inception, East Timor's rated level of democracy was second only to Namibia within our sample (though its democratization progress has since slowed down due to a lack of capacity). This suggests that the process of democratization, once freed from the tutelage of the international community, is at least to some extent shaped by idiosyncratic domestic factors. For reasons that we cannot explore in this chapter, the political culture has been more conducive to democracy in East Timor than in Kosovo.

## Conclusion: More Is Not Enough and Sometimes Worse

In this chapter, we have demonstrated that "more" is rarely better, and we have identified two causal mechanisms that help explain this observation. First, where the cost of adopting democracy is atypically high, for example in Rwanda, Afghanistan, and Bosnia, political regimes will not choose democratic governance because peacebuilders cannot offset its steep price—even with a heavy mission footprint. Ethnic mistrust, security concerns, and an entrenched secondary elite who oppose reform make for atypically high adoption costs.

Second, and perhaps more surprising, we also find that a highly intrusive mission can actually harm a democratization project. In our sample, East Timor, Kosovo, Bosnia, and Afghanistan typify highly intrusive missions. In all of these cases, an initially cooperative peacebuilding process deteriorated into open confrontation between peacebuilders and domestic elites. This is because greater mission intrusiveness and external tutelage *in and of themselves* generated domestic resistance and spurred demands for local ownership and self-determination. A system of "benevolent autocracy," aimed at creating democracy, caused ends to collide with means. Due to this normative inconsistency, peacebuilders in highly intrusive missions risk losing their credibility, which seriously impairs their relationship with both domestic elites and the population at large. When ordinary people resist peacebuilders and their policies, as they did on various occasions in Afghanistan, Kosovo, and Timor, peacebuilders adjust their agenda by giving in to domestic demands for increased autonomy. In so doing, peacebuilders trade away some of the leverage they acquired through mission intrusiveness in exchange for a less confrontational relationship with domestic elites. In consequence, the fate of the democratization project becomes hostage to the political will of domestic elites, who are seldom eager to pursue democratic reform.

Another mechanism that helps explain why highly intrusive missions can impede democratic outcomes is that intrusive missions give peacebuilders far-reaching legislative and executive power. This allows domestic politicians to shift responsibility for unpopular democratic reforms to external actors; local elites recognize that, if they drag their feet, peacebuilders will ultimately enforce any changes deemed necessary. This accountability gap negates the ownership that is essential to a democratic system. Bosnia exemplifies this mechanism. Domestic elites were quite content to let the OHR take unpopular decisions, while at the same time investing in their informal networks of power.[18]

Because of these mechanisms, mission intrusiveness is governed by the rule of diminishing returns. More intrusive missions do not bring more democracy because high levels of intrusiveness can create a backlash against democratization or reduce government accountability.

At the extremes of the adoption costs spectrum, mission footprint seems to matter little. In cases where adoption costs are low, even a relatively light-footprint mission ensures a successful postwar democratic transition. Examples are Namibia, Macedonia, and Mozambique. In East Timor, adoption costs were also low, and the mission's footprint quite heavy. In all of these cases, the relationship between the peacebuilders and local state elites was generally cooperative because interests were, for the most part, closely aligned. In Namibia, domestic elites fully cooperated with peacebuilders because they had a huge interest in free and fair elections as part of the journey toward independence. Domestic elites similarly embraced the objective of peaceful democracy in East Timor and Mozambique. Although elites occasionally slowed the reform process to extract additional resources and concessions from external actors, their commitment to the overall democratization agenda was genuine.

There are also cases where the high ratio between adoption costs and leverage clearly favors the status quo. These cases seem in hindsight overdetermined and hopeless. An example is Tajikistan, where peacebuilders lacked credible leverage over a government that was able to count on Russian support. Rwanda is a second example, but here the absence of leverage was a product of far-reaching overtures to domestic elites who favored the status quo.

Thus, for the "easy" and the "hopeless" cases, the ratio between adoption costs and leverage is an important factor, even though the process of post-war democratization is to a very large extent driven by adoption cost. The situation differs in cases where relatively high adoption costs meet a heavy footprint mission, as we have seen in Bosnia, Afghanistan, and to some extent Kosovo (though adoption costs in this case were lower than in Bosnia and Afghanistan). Here we find that high adoption costs cannot be offset by highly intrusive missions. This is perhaps to be expected, given the many challenges peacebuilders have faced in attempts to reconcile deep ethnic divisions in Bosnia or in their statebuilding faceoff against a broad and amorphous secondary elite in Afghanistan.

One might argue that the preceding conclusions are a result of selection bias—that heavy footprint peacebuilding operations fail to bring democracy to war-torn countries precisely because only the thorniest cases are served with highly intrusive missions. If this is true, then a heavy-footprint mission might still be more effective than a lighter footprint; the reason for failure is due to the atypically difficult context rather than mission intrusiveness. According to this reasoning, if one were to control for difficulty, then highly intrusive missions would fare better than less intrusive missions. But such an argument, which follows the logic of quantitative research, is flawed. Our empirically thick descriptions of Afghanistan, Kosovo, Bosnia, and East Timor suggest that highly intrusive missions have a tendency to harm, rather than help, democratic development. This is due, at least in part, to the fundamental inconsistency between means and ends.

It is the "intrusiveness" itself that contributes to an undemocratic outcome. In highly intrusive missions, cooperative relations between peacebuilders and domestic elites often become strained. This was true even in cases where the relationship between peacebuilders and domestic elites was initially cooperative and based on shared objectives. This demonstrates a paradox in the very idea that heavy external oversight can produce autonomous and self-governing democratic regimes. And indeed, our cases demonstrate that domestic elites tend to resist paternalism on their journey to self-determination and democracy.

Domestic elites resist the tutelage of external actors in many ways. The most efficient method is to threaten renewed violence. This violence can be directed toward rival group(s) in the country (that is, the former wartime enemy), at peacebuilders directly, or to both at the same time. When faced with the threat of violence, peacebuilders are often willing to adjust their democratization agenda, be it explicitly or through a tacit understanding that domestic elites cannot be counted on to implement liberal reforms. Peacebuilders substantially revised their expectations in Afghanistan, Bosnia, and Kosovo, and to a lesser extent in East Timor. In each case, revisions were prompted by fears of an escalating security situation. Afghanistan also profited from it important strategic position, which prompted the United States to grudgingly tolerate President Karzai's refusal to embrace prescribed policies for good governance. It also profited from the fact that peacebuilders were highly dependent on domestic elites and were therefore inclined to tacitly accept a revision of the peacebuilding contract.

Finally, highly intrusive missions tend to last a long time. The average duration of such missions in our sample was 118 months, compared to forty-two months for light-footprint missions. In a paradoxical twist, longer missions favor domestic elites. Peacebuilders' leverage is greatest at the time of deployment. Once deployed, however, they become "invested" and face certain constraints that may temper their zeal for the radical reforms necessary to achieve their objectives. Peacebuilders operate under time constraints because they have to present rapid success stories to their home constituencies. They must minimize casualties; otherwise their governments will lose electoral support. Consequently, peacebuilders prioritize stability over the kinds of structural reforms that are posited to produce the kind of liberal peacebuilding they desire. Often, peacebuilders are highly dependent on domestic actors because their cooperation is essential for the smooth and stable implementation of their projects. All of this creates an incentive for peacebuilders to accommodate domestic elites in their resistance to some aspects of the peacebuilding mission. Hence, the longer a mission, and the more peacebuilders invest, the more vulnerable they become to renegotiation of the peacebuilder contract. It is therefore not only high adoption costs that limit the democratic success of intrusive missions. A heavy footprint tends to generate a backlash that often prompts peacebuilders to cede some of their leverage. This complex mission offers domestic elites greater opportunity to revise the contract, and, as a result, "more" often becomes "less."

# 5   Aid

THIS CHAPTER EXPLORES THE IMPACT THAT AID, AND ESPE-
cially aid for democracy, has on democratic outcomes in postconflict peacebuilding. We argue that the factors normally expected to affect
postconflict peacebuilding outcomes, and democracy in particular, do not affect these outcomes directly. Instead, they affect outcomes by influencing the
adoption costs of democracy for domestic political actors.

Thus, donors might use aid funds to reduce the cost of participation in a
democratic political settlement for potential spoilers and to increase the rewards for those already disposed to participate. They might also use aid resources to punish spoilers and raise the cost of exit from the settlement. If
donors consistently punish spoilers and reward cooperators, they can strengthen
their reputation as credible guarantors of a democratic political settlement. As
such, donors could theoretically reduce the adoption costs of democracy for
domestic political actors.

Using aid in this way, however, requires that donors condition aid on the
democratic behavior of domestic political actors. Effective use of aid conditionality is rare. It requires that donors have solid knowledge of the local context, that they be able to separate aid interventions into discrete parts that can
be linked effectively to action by domestic political actors, and that different
donors be willing and able to coordinate the conditional use of aid. These requirements are seldom met.

The Paris Declaration on Aid Effectiveness, the OECD (Organisation for Economic Co-operation and Development) Principles for Good Engagement in Fragile States and Situations, and every subsequent collective donor effort to improve aid effectiveness have underscored the need to improve coordination among donors, align initiatives with local priorities, and improve understanding of the local context. Despite this acknowledgment, however, little has changed in practice. Individual donors remain torn between multiple and often competing goals, different donors have different priorities, and domestic political elites have little interest in the goals that donors urge on them.[1]

Our own findings confirm that aid per se has a limited impact on democratic outcomes. Instead, we find that aid relationships influence outcomes in more complex and nuanced ways. These relationships allow donors to exercise conditionality and can facilitate the trust between donors and domestic political actors that underpins peacebuilder leverage. These positive effects do not result from aid in and of itself but through the relationships formed over time between donors who contribute to and participate in peacebuilding missions and domestic political actors.

It is rare that conditionality is effectively employed, however. Mozambique provides us with the clearest examples of its positive effects, while Afghanistan illustrates how flooding a country with aid when relationships and mutual confidence between donors and the recipient country are weak can have quite negative consequences for democracy. Finally, the case of Rwanda shows how other factors can mitigate the influence of aid despite long-standing relations between donors and local actors and high levels of aid overall. In this case, donor reluctance to condition aid on democracy undermined peacebuilder leverage.[2]

The experience of these three countries indicates that aid matters when (1) donors have preexisting relationships and credibility with local actors due to their history in the country and (2) donors are willing to translate these assets into leverage, through the use of implicit or external conditionality that demands progress on peacebuilding in exchange for continued support. These conditions are rare. More commonly, we find that donors tend not to exploit aid for leverage due to other priorities and the absence of coherence among them. Where conditions are imposed, domestic political actors are often able to circumvent them.

This chapter proceeds as follows. We begin with a brief overview of the academic and policy literature on the use of aid to support democratization. The most recent policy literature, much of it commissioned or written by donors, makes clear that, after two decades of promoting both democracy and good governance as remedies for poor economic performance, donors are now placing a clear emphasis on governance rather than democracy. This more nuanced approach attempts to grasp and use the existing incentive structures that drive political behavior and policy choices as an essential point of departure in addressing the problems of state building. Based on two decades of postconflict state-building experience, this approach supports the theoretical argument of this book—that democratic outcomes depend on adoption costs.

We then empirically examine the effects of aid on democratization in our nine cases. We first describe patterns we observe in these cases, looking both at general aid and also at aid targeted at building democratic processes and institutions. We map levels of aid and temporal and sectoral patterns of aid distribution to postwar countries. Our objective here is to discover whether more aid leads to more democratic outcomes, a finding that would suggest that aid may have a positive impact on democratization. We then address whether and to what extent aid targeted specifically at democracy promotion has affected democratic peacebuilding outcomes. We conclude by returning to the theoretical argument at the core of this book, discussing whether and how aid affects both the adoption costs of democracy for domestic political actors and the leverage that peacebuilders bring to the table.

Before proceeding further, a clarification is in order. In contrast to Chapter 4, where we focused on UN peace operations, this chapter explores the impact of *bilateral aid* on postconflict peacebuilding—specifically bilateral aid focused on democracy promotion. Bilateral donors fund UN and other multilateral peace missions directly. But they also provide funding separately from the multilateral peace mission. It is in this capacity that we suspect they may be influential actors over and above their impact on the design and resourcing of the peace mission itself. We thus include donors under the label of "peacebuilders," which refers to all external actors directly engaged in the postconflict peacebuilding process. In doing so we assume that, while the specific objectives, priorities, and methods of individual donors may not always be consistent with those of the mission or of one another, all of these actors share the goal of implementing a broadly defined peacebuilding agenda that includes the establishment of a democratic political system and an enduring peace.

## Overview of the Literature

Aid for democracy is a relatively recent and controversial idea. The notion that democratization could be externally crafted and applied as a remedy for what ails underdeveloped or conflict-prone states gained currency in the early 1990s with the collapse of the Soviet Union and the end of the Cold War. Previously, financial support for democratization was considered neither desirable nor likely to be effective.

While good governance was initially championed as a response to systematic economic mismanagement in poor countries, by the late 1990s democratization and good governance became ends in themselves for many major aid donors.[3] Such was the legitimating power of "democracy" as a basis for regimes emerging from conflict that virtually every negotiated peace settlement signed after 1989 had democratization at its core. Peacebuilding missions after the Cold War were launched with a clear expectation that stability and peace required a democratic system of governance to be in place. Democracy aid as an explicit form of external intervention thus became central in the peacebuilding package.

The terrorist attacks of September 11, 2001, and their aftermath tested the limits of the notion that democratic governance could serve as a basis for long-term peace and stability. During the administration of U.S. President George W. Bush, American military intervention in Iraq and Afghanistan was justified, in part, by the claim that democratization of despotic regimes was an essential component in the "war on terror." Democracy in the Middle East became a U.S. national security imperative.[4]

It is clear that support for democracy has, since the end of the Cold War, become a pillar of Western aid policy. And yet the question of whether democracy aid produces democracy has been the subject of considerable controversy. Some who argue in favor of democracy aid assume that it works differently than general aid. They argue that democracy aid focuses on agent-centered assistance that empowers individuals, groups, and political institutions in a recipient country and therefore has a direct impact on democracy, whereas generic aid may have an impact on various economic and social factors, which would only indirectly and in the long term produce conditions more conducive to democracy.[5]

Two recent quantitative studies have put this assumption to the test.[6] Both studies estimate the impact of USAID's (the U.S. Agency for International

Development's) support for democracy on democratization, and both find a statistically significant impact. Scott and Steele base their finding on disaggregated aid data, focusing only on one type of aid (democracy aid), given by one donor (USAID), whereas previous studies that found no significant positive impact often used official development aid (ODA) to predict democratization. They see the use of ODA as "problematic because it is an aggregate figure lumping together multiple aid programs offered for a variety of policy objectives."[7]

Other authors are far more skeptical with regard to the effectiveness of democracy aid. Summing up a widespread sentiment, de Zeeuw and Kumar write that "[the international community] has no illusions about its role in crafting democracy. International policymakers recognize that they can only help and prod—nothing more."[8] Two recent collections of studies come to similar assessments of the limited impact of democracy aid,[9] while others argue that efforts to promote democracy are not only unlikely to succeed but are likely to compromise other state-building goals as well.[10]

Scholars have identified several issues that may reduce the potential impact of democracy aid. One problem is that democracy is often of less concern to external actors than other geostrategic or developmental interests. Aid has long been used to further the geostrategic interests of donor countries,[11] and, since 2001, this strategic dimension has become significant once again, as donors increasingly use aid to address issues of security and conflict.[12]

The effectiveness of aid is also undermined by a lack of knowledge of the regional context. In the early years of democracy promotion, there was little understanding by aid agencies of underlying political systems and tensions in many developing countries; democracy experts were rarely involved in program design, and the work of democracy promotion was largely a technical exercise.[13] While scholars were concerned about the lack of structural underpinnings for democracy (capitalism, literacy, a civic culture) and the lack of agents to introduce it (weak middle classes, often co-opted into an authoritarian system; weak working classes)[14] the aid industry continued to churn, largely oblivious to the realities of the social structures they were supporting.[15]

Other scholars maintain that aid often has focused primarily on "the visible trappings of democracy," notably on the electoral process, rather than on the political foundation necessary for meaningful elections.[16] Many evaluations of American democracy promotion conclude that the United States tends to emphasize elections and related procedures to the exclusion of other substantive elements of democracy, often to the detriment of effective support for democratization.[17] With regard to U.S. democracy assistance policy, Carothers points to the sometimes inappropriate adherence to a preconceived democracy template that often renders democracy assistance ineffective.[18] Similar arguments have been raised by Burnell and, with regard on EU democracy promotion, Youngs.[19] The legitimacy that elections can bestow on a regime, along with the fact that elections are a very tangible "output" of donor activity, has made support for elections a favorite domain for aid organizations. But the formal trappings of democracy may not always translate into real democratic progress, and many scholars maintain that elections or other technocratic dimensions of political reform have been unduly stressed. They argue that holding an election does not necessarily lead to embedded democratic practices supported by societal norms, high citizen participation, or genuine local demand for democracy.[20] Wright, for example, contends that aid promotes democratization only when political leaders expect to win elections anyway.[21]

Another contentious issue is the question of aid conditionality.[22] Conditionality is, at least potentially, a key instrument of donor leverage to push recipients down particular paths. However, conditionality has rarely been applied effectively, and, in any case, some scholars question its wisdom. Focusing on democracy promotion in Africa, Brown highlights how "many African governments quickly learned how to make the minimum necessary reforms to retain their levels of aid: allowing opposition parties to compete, but not win; permitting an independent press to operate, but not freely; allowing civil groups to function, but not effectively; and consenting that elections be held, but not replace the ruling party."[23]

Furthermore, difficulties of donor coordination also tend to constrain the effectiveness of democracy assistance. At least in the early period of democracy aid, donors tended to respond to particular situations on an ad hoc basis and with little coherence, rather than preparing a systematic and cooperative response built on evidence-based reasoning. This helps to explain the varied levels of support by donors for democracy in different countries, as well as the differences in outcomes across cases where aid levels have been similar. In addition, within the debate among scholars and practitioners there is tension between the familiar desire to standardize "best practices" that could apply to a broad range of cases and an appreciation of the context-specific and contingent nature of effective democracy promotion.[24]

Finally, one strand of literature on aid and democracy suggests that aid can have an outright negative effect by undermining the domestic legitimacy of a regime through a focus on institutions rather than the exercise of democratic voice[25] or by underwriting undemocratic practice.[26] Trade-offs between short-term and long-term goals can have far-reaching detrimental impacts. For example, a drive for early elections to tick the legitimacy box may undermine the slow nurturing of a democratic culture, which is particularly problematic in postconflict situations.[27] A range of authors stress that, fundamentally, large influxes of aid cannot offset the need to nurture a local democratic process, which requires smaller and steadier commitments of aid over a long period of time.

To sum up, those who are skeptical that aid can effectively foster democracy point out that democracy promotion is often not the primary objective of donors; that donors often lack regional knowledge and that their efforts suffer from lack of coordination; that aid focuses too much on the formal trappings of democracy; that conditionality is either not applied or not effective; and that aid can do more harm than good. By contrast, those who think that aid can contribute to democratization assume that aid can help local actors to develop basic capacities for governance and that aid can motivate local actors to pursue democracy by offering much needed material rewards and by signaling peacebuilders' high commitment to promoting democracy. The most recent attempts by donors to examine the impact of aid on state building suggest that aid is likely to affect state-building outcomes to the extent that it affects the incentives of key domestic political actors and societal groups. As we will discuss in more detail in the following pages, our research supports this argument.

Most recently, donors themselves have begun to question the centrality or even the desirability of democratization for successful postconflict peacebuilding. It is no longer taken for granted that military conflict can be transformed into peaceful political competition through the magic of the ballot box. This is reflected most obviously by the definition of state building as a process that enables states to provide essential services to their citizens and encourages them to adopt policies that effectively promote economic development.[28]

First, there is a strong emphasis on governance rather than on competitive electoral politics and other aspects of democracy. For example, the 2011 World Development Report highlights the need for states that can deliver on three areas of critical concern to citizens: "citizen security, justice, and jobs." The report makes clear that supporting states' ability to deliver in these areas does not necessarily mean support for democracy and that indeed the latter may impede the achievement of these goals, at least in the short term.[29] Donor policy statements now caution that "donors risk doing harm to statebuilding by promoting elections where major political organizations, or elite factions, are excluded from the process, or where incentives remain in place for political organizations and powerful elite interests to exit and engage in violent confrontation."[30]

This shift away from explicit democracy promotion is at least in part due to an increasing appreciation for the *political* aspects of democracy over and above the implementation of a series of procedural and institutional reforms. After two decades of engagement in postconflict peacebuilding, many donors have gained a more nuanced understanding of the politics of these transitions. Donor group policy documents recognize state building as "a highly political and contentious process" driven by the interests of domestic political actors.[31] Simply put, "State building is difficult, messy and ultimately led by endogenous factors."[32] Policy documents stress that state building is a long-term process that includes not only building institutions and establishing new political processes but also building the political consensus around those institutions and processes to secure legitimacy.

Moreover, democracy promotion can undercut other goals of postconflict state building, including not only good governance but also peace. The 2010 OECD DAC (Development Assistance Committee) Fragile States Group report on international state building therefore urges donors to inform their support for state-building processes with a thorough understanding of domestic political dynamics:

> The way donors intervene can affect the incentives elites face to buy in to or opt out of peacebuilding processes. The consequences of not understanding the shape of a political settlement can lead donors, often unknowingly, to do harm to statebuilding.[33]

In particular, the report argues that the outcome of democratic transitions depends very much on whether or not key security issues have been settled. For example, the authors argue that, in Afghanistan and Rwanda, "security parameters were decisive in affecting the divergent trajectories of democratic transition."[34]

This shift away from the short-term electoral fix and toward a more nuanced understanding of the politics of postconflict state building supports the theoretical argument advanced in this book. Donors with long experience on the ground in postconflict settings are beginning to cast the central problem of building effective states (which provide basic public services) as one of creating political will as well as building capacity. Moreover, insecurity is seen to stem from political settlements that either exclude key political factions or societal groups or that entrench the power of "spoilers" who lack incentives to make peace work. Thus, both fully competitive elections and noncompetitive power-sharing arrangements pose dangers to peace and the construction of a strong and capable state.

Recent work on state building for development focuses on relations between political elites and the circumstances under which "a country's ruling elite come to an explicit or implicit agreement that their interests lie in enlarging the national economic pie and making choices with a view to the long term."[35] The problem of building a state whose leaders are willing and able to pursue policies that will lead to economic development is cast as a collective action problem: "Given the way political competition works, especially but not only in ethnically divided societies, the incentives to engage in short-term clientelistic strategies for gaining votes and seeking legitimacy are overpowering."[36] According to this perspective, the role of external donors is to help domestic political actors overcome barriers to change.

Political arrangements also affect the incentives of domestic political actors. According to the OECD report, the key for donors in deciding "how far to rely on elections as part of a statebuilding process is whether or not an electoral process is likely to establish or make progress towards a more inclusive political settlement, where previously contending elites have positive incentives to buy into statebuilding."[37] There is considerable debate in the literature on democracy about the positive effects of democracy on more inclusive settlements.

However, the key point for our purposes is that, as donors have recently begun to emphasize, elite incentives matter. It is no longer safe to assume that elections or democratic constitutions will legitimize a political settlement.[38] Indeed, the OECD report states that "the clearest insight that emerges from these case studies is that donor support for democratization or advocacy of elections, without a sound understanding of the impact their support may have on a reigning political settlement, risks doing harm to statebuilding."[39]

Instead, "the challenge for the international community is to ensure that its engagement does not distort the 'political marketplace' in a way that reduces the incentives for peace."[40]

We argue that adoption costs can be captured by looking at the threat to the security of domestic actors and the threat to their primary objective in the postconflict period. This is consistent with policy literature that draws on two decades of state-building experience and finds that security considerations and political incentives are key to understanding state-building outcomes. To what extent can aid help to reduce these threats and thereby reduce the adoption costs of democracy?

In the rest of this chapter, we explore the empirical evidence from our nine cases. We first describe the patterns of overall aid disbursements. Next, we look at the distribution of democracy aid. Finally, we return to our theoretical argument to examine the impact of aid on adoption costs and on peacebuilder leverage.

## Patterns of Aid Distribution after War

In this section, we examine whether there is any observable relationship between levels of aid provision and the democratic peacebuilding outcomes in our nine cases. We begin by describing the patterns of aid disbursement for our cases using two different data sources. First, we gathered the data available through the OECD-DAC creditor reporting system (CRS) and included disbursements and commitments for overall aid, humanitarian aid, and democracy aid. The CRS categories we counted as "democracy aid" were as follows: (1) education general; (2) government and civil society general; (3) conflict prevention and resolution, peace, and security; (4) communications; and (5) support to nongovernmental organizations. For all countries, data were gathered for the first five years following the start of the external intervention.

To cross-check the validity of the DAC data and to get more fine-grain data, we also collected original aid data for each country in our sample within the framework of this research project (henceforth "project data"). These data were drawn from official government statistics, documents, and reports, as well as statistics available from international and bilateral aid agencies. We collected project data on overall aid disbursements as well as democracy aid in particular. We define democracy aid as investment in elections and political process, rule of law, accountability, anticorruption, human rights and minority rights, institutional infrastructure (parliamentary and public administration, decentralization, administration capacity), civil society, media, civic education, empowerment, civil–military relations, DDR (disarmament, demobilization, and reintegration), and security sector reform. We consider these categories to be more detailed and precise than the DAC categories. Consequently, our data and DAC data on democracy aid refer to different subcategories and are thus not directly comparable. Also, the DAC data include spending by OECD countries on the UN peace mission itself, while the project data do not. As Tables 5.1 and 5.2 show, the overall amounts for each country differ between DAC and project data.

It is notoriously difficult to gather reliable aid data. Data collection was hampered by variations in aid categories both over time and among different donors, as well as wide variation in archiving and record-keeping practices among donors. In the early 1990s, aid categories referring explicitly to democratization often did not exist, thus no disaggregated data on democracy aid are available for the earliest cases in our sample (Namibia and Mozambique especially). The data that do exist are unlikely to capture all donor activities

**TABLE 5.1.** Overall aid (five years average) and democratic outcomes.

|  | Namibia | | Macedonia | | Timor-Leste | | Mozambique | | Bosnia |
| --- | --- | --- | --- | --- | --- | --- | --- | --- | --- |
| Time period–five years after intervention start | 1989–1993 | | 2001–2005 | | 1999–2003 | | 1992–1996 | | 1996–2000 |
| Source of data | Project | DAC | Project | DAC | project | DAC | project | DAC | Project |
| Total aid in millions, five-year average | 228 | — | 268 | 322 | 150 | 339 | 983 | 985 | 1121 |
| Aid per capita, five-year average | 154 | — | 132 | 159 | 173 | 403 | 67 | 61 | 321 |
| Freedom in the World Score | 2.5 | | 3 | | 3 | | 3.5 | | 4.5 |
| Polity IV score | 6 | | 9 | | 6 | | 6 | | –66 (foreign interruption) |
| Outcome | Democratic | | Democratic | | Democratic | | Democratic | | Nondemocratic |

SOURCES: DAC data provided by the OECD-DAC creditor reporting system (CRS); project data was collected from various sources by case study authors during fieldwork.

Democratic: Coded as an electoral democracy by Freedom House.

that would currently be labeled as "democracy promotion." Both the DAC and the project data are incomplete for several reasons. First, there were no project data for Afghanistan, and the project data from Tajikistan were only partial. Second, DAC data do not include aid from non-OECD countries, notably Russia and China, and sometimes assistance is provided in kind or as loans or alternative forms of finance. One example where this is particularly problematic is Tajikistan, where Russian in-kind assistance was substantial and where China provided the most substantial loans, primarily though infrastructure projects undertaken by Chinese companies.[41] None of this in-kind support is reflected in the available data on aid flows. In East Timor, data for the period of UN transitional administration were available only for funds channeled through the transitional administration, which likely do not capture the overall picture.[42] Finally, comparing commitments and disbursements is impossible based on the available data. Project data were available sometimes for commitments and sometimes for disbursements, while DAC data on disbursements were available only from 2002 onwards, which is too late for most of our cases. Hence, conclusions derived primarily from aid data

| | Afghanistan | | Kosovo | | Tajikistan | | Rwanda | |
|---|---|---|---|---|---|---|---|---|
| | 2002–2006 | | 1999–2003 | | 1997–2001 | | 1993–1997 | |
| DAC | Project | DAC | project | DAC | project | DAC | project | DAC |
| 1,072 | — | 3,159 | 531 | — | 45 | 171 | 506 | 389 |
| 305 | — | 133 | 280 | — | 7 | 28 | 89 | 68 |
| | 5 | | 5 | | 6 | | 6.5 | |
| | −66 (foreign interruption | | No data | | −1 | | −6 | |
| | Nondemocratic | | Nondemocratic | | Nondemocratic | | Nondemocratic | |

**TABLE 5.2.** Democracy aid and democratic outcomes.

| | Namibia | | Macedonia | | Timor-Leste | | Mozambique | | Bosnia |
|---|---|---|---|---|---|---|---|---|---|
| Time period–five years after intervention start | 1989–1993 | | 2001–2005 | | 1999–2003 | | 1992–1996 | | 1996–2000 |
| Source of data | Project | DAC | Project | DAC | project | DAC | Project | DAC | Project |
| Democracy aid in millions, five-year average | — | — | 94 | 52 | 94 | 44 | — | 36 | 24 |
| Democracy aid per capita, five-year average | — | — | 44 | 26 | 68 | 52 | — | 2 | 7 |
| Democracy aid as percentage of total aid | — | — | 36% | 18% | 42% | 13% | — | 4% | 2% |
| Outcome | Democratic | | Democratic | | Democratic | | Democratic | | Nondemocratic |

SOURCES: DAC data provided by the OECD-DAC creditor reporting system (CRS); project data were collected from various sources by case study authors during fieldwork.

Democratic: Coded as an electoral democracy by Freedom House.

should be treated with caution. We use DAC data for the sake of trend analysis and comparison, but we also use project data for the narratives drawn from our cases in the second part of this chapter.

In what follows, we will briefly describe the overall levels of aid, the per capita levels of aid, and the temporal and sectoral patterns of aid distribution. We first examine the overall aid flows (Table 5.1). In absolute terms, Afghanistan, followed by a wide margin by Bosnia and Mozambique, received the lion's share of aid. Rwanda and Kosovo sit in the middle, and Macedonia, Namibia, Timor, and Tajikistan trail behind the other cases. In terms of aid per capita, East Timor, Bosnia, and Kosovo benefited most from external support, receiving roughly US$300 or more annually in the first five years. These are also the cases where intervention in general was most intrusive, with external actors taking over government responsibilities de jure in East Timor and Kosovo and de facto in Bosnia (see Chapter 4 on mission intrusiveness). Tajikistan, Rwanda, and Mozambique received the least aid per capita.

The data also reveal that more recent missions (Afghanistan, Timor, Bosnia, and Kosovo) tend to receive more aid than missions launched in the immediate aftermath of the Cold War (Rwanda, Mozambique, and Namibia).

| | Afghanistan | | Kosovo | | Tajikistan | | Rwanda | |
|---|---|---|---|---|---|---|---|---|
| | 2002–2006 | | 1999–2003 | | 1997–2001 | | 1993–1997 | |
| DAC | Project | DAC | project | DAC | project | DAC | project | DAC |
| 41 | — | 430 | 102 | — | 1 | 6 | 32 | 33 |
| 12 | — | 18 | 54 | — | 0,11 | 1 | 6 | 6 |
| 12% | — | 13% | 18% | — | 2% | 3% | 7% | 9% |
| | Nondemocratic | | Nondemocratic | | Nondemocratic | | Nondemocratic | |

As we have seen in Chapter 4, earlier missions are also less intrusive. Hence, the data suggest that more recent and more intrusive missions tend to attract greater aid disbursement.

This does not necessarily indicate that donors have become more willing to provide resources for postconflict countries, however. It is more likely that interveners have specific interests at play in particular conflicts. The Balkan countries are in the direct neighborhood of the European Union, and stability in the region was an immediate concern for the EU and its member states. And while East Timor is a small country far from the United States and Europe, it was seen by Australia (a major intervener in this case) as part of an "arc of instability" in Southeast Asia, and international public outrage after the violence that followed the 1999 referendum helped to spur hitherto reluctant governments (Australia and the United States) to act.[43] The large amount of aid that went to Afghanistan should be seen within the context of the "war on terror."

Figure 5.1[44] provides an overview of per capita aid flows in the first ten years of intervention in the seven cases for which we have enough data (we lack data from Namibia and Mozambique). In four cases (Bosnia, East Timor, Kosovo,

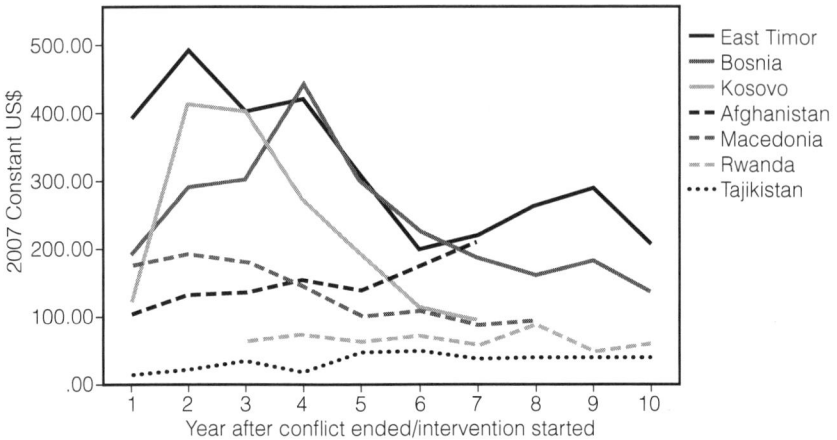

**FIGURE 5.1.** Aid per capita, DAC data.

and Macedonia), aid peaked during the first five years of the mission, supporting the notion that aid tends to be front loaded in the first years after conflict.
Aid then steadily declined, except for a small peak in East Timor in 2006 and
2007. This was due to an increase in humanitarian aid after the crisis of 2006,
when divisions between political elites as well as the police and the army led to
violent protest and fights between various factions of the security forces.[45] In
three other cases, we find that the aid curve remained flat (Rwanda and Tajikistan) or aid continually increased (Afghanistan), as the initial "light footprint"
approach was replaced by a more heavy-handed intervention.

Finally, with regard to the different sectors in which aid was spent, there
are considerable differences among our countries, indicating that no such
thing as the "typical postwar aid package" exists.

Similar across most cases is the fact that humanitarian aid, which was already provided during the war, was gradually phased out at the war's end,
giving way to support for institution building and reform. This explains the
overall decline in total aid disbursements over time, which is a common pattern across all cases.

For all these reasons, some caution is in order when interpreting these figures. Nevertheless, the data offer three important insights. First, aid packages
tended to become larger as missions grew more intrusive. But, second, there
is no such thing as the typical peacebuilding package. The temporal sequence,

the overall amounts, and the sectoral distribution of aid differed widely across the cases. This implies that the international donor community, rather than following a standard pattern based on experience and lessons learned, reacted on a case-by-case basis. The contents of the aid packages are also dependent on the strategic importance of the country.

Finally and most importantly, the data show no correlation between levels of received aid, either in absolute terms and per capita, and democratic outcomes. Of the four countries that received most overall aid (Afghanistan, Bosnia, Mozambique, and Kosovo), only one, Mozambique, is reasonably democratic. When looking at aid per capita, among the four countries that received most aid per capita (East Timor, Bosnia and Kosovo, and Afghanistan), again only one, East Timor, is democratic. Among those that received the least aid per capita, we have one case of a democratic outcome and two nondemocratic outcomes. This insight is drawn from a rather crude comparison of aid levels and democratic outcomes across cases; hence the evidence is far from robust. However, the intuition from the data is that levels of aid and democratic outcomes are not associated, which supports the widespread skepticism in the literature about the effectiveness of aid. In the next section, we will focus on the effects of aid specifically targeted for democracy. We start with a brief overview over the literature and then analyze the evidence from our cases.

### Democracy Aid

This rough-and-ready comparison of aid levels and democracy outcomes across our nine cases suggests that overall aid levels do not correlate with positive outcomes. But even if aid in general is not consistently related to democratization, aid specifically earmarked for democracy might still be effective. In this section, we describe the observable patterns of democracy aid disbursement across our nine cases. We analyze these patterns and scan them for potential causal mechanisms that link democracy aid to specific outcomes. We then take a closer look at the insights that our case studies offer about the effects of aid on democracy, taking into consideration the environment and context in which aid is provided and how it is used in the interaction between domestic political actors and peacebuilders. Specifically, we examine whether our case studies support the overall theory of democratic change advanced by this book by investigating whether aid for democracy can increase peacebuilder leverage over domestic political actors or offset the costs domestic political actors incur by adopting democracy.

## Democracy Aid in Practice

We now turn to a brief description of aid specifically earmarked for democracy in our cases. In all nine cases, democratization was one of the objectives of the peacebuilding mission, but its importance varied. In some cases democracy was clearly a top priority, as in Mozambique and Namibia, while in others democratization was just one aim among many. For example, in Afghanistan military intervention was designed to achieve democracy through forced regime change. Where democracy and stability were conflicting goals, stability took precedence. In Bosnia, preserving the integrity of the Bosnian state was the central aim of interveners; democratization was "icing on the cake."[46]

Surprisingly, these differences do not necessarily influence aid spending patterns. In terms of the absolute quantity of democracy aid, Afghanistan again leads the pack with around US$400 million on average in the first five years, followed by Kosovo and East Timor. The least democracy aid went to Rwanda, Tajikistan, and Mozambique. Democracy aid per capita was highest in East Timor, Kosovo, and Macedonia, and lowest in Tajikistan, Rwanda, and Mozambique. In terms of democracy aid as a percentage of total aid, we find that in Kosovo and Macedonia democracy aid accounted for almost 20 percent of total aid. In Afghanistan, Bosnia, Rwanda, and East Timor, democracy aid accounted for around 10 percent, and in Mozambique and Tajikistan democracy aid made up less than 5 percent of overall aid.

With regard to patterns of aid disbursement over time, the data reveal that financial support for democratization was higher in later missions as a percentage of total aid spending (with the exception of Tajikistan). This is consistent with the more expansive donor rhetoric on democratic peacebuilding that was characteristic of the late 1990s, but it might also be a reflection of greater donor interest in these countries compared to earlier interventions in Namibia or Mozambique. Gaps in the data for the earlier cases might also distort the picture. Thus, while peacebuilders had different priorities for different missions, this was not reflected in spending patterns. The only clear pattern is that recent missions received higher levels of democracy aid than earlier ones.

In most cases we also find a heavy focus on elections (particularly in election years) and on building the formal institutions of democracy. In cases such as Kosovo, Bosnia, Macedonia, and Mozambique, democratization and early elections were a focus of intervention, and there was a large input into the election process accordingly in the initial five-year period. On the other end of the spectrum is Namibia, where available evidence suggests little aid for the democratization process beyond some very small-scale ad hoc initiatives such as support from political foundations in Germany.[47] The other cases fall somewhere in between, in which aid was provided for a range of activities loosely connected with democracy throughout the period of the intervention and beyond, with no obvious focus or agenda.

Not surprisingly, a dominant share of democracy aid in many cases was diverted to institutional infrastructure. This was particularly true in Afghanistan, East Timor, and Kosovo, where the international community attempted to build states largely from scratch, and in Macedonia, where decentralization and reform of the public administration were key provisions of the Ohrid peace agreement. In Afghanistan and East Timor, for example, institutional infrastructure accounted for around 70 percent of total democracy aid in the three years after intervention and somewhat less afterwards. Initially in Tajikistan and in Bosnia, donors placed a heavy emphasis on funding civil society, while in Rwanda aid for the rule of law and the justice sector dominated the agenda. Afghanistan stands out from the overall pattern in that support to the security sector in the early part of the intervention outstripped all other forms of aid. In the first year, 84 percent of aid was focused on the military, 9 percent on relief, 4 percent on the International Security Assistance Force, and 3 percent on reconstruction.[48]

The timing and sequencing of democracy aid varied. In some cases, democracy aid really took off only several years after the immediate postwar period. In Bosnia, for example, the importance of democracy aid increased substantially seven years after the conflict, in 2002. Support increased from below US$20 per capita to between US$30 and US$40 per capita in the following years, when the focus of the international community shifted to institution building. In Tajikistan, aid for democratization increased only in 2001, together with a general increase in external aid. While overall democracy aid remained relatively constant in Rwanda, support for the electoral process as a share of democracy aid took off only in 2003.

As we mentioned earlier, we should be cautious when interpreting these numbers. But bearing this caveat it mind, the available data do not seem to support the notion that "more is better"; more aid, be it overall aid or democracy aid, is not consistently associated with more positive democratic outcomes. Of those cases that received atypically high levels of overall aid per capita in the first five years after the war (Bosnia, Kosovo, and East Timor), only East Timor emerged as relatively democratic five years after the war.

Afghanistan, the case with most overall aid and still more substantial amounts of aid in per capita terms, not only did not democratize but also slid back into civil war. By contrast, Mozambique, which is often seen as a democratic success story, received the lowest contribution of aid per capita.

When we view democracy aid as a percentage of overall aid, we again see no evidence linking aid levels to outcomes. Of the four cases that were comparatively successful at democratization (East Timor, Namibia, Macedonia, and Mozambique), substantial amounts of democracy aid were available only to East Timor and Macedonia, while little aid was explicitly targeted to democratization in Namibia and Mozambique (although, as previously noted, democracy aid may be slightly underreported in the latter cases due to less systematic reporting during this period). Large amounts of democracy aid went to Kosovo, and, although these contributions played an important role in enhancing the professionalism of the interim government, full-fledged democratization was not achieved. Afghanistan is another example of substantial contributions of democracy aid, yet Afghanistan clearly did not emerge as a democracy. At least in these two cases, a lack of resources for democratic reform does not explain their limited success.

The data also suggest that aid packages made available to postwar countries differ greatly with regard to overall quantity, to the sectors that receive most aid, and to the temporal patterns of aid disbursement. We think this finding reflects the fact that aid policies toward various postwar countries were based not so much on theoretically informed conceptual planning but rather on ad hoc decision making, guided by the parochial interests of primary donors and the dynamics within the donor coalition. The lack of an identifiable pattern suggests, in our view, that there is no learning curve. Aid over the years has not become "smarter."

However, like aid overall, aid for democracy has increased over time. Recent missions show higher levels of democracy aid, both in absolute and in relative terms. For now, we do not know whether this shift in spending patterns reflects a shift in strategy, as donor rhetoric would lead us to expect, or merely reflects the specific nature of recent peacebuilding missions (and is thus a result of a selection bias).

To conclude, the lack of an observable association between aid patterns and democratic outcomes suggests that the impact of aid is overshadowed by other factors. Aid trends across our cases shed little light on possible causal mechanisms that might link aid to democratic outcomes. To understand how aid can shape the interaction between peacebuilders and domestic political actors, we must look deeper into the context in which aid is provided.

## Aid and Peacebuilder Leverage

As we have seen, our data suggest that there is no direct association between aid and democracy. Aid figures alone fail to tell a compelling story. However, we theorize that aid does have an *indirect* effect via the leverage it gives peacebuilders over political elites. This leverage can take both positive (motivational) and negative (coercive) forms, and it is not directly related to the *amounts* of aid provided. Instead, aid affects peacebuilder leverage in three important ways, all of which relate to the ability of donors to reduce the risks and increase the rewards of adopting democratic politics.

First, aid builds relationships and shapes expectations—both among a country's major donors as well as between donors and recipients—often years before a peacebuilding intervention begins. This improves the likelihood that donors can serve as credible guarantors able to overcome the kinds of collective action problems that can raise the cost of adopting democracy for domestic political actors. Second, aid allows donors to take ad hoc actions during the peace implementation process that smooth over rough patches or fill in gaps that were overlooked in the planning and funding of a UN mission and that can likewise reduce adoption costs. Third, the provision of bilateral aid alongside a peace mission allows donors to link their funding to discrete elements of peace implementation and democratization (conditionality), potentially raising the costs of noncompliance with a democratic peace settlement.

Aid relationships affect the level of trust that exists between various local elites and donor countries that are key actors in peacebuilding. A track record of consistent support during a humanitarian crisis brought about by war, for example, can give a donor group credibility with local elites. Trust in external peacebuilders can lower elite adoption costs by reducing perceived threats posed by the democratic political settlement. Moreover, where donors have a history of working together in a country before or during war, they are able to more easily overcome the coordination and cooperation challenges that plague many peace missions. Donor cooperation during a humanitarian emergency can provide a precedent and even an institutional template (such as donor working groups) for cooperation during the peace process. Coherence among donors reduces the ability of local actors to "divide and conquer" external actors during the peacebuilding process to evade provisions they dislike. And it increases donor ability to implement conditionality, thereby increasing peacebuilder leverage.[49]

Second, during the peace intervention itself, the types and levels of aid available will affect whether and how donors can respond to hiccups in the peace process with the necessary resources and in a timely fashion. Third, where bilateral donors are heavily involved in designing, funding, and overseeing the implementation of a peace mission, they may be better able to link their own funds to discrete, observable actions by domestic political actors that are necessary for the democratization process to advance. This is in contrast to missions where the bulk of funding for a peace mission, along with the primary responsibility for implementing often conflicting goals, falls under the sole authority of the UN mission.

We argued in Chapters 1 and 2 that the success of democratic peacebuilding efforts depends on how local elites calculate the costs and benefits of adopting democracy and on the leverage peacebuilders can bring to bear on local elites who find adoption costs prohibitive. In our simplified version of this calculus, local elites consider the potential threats to their physical security and their ability to achieve their primary goals, whatever these might be. They also consider the costs of *not* adopting democracy. Here is where peacebuilder leverage begins to weigh in. To what extent do local elites fear negative consequences if they fail to embrace the democratic reforms urged on them by the international community? Are they likely to lose vital economic resources? Governments in aid-dependent countries might consider this possibility carefully. Do they depend on international legitimation or political support to achieve a key goal, such as national independence, as in the cases of Namibia, East Timor, and Kosovo?

As we have discussed in the preceding chapters, local elites in Macedonia, Namibia, Mozambique, Kosovo, and East Timor faced low adoption costs. Local elites in these countries could reasonably expect that embracing democracy did not pose a serious physical security threat or loss of political power. Moreover, in each of these countries the costs of *not* adopting democracy were relatively high. Local elites in Namibia, Kosovo, and East Timor required the active support of the international community in general and of peacebuilders in particular in order to achieve a key goal: independence. And in Macedonia and Mozambique, local opposition elites depended on support from the international community to strengthen their bargaining position vis-à-vis the government, while government actors in both countries needed external legitimation and resources to maintain forward economic progress. In Mozambique, the government received more than half of its budget from donors. Macedonia hoped to join the European Union, a goal that could be achieved only with the approval of the same external actors who played a key role in the peacebuilding process.

By contrast, in Afghanistan, Tajikistan, and Rwanda, the costs to domestic political actors of adopting democracy were relatively high, while the costs of failing to do so were low. Democracy in Afghanistan threatened both the political and to some extent the physical security of ruling elites. In Rwanda, victory on the battlefield gave the Rwandan Patriotic Front little incentive to compromise, and the genocide gave credence to RPF claims that democratization could endanger Rwanda's security. At the same time, the genocide reduced the leverage of international peacebuilders because they had failed to intervene militarily to stop it.[50]

Do aid levels and adoption costs match up? Not entirely. Kosovo, East Timor, and Macedonia are the highest recipients of aid per capita and in terms of democracy aid as a share of overall aid. At the other end of the spectrum are Tajikistan, Rwanda, and Mozambique. In countries with high levels of aid in our sample, we find low adoption costs. This might suggest a correlation between the two, though we can draw no definitive conclusions from our small sample size. On the other hand, the three countries that receive the least aid per capita, or that receive the least democracy aid as a share of overall aid, include one country with low aid levels and low adoption costs (Mozambique), and two countries with high adoption costs and low levels of aid (Rwanda and Tajikistan).

Thus we have some limited evidence that aid affects adoption costs, but not uniformly. We suspect this is because aid affects adoption costs only indirectly or, to be more precise, that the act of providing aid can have various incidental consequences partially independent from the amounts of aid given. These serve to raise or lower adoption costs for local elites, as well as to increase the leverage of peacebuilders. Aid interventions promote democratic outcomes where they lower adoption costs and where they reduce barriers to collective action for donors, because collective action challenges so often reduce donor leverage.

For example, in Mozambique a wide range of bilateral donors had established working relationships with local elites on both sides of the war while providing aid during the humanitarian emergency brought on by drought. Donor involvement in humanitarian aid also led to the formation of a number of ad hoc donor working groups created to coordinate aid delivery. Both sets of relationships—between donors and local elites and among donors themselves—set the stage for a balance of adoption costs and peacebuilder leverage that weighed in favor of a democratic peace. Local adoption costs were already relatively low, as the political settlement did not pose a serious threat to the physical security or political power of local elites. Because donors had demonstrated their commitment and an ability to deliver resources over the preceding decade, they were able to serve as credible guarantors of the settlement. Years of work experience in the country gave donors experience working together, as well as a good understanding of the incentives and challenges facing local actors. Thus they were able to minimize coordination problems and present a relatively united front on key issues. Perhaps more importantly, donors were able to insert themselves into the design and implementation of the transition from war to peace, successfully advocating for increased funding and attention to transitional elections, creating a trust fund to enable Renamo, the armed opposition group, to transform into a functioning political party, and stepping in at various points with resources and good offices when the peace process stalled.[51]

For example, shortly after the peace agreement was signed in 1992, a group of major bilateral and multilateral donors formed the Democracy Assistance Group (succeeded by the Electoral Process Monitoring Group). This group aimed to facilitate and coordinate funding to implement the peace process, including technical and logistical support for elections, electoral and civic education, and democratization programs. Donors paid US$55 million of the US$60 million cost of the 1994 elections, while the government of Mozambique paid the remaining US$5 million. They created a US$17 million trust fund to facilitate Renamo's transition to the political arena, as well as another, smaller fund to support the rest of the country's nascent opposition parties. Thus, although Mozambique received little aid relative to our other cases in the first five years after war, the fact that it had historically received large amounts of aid and had a core group of highly committed and experienced donors provided external actors considerable leverage over local elites in the "peacebuilder's game."

Where aid seemed to have no impact, we observed two broad patterns in our case studies: examples of negative conditionality, where intrusive enforcement helped arrest undemocratic behavior but did not encourage positive behavior (Bosnia, Kosovo); and a hands-off, low-pressure approach that likewise had limited impact (Rwanda, Tajikistan).

Turning to the former examples first, in Bosnia, "conditionality was a key component of the [international community's] tool box for statebuilding."[52] As in Kosovo, there was an extremely direct and intensive exercise of authority by external actors over the implementation process that went well beyond traditional conditionality. Those who failed to comply could be and were removed from office. When the legislatures failed to pass laws, the Office of the High Representative passed them on their behalf. Local government aid was tied to allowing minority return, and there were demands for compliance with war crimes tribunals and the like. Nevertheless, there was no question that the mission would end because of noncompliance with stipulated conditions. Instead, rebellion begot more direct intervention, which led to a situation in which the more the international community built state structures, the more it was obligated to keep them functioning. Consequently, we can see that conditionality was used to enforce particular governance practices but did not succeed in building a positive democratic culture.

The second pattern is best illustrated by the more authoritarian examples, namely Rwanda and Tajikistan. In both countries, the government resisted donor pressure to democratize; public verbal retaliation was used against donors who supposedly pushed the issue of democracy too aggressively. But this has not significantly affected aid flows. This outcome might be surprising because one might expect that peacebuilders would have greater leverage in aid-dependent countries.

Aid dependency means that recipient governments need to keep donors on board. It leads to considerable donor influence over policy processes; involves high levels of foreign technical assistance in some areas of administration; and potentially limits the ability of recipients to make their own policy choices. Yet punitive conditionality has rarely been applied in relation to democracy.[53] Rhetorical threats outweigh concrete action.[54] And where conditions have been applied, the impact has been insignificant. For example, much pressure was placed on the Rwandan government in the run-up to the general elections of 2003, including reductions in aid for the election process. Yet the government found the money from domestic sources—a combination of private contributions and public revenue—and proceeded with the vote. The ensuing elections were condemned as not free and fair by some observers but were generally accepted by the international community.

Aid conditionality, as well as these other forms of pressure and persuasion, can have unintended and negative consequences. This can occur when donors purposefully ignore democratic discrepancies and fail to follow through on threats to withhold aid. Or it can take the form of choosing to back particular groups, in the belief that these groups are more committed to democracy than others. In Kosovo, external actors concentrated their aid and cooperation on partners chosen from the Kosovo Albanian majority population, especially during the humanitarian emergency phase in 1999–2000. UNMIK and KFOR favored the prewar political elites from the LDK (Rugova) and the UCK–PDK (Thaci); they also selected moderate leaders from minority groups while potential spoiler groups such as veteran associations and resistance groups were sidelined. However, such a strategy can also ignore the real power wielders to catastrophic effect, as the Rwandan example demonstrates. Here, the position of extremists was strengthened by their exclusion from peace negotiations. More effort to engage with *all* parties to the conflict might have helped the peace process to work.

The Mozambique example demonstrates how the leverage of external actors can be enhanced when they work together toward a common goal. We saw a similar situation in Macedonia, where peacebuilders supported full implementation of administrative and economic reforms laid out in the peace agreements.

Coherence alone is not enough, however. In both Bosnia and Kosovo, external actors were agreed on a set of goals; in Bosnia they agreed that the Dayton peace agreement was inviolate, and in Kosovo external actors were working toward the goals laid down in UN Resolution 1244. However, as we have already seen, in both these countries a coherent approach to conditionality did little to enhance the democratization process, and in Kosovo there was insufficient coherence in aid delivery and policy at the start of the intervention. Moreover, a coherent approach requires the inclusion of *all* key external players. This was particularly problematic in Tajikistan, where Western donors did not work well with Russia, which had significant leverage over the government. Donors lost the opportunity to forge a common agenda, giving the government an alternative source of support.[55]

Rwanda and Afghanistan provide particularly good examples of the impact of *in*coherence among donors. The run-up to Rwanda's first legislative and presidential elections after the genocide, held in 2003, saw the inaugural application of conditions to aid directly related to democracy. A clampdown on opposition parties and voices as well as human rights abuses led several donors to withhold or threaten to withhold aid, including the European Commission, the United Kingdom, and the Netherlands. The UK arrested aid to the media sector when the government refused to liberalize its airwaves; the European Commission initially refused to disburse aid promised for elections (but released funds after elections had taken place); and the Netherlands ultimately withheld its aid for elections. This action was undermined by other donors who came out in support of the government and maintained the flow of aid.

This varied response by donors reflects their diverging opinion about the Rwandan government. Throughout the first five years after the conflict, donors were almost divided into two opposing camps: those who were positive about the new regime (often new donors who had a limited history of bilateral relations with the country, such as the Netherlands, Sweden, and the UK) and those who were negative about the new regime (those who had enduring ties to the country and thus its former regime, such as France and Belgium). Positions became less polarized as time passed, but aid in the early years after the conflict was affected by this uneven donor stance. The government was able to rely on certain friends and could therefore afford to ignore demands made by some donors.[56]

In Afghanistan, attempts at structured coordination, with donors taking responsibility for specific activities based on their interests, created different problems. The emphasis on counterterrorism and security led to much aid being provided in a supply-driven manner according to the sectoral or geographic priorities of donors. The UK and Canada, for example, worked to secure the southern parts of the country, where their troops were concentrated. A pillar-based approach was taken to security and justice-sector reform, with responsibilities parceled out, such as Germany for the police, the United States for the Afghan National Army, the UK for counternarcotics, and Italy for the judiciary. While this sort of approach was successful in Kosovo, in Afghanistan it led to imbalances in how state institutions were supported, leading to uneven and uncoordinated development.

Leverage is also undermined when local elites are aware that donors may not follow through on threats to apply conditions to aid or may not react to digressions. In other words, where local elites recognize that external actors have either too much or too little at stake to enforce conditions, donor leverage is weakened. Threats by the EU in Tajikistan (referred to in the preceding paragraphs) were primarily symbolic and aimed at preventing further deterioration. Thus, donors implored the government not to ban political parties based on religious affiliation, not to adopt a draconian law on religion, not to harass media and civil society, and not to ban NGOs from receiving grants from abroad. Yet, when ignored, donors continued to provide aid and were criticized for appearing to tolerate human rights abuses.

Similarly, donors continued to support the Rwandan government with ever-increasing amounts of aid, despite its repression of political rights, on the grounds that the country was moving in the "right direction." In East Timor there have been tensions between the government and UN actors over war crimes indictments and human rights abuses but no knock-on effects for aid; bilateral donors have refused to push the impunity issue to preserve their relations with Indonesia, and although "concerns" have been expressed about democratic digression, there is no evidence that conditionality has been applied.

In Afghanistan, conditionality was not even threatened, let alone applied, in the face of clear breaches of democratic principles, such as the vetting of election candidates and human rights abuses or requested reforms not being carried out.[57] In Kosovo, local actors were confident that external aid would continue and were therefore under limited pressure to comply with peacebuilder demands. The situation was similar in Macedonia, where aid was guaranteed under the Stable Relations Agreement. Likewise, in Bosnia the mission was "too big to fail" and required the cooperation of local actors, who were well aware of their bargaining power.

Part of this inconsistency can be traced to the differing goals and priorities of donors and to whether democracy was really central to their agenda, again an issue raised in the literature. In Mozambique, democratization was crucial to the peace process; in many other cases, it has been just one priority among many, which undermines peacebuilder leverage through aid. In the early years after the Rwandan genocide, donors acted under a heavy cloud of guilt brought about by the failure to prevent or halt the slaughter; democracy was not the central objective. In Tajikistan, the United States was keen to make a new "friend." Because there was no strategic interest in isolating the country, its "disappointment with Tajikistan's 'democratic development' did not affect the amount of assistance."[58] In both of these countries, aid for democracy was limited during the first five years after the conflict. There was support for humanitarian relief, reconstruction, and institution building, but aid was not used to strongly influence the restructuring of domestic power. Multiple and competing objectives (within the programs of individual donors and among them), as well as strategic considerations, were particularly strong in the case of Afghanistan.

We have already mentioned the problems that arise when donors look the other way. A final hindrance to the potential leverage offered by aid occurs when donors fail to recognize and act on particular windows of opportunity where they could have made a difference or when well-intentioned acts backfire. In Namibia, the international community's attitude has been described as one of "benign neglect," in that they overlooked the weaknesses of the young democracy and failed to entrench democratic principles through targeted aid.[59]

In Bosnia the international community forfeited some of its initial leverage by holding elections quickly and by confirming the war's victors as legitimate state leaders. The international community retracted some of its powers in 1997, but constant showdowns did little to build a culture of responsibility among local politicians. Donors were reluctant to take decisive steps that might advance democracy but destabilize the peace—such as removing war criminals from politics—although eventually they did take such steps. They gradually built structures that gave them legal authority to remove politicians who did not respect the new democratic rules of the game or who refused to honor the peace settlement. Yet, in doing so, the international community accepted full responsibility for the external authority structures it erected, creating a spiral of dependency.

The failure of donors to frontload democracy aid in Tajikistan when they could have made a real difference is considered aid's main weakness in that country. Leverage was high when the leadership was most vulnerable and desperately in need of aid. By the time aid was increased, donors had alienated the government by ignoring its stated priorities and by failing to cooperate with Russia. A similar situation prevailed in Afghanistan, where a failure to provide substantial aid in the first two years after the conflict contributed to peacebuilders' inability to secure peace and generate political transformation.[60] In Rwanda, by not addressing the ongoing security threat posed by opposition groups camped on the border, a threat that was certainly recognized by several donors as legitimate in the late 1990s, international actors helped to embed a strong national security discourse that was later used by the Rwandan government to repress political opposition.

## Conclusion

In this chapter we have sought to isolate the impact of aid, or more accurately, of aid *donors*, on democratic outcomes in postconflict peacebuilding interventions. Although data on democracy aid are incomplete, we have filled in the picture through a careful examination of aid's effects in our nine cases.

The empirical evidence in these cases suggests that the impact of aid on democratic peacebuilding outcomes is mediated by the relationships among donors and between donors and local elites and by the degree to which aid provision is structured to allow donors to make timely interventions on the ground that either lower the costs to local elites of adopting democracy or raise the costs of not doing so. The amounts and types of support for democratization, which at first glance might seem important, are in fact secondary.

First, leverage from aid depends on the *relationships* that aid provision creates over time among donors who fund and/or implement key aspects of peacebuilding and between these donors and local actors. These relationships, which precede interventions, are important because they affect mutual confidence between peacebuilders and local elites and hence add to or subtract from the credibility of donors as external guarantors. They also add to or subtract from donors' ability to coordinate with one another and determine the degree to which donors have local knowledge about political, social, cultural, and other conditions that could affect the peacebuilding process.

Second, aid increases leverage where it is structured in such a way that it enables donors to be flexible and responsive to unforeseen challenges in the peace process. It is most effective when individual donors are able to tie their own contributions to actions they require of local elites to move the democratization process forward. Donors with resources and the organizational capacity to make timely interventions using those resources had more leverage than those who did not.

Aid is *not* effective in increasing leverage or mitigating the adoption costs of democracy when donors are unable or unwilling to apply conditionality; when they lack a clear commitment to democracy over other concerns; when they lack the coherence necessary to act decisively and predictably; and when they lack the local knowledge and connections necessary to take advantage of opportunities to gain leverage.

When donors used aid to make an unpredictable security or political environment for local actors a little bit more predictable, they lowered the cost of adopting democracy for local elites (or at least clarified these costs). Thus, financial support for Renamo in Mozambique lowered adoption costs for the party leadership, and donors' willingness to shoulder the cost of elections similarly lowered adoption costs for Mozambique's political elites. In Macedonia, Bosnia, and Kosovo, democracy aid was aimed at, among other things, helping governments conform to the requirements necessary to join the EU. This carrot gave donors, and thus peacebuilders, some measure of leverage. Where donors were not able to mitigate high adoption costs by influencing security or political environments or by dangling tangible rewards conditioned on democratization, aid appears to have made little difference to democratic outcomes, no matter how much was given. This is evident from an examination of Tajikistan, Afghanistan, and Rwanda.

# 6   Neighborhood

SCHOLARS AGREE THAT THE GEOGRAPHIC LOCATION OF A country has a significant bearing on its propensity for war or peace and its quality of governance. No country is immune to flows of people, goods, money, or ideas from nearby countries. Clearly, transnational factors—which originate in one country but affect developments in adjacent countries—can contribute to democratization and stabilization, and many scholars have observed that countries with relatively high levels of democracy often cluster together, as do countries with a high propensity for war.[1]

Neighborhood matters, and in this chapter we investigate the impact of neighborhood factors on postwar democratic transitions. As we have described in previous chapters, we assume that peacebuilding outcomes depend on the interactive process between domestic elites and peacebuilders and that the preferences of domestic elites are to a large extent determined by the costs of adopting democracy on the one hand and by peacebuilders' leverage on the other. We assume that neighborhood factors influence the adoption costs borne by domestic elites, but also the capacity and willingness of peacebuilders to mobilize resources, and we put this assumption to a test, using empirical evidence from nine recent peacebuilding operations.

We proceed as follows. We begin with a brief literature review, summarizing how neighborhood factors are believed to increase or diminish chances for peace and democracy in a given environment. Scholars typically treat peace and democratization as separate issues, a division that is reflected in our discussion. We then discuss what the literature has to say on the effects of neighborhood on democratization, and next we synthesize the two strands. Finally, we turn to our empirical evidence and examine whether and how neighborhood factors affected the democratic outcome of peacebuilding.

## Neighborhood Effects on Civil War

Perhaps the most straightforward of all neighborhood factors is the transnational spread of ethnic violence.[2] Violence in one country can spill into a neighboring country. For various reasons, belligerents in one country may decide to widen the scope of their battle, contributing to a spatial escalation of the conflict. This is often referred to as "contagion."[3] Of course, ethnic violence can also spread unintentionally; Lake and Rothschild refer to this as "diffusion." Generally speaking, diffusion occurs when ethnic violence in one state increases the probability of conflict in another. For example, events linked to violent conflict in State A may upset the delicate balance of power and economic opportunity between various ethnic groups in State B, igniting a second war. This can happen when large refugee flows change the demography of a country or when insurgents from a neighboring state disrupt an equilibrium between rival ethnic groups.

The ethnic balance—or, more generally, the balance of power among the various elites groups on which stability depends—can also be upset if one party to the conflict receives support from external actors. Rogers Brubaker argues that ethnic groups with kin in an adjacent country are more likely to engage in ethnic and national mobilization because they expect outside support.[4] This mechanism was clearly at work in the former Soviet Union and Yugoslavia, and it can also be observed in other regions where ethnic politics matter and where international borders were created without regard to the settlement pattern of ethnic groups. But ethnic groups are not alone in upsetting preexisting power balances. Civil wars in Bosnia, Afghanistan, Rwanda, and Tajikistan were to no small degree caused by the support that external regional powers lent to one party of the conflict or the other.

Conflict may also spread beyond the borders of one country due to the "demonstration effect," which, at its most basic level, refers to a situation in which one group updates its beliefs about the cost and benefit of war after observing the success or failure of a foreign group pursuing similar ends. For example, a group in one state may witness how another group mobilizes to demand a redistribution of power. The observing group may then conclude that mobilization is worth the associated risks. Thus, ethnic mobilization may lead neighboring groups to reevaluate the safeguards contained in their own political system and/or rethink the resilience of the elite group that controls the state.[5] Many ethnic groups in the former Soviet Union, for example, watched the early mobilizers in Estonia, Latvia, and Lithuania. When they concluded that the Communist Party did not intend to crack down at full force, they themselves began to mobilize. The result was a spiral of ethnic mobilization fuelled by transnational demonstration effects.[6] According to Fearon, groups can also mobilize out of fear.[7] When a group observes an ethnic conflict across its border, it may conclude that conflict is imminent at home. In response, the group may mobilize for defensive purposes, or even consider a preemptive strike.

Elites can also update their beliefs about the feasibility of violence. For example, if a leader can successfully instrumentalize ethnicity to cement his or her hold on power, other leaders may pursue a similar strategy.[8] It is perhaps not surprising, then, that Gleditsch and Gleditsch and Buhaug find that the political support of a neighboring ethnic group, the general level of regional democracy, as well as a country's integration in international trade all influence a country's chances of remaining at peace.[9]

## Neighborhood Effects on Democratization

The literature on civil war is predominantly concerned with bad, as opposed to good, neighborhoods. Contagion, external support for one party, or demonstration effects are all seen as mechanisms that can contribute to a country's destabilization. By contrast, the literature on democratization puts considerable emphasis on the *positive* incentives that transcend borders and inspire democratic change.[10] Some scholars have noted that democracies tend to cluster in space, suggesting that democratization is diffused across borders.[11] One mechanism that might account for such diffusion is the demonstration effect. For example, positive demonstration effects are believed to have contributed to the waves of democratic transitions following the collapse of the former Soviet Union and Yugoslavia;[12] the so-called colored revolutions in Ukraine, Georgia, and Kyrgyzstan between 2003 and 2005; and the "Arab Spring" that shook Tunisia, Egypt, Bahrain, and Libya in early 2011. Scholars argue that news coverage of a democratic transition can inspire new challenges to autocracy abroad and that a successful democratic change can lead groups to update their perceptions of the possible. Groups also learn from each other—how to organize rallies, how to instrumentalize domestic and international media, and how to brand a movement—leading to such catchy names as the Rose Revolution in Georgia, the Orange Revolution in Ukraine, the Tulip Revolution in Kyrgyzstan, or the Jasmine Revolution in Tunisia.

While the literature typically highlights positive demonstration effects, it should be noted that these effects can run both ways.[13] Negative demonstration effects can occur when leaders observe that democratization in a neighboring country has led to chaos and civil unrest or jeopardizes an elite's hold on power, or, conversely, when leaders see that an autocrat successfully employs authoritarian means to resist domestic or international pressure to democratize. Clearly, the influence of "successful" authoritarian models such as China and Russia has grown recently, and against such role models the liberal democracy prescribed by the international community may seem less attractive to some observers.

Apart from the demonstration effect, democratization can also be promoted if sympathizers receive financial aid and/or political support. As with the demonstration effect, however, external support can run both ways; an autocratic hegemon may opt to promote authoritarian politics in neighboring countries and support an authoritarian regime that can complicate or even doom a democratization effort.[14]

Finally, democratization may also be influenced by its existing ties—economic, cultural, and political—to other countries. For example, transnational networks may promote democratic reforms in authoritarian societies, diffuse democratic principles, support domestic allies, and exert pressure on authoritarian regimes.[15] Steve Levitsky and Lucan Way have argued that regimes have pursued different political pathways in accordance with their relationship to the West.[16] The post–Cold War international environment, they say, does not affect all countries evenly. External democratizing pressures, in the form of diplomatic or military pressure, multilateral political conditionality, democracy assistance programs, and the activities of transnational human rights and democracy networks are more intense and sustained in some regions (Central Europe, the Americas) than in others (sub-Saharan Africa, the former Soviet Union).

Levitsky and Way argue that there are two dimensions of international relations that affect democratic processes. The first one is "linkage to the West":

that is, the density of a country's economic, social, and communication ties to the United States, the European Union, and Western-led multilateral institutions. The second dimension they call "Western leverage." This dimension refers to a government's structural vulnerability to external pressure. In general, the West has reduced leverage in countries with a large economy, major oil deposits, nuclear weapons, the support of a major non-Western power, and countries that are of strategic security interest.[17] (Note that this concept of leverage is different from the one that we use throughout this book. Our definition refers to a specific situational leverage that peacebuilders may hold over domestic elites when they depend on the resources and security guarantees that peacebuilders can offer and because they require the support of peacebuilders to obtain their prime political objective. "Leverage" as used by Levitsky and Way refers to a structural and general vulnerability of a state to the interests of Western powers due primarily to economic factors.) Both leverage and linkage can raise the cost of authoritarianism. Interestingly, Levitsky and Way find that the mechanisms of leverage are in themselves rarely sufficient to democratize autocracies; rather, the more subtle and diffuse effects of linkage seem to contribute more consistently to democratization.

One political entity that is believed to radiate both leverage and linkage is the European Union. It is said the EU has a "gravitational pull" in significant parts of Central and Eastern Europe[18] owing to its ability to increase linkages and information flows to reformist countries and to offer them significant benefits such as admission to the EU market, access to the EU system of transfers, and guarantees of political stability and security. One study of the interaction among ruling illiberal elites, opposition forces, and the European Union describes how EU influence undermined the "asymmetries enjoyed by illiberal rulers."[19] Other authors have focused on how democratic conditionality influenced elite behavior in new and aspiring member states.[20]

This brief discussion has shown that spatial effects, transborder in nature, can contribute to an environment that either enables or constrains postwar democratic transitions. The literature has identified a number of mechanisms—contagion, demonstration effects, linkage, leverage, and support—that account for a country's propensity to war or democratize. All of these mechanisms are highly compatible with our conceptualization of peacebuilding as an interactive process between domestic elites and peacebuilders. These mechanisms also align with our concept of adoption costs because each can shape domestic elites' preferences and influence adoption costs. Violent con-

TABLE 6.1. Possible causal mechanisms of neighborhood effects on postwar democratization.

|  | Mechanism | Effect |
|---|---|---|
| Contagion and diffusion | Triggers war or increases perceptions of threats of war | Increases adoption costs |
| Support to one party | Changes power balance | Increases/reduces adoption costs |
| Demonstration effect | Adapts beliefs | Increases/reduces adoption costs |
| Linkages | Shapes preferences | Reduces adoption costs |
| Leverage | Offsets some adoption costs | Reduces adoption costs |

tagion, or the fear of it, will increase costs; external support to domestic elites will affect the balance of power within a country and hence adoption costs; demonstration effects can lead groups to update their beliefs about the feasibility and desirability of authoritarian or democratic policies; finally, linkages and leverage can reduce costs. Table 6.1 offers an overview of the neighborhood factors so far discussed and the causal mechanisms by which they might shape outcomes.

The remainder of this chapter relies on empirical observations from our nine case studies to uncover how these five mechanisms practically shaped postwar democratic transitions after the Cold War. We find that neighborhood matters, but it matters in different ways in different locations. In three cases—East Timor, Namibia, and Mozambique—neighborhood factors helped create an environment conducive to the war's conclusion. However, neighborhood factors did not shape the ensuing interaction between domestic elites and peacebuilders, which in all three cases led to successful democratization.

In the remaining six cases, neighborhood factors significantly shaped domestic elites' preferences for or against democratic reform. Neighborhood also accounts for some of the leverage that peacebuilders had over domestic elites in these cases. But, importantly, the effects of neighborhood are predominantly negative: In three cases—Afghanistan, Tajikistan, and Rwanda—neighborhood factors significantly constrained democratization; in two cases—Bosnia and Kosovo—neighborhood factors provided a mixed environment for democratization; only in one case—Macedonia—did neighborhood factors contribute to an environment that was clearly favorable to democratic development.

## Enabling Peace: East Timor, Namibia, and Mozambique

In East Timor, Namibia, and Mozambique we observe that neighborhood factors, although crucial for the transition from war to peace, did little or nothing to shape the transition toward a more democratic regime. This suggests that transitions from war to peace, and from a nonliberal postwar regime to a more democratic one, are driven by different sets of factors. Moreover, democratic transitions are much less affected by external factors than are transitions from war to peace.

A case in point is East Timor, where neighborhood factors helped create an environment where the country could begin its pursuit of democratic development. Only when Indonesia cautiously adopted democratic reforms under the leadership of President Suharto's successor B. J. Habibie did East Timor stake out its independence and begin its democratization process. While this process was aided by the United Nations and other international actors, including one regional power (Australia), the main factors that account for the democratic outcome were domestic. These include local domestic actors' high demand for democracy, their reliance on the international community in their bid for independence, the fact that the new leadership faced little domestic opposition, and a relatively generous yet unintrusive peacebuilding mission. Neighborhood factors do not explain domestic demand for democracy, but it is true that the democratization process was facilitated by the support of Indonesia and Australia.

Transitions in Mozambique and Namibia bear much resemblance to East Timor. In each case, a favorable neighborhood helped ease protracted conflicts, yet the factors that account for democratic success were predominantly domestic. In both countries, the democratic opening of South Africa (the regional hegemon) facilitated the transition to peace. Specifically, South Africa's willingness to implement UN Resolution 435 in 1990 allowed Namibia to achieve independence. This independence was negotiated in a manner that required democracy and guaranteed South African interests. Yet, once the new government came into power, South Africa's influence rapidly diminished. The UN mission in Namibia did foresee a special role for South Africa as a partner in the peace process, but the hegemon's role in Namibia's ensuing shift to democratic governance was clearly minimal compared to domestic factors.

The end of apartheid in South Africa also contributed to peace in Mozambique and to its ability to hold multiparty elections. South Africa's new democratic leadership stopped aiding the Renamo rebel group, backed Mozambique's peace agreement, and supported the peace process. This allowed Mozambique to embark on postconflict democratization, but, as in Namibia, the adoption costs of democracy were primarily driven by domestic politics. While international donors and the UN mission to Mozambique were aware that success in Mozambique depended on regional stability, the focus remained on Mozambique alone, and the mission mandate did not address regional issues.

Thus, in Timor, Namibia, and Mozambique, neighborhood factors helped ease warring factions out of war but greatly diminished in importance once a truce was reached. The subsequent interaction between the domestic elites and the peacebuilders was predominantly shaped by domestic factors.

## Constraining Environments:
## Rwanda, Tajikistan, Afghanistan

In Namibia, Mozambique, and East Timor we observe that neighborhood factors did not *cause* a democratic outcome but rather *enabled or unlocked* other factors that did have a benevolent effect. Three other cases from our sample—Afghanistan, Tajikistan, and Rwanda—demonstrate the potential negative impact of neighborhood on democratic postwar transitions. In each case, neighborhood factors increased the adoption costs for elites. The resources and leverage peacemakers were willing and able to muster proved insufficient to offset these high costs or create local demand for democracy.

In Rwanda, elites feared a spillover of ethnic violence from Burundi and the Democratic Republic of Congo (DRC). The high tensions among Burundi, Uganda, the DRC, and Rwanda created a neighborhood of insecurity and conflict. Hutu rebels launched attacks on Rwandan territory from the neighboring DRC after the Rwandan Patriotic Front (RPF) seized power in 1994. Skirmishes erupted between Rwanda and Uganda after both countries deployed troops to fight in the Second Congo War between 1998 and 2002. The civil war between Hutus and Tutsis in Burundi (1993–2005) further destabilized the region. Movements of displaced persons and refugees in the aftermath of the genocide stressed the capacities of state authorities beyond their limits. In essence, the region was in a constant state of flux—in the midst of conflict or close to it while confronting pressing humanitarian emergencies. This regional context, combined with a lack of credible democratic role models, reinforced deep-seated reservations on the part of Rwandan elites, convincing them that democratization as defined by the West was a potentially dangerous and destabilizing process.

Despite the fact that Rwanda's overwhelming aid dependence gave peace-builders significant potential leverage, Western powers were inclined to tolerate Kigali's preference for authoritarianism. They accepted President Kagame's prioritization of stability, humanitarian relief, and reconstruction and channeled most resources into these areas. This decision was partly influenced by a genuine desire to stabilize Rwanda and the Great Lakes region in general, but, as most observers believe, was also due to feelings of guilt and responsibility for the 1994 genocide.

Tajikistan is another case where neighborhood factors clearly constrained the prospects for postwar democratic transitions. In 1997, five years after the start of the peacebuilding mission, Tajikistan was a solidly authoritarian state with a Freedom House score of 6 (and has not since improved its rating). A number of neighborhood factors have played into this outcome.

First, the elite that emerged victorious after the bloody civil war received substantial support from Russia and Uzbekistan. Neither of these states supported democracy. Russia, the regional hegemon and a significant backer of the peace process, was not interested in sponsoring a democratic opening but preferred to stabilize the region by supporting secular parties in Central Asia as bulwarks against Islamic radicals. For similar reasons, Uzbekistan also favored an authoritarian and secular regime.

Furthermore, as described by Matveeva, a "negative demonstration effect" may also have played a role in shaping the antidemocratic preferences of Tajik elites (and large parts of the Tajik public).[21] The economic success and political stability of Russia as well as Kazakhstan, Central Asia's powerhouse, provided the public and leaders with "functioning alternatives" to democracy, further undermining any domestic demand for liberal democracy.

Fear of contagion also incentivized autocracy. The Tajik government was wary of spillover violence from neighboring Afghanistan. During the Tajik civil war, swaths of the Afghan–Tajik borders had become highly porous; armed fighters, weapons, and above all narcotics traveled freely. Opium from Afghanistan was exported via Tajikistan. Fighters from the Tajik opposition found shelter in Afghanistan, and fighters from the Afghan Northern Alliance found shelter in Tajikistan. The Tajik government repeatedly suggested that democracy would be risky because it would allow violence in Afghanistan to permeate Tajikistan. In their eyes, an authoritarian regime was a bulwark against contagion, in the same way that it guarded against radical Islamists at home.

Finally, few linkages bridged the West and Central Asia in general—and Tajikistan in particular; Tajikistan, the poorest and smallest of the Central Asian states, was isolated from many of the changes happening in the western areas of the former Soviet Union. Prior to the terrorist attacks of September 11, 2001, Tajikistan was off the radar of Western foreign policy. Afterwards, aid flows to Tajikistan grew precipitously. Aid as a percentage of central government expenditures climbed from 5 percent in 1993 to 37 percent in 2004, while official development assistance in 2004 reached US$240 million, compared to US$180 million in general government final consumption expenditure.[22]

Tajikistan's newly acquired strategic importance in Central Asia had the effect of reducing peacebuilders' de facto leverage. Leaders in Tajikistan knew that Western powers were keen to enlist Central Asian elites in their struggle to defend secular regimes against the assaults of radical Islamists. Furthermore, the war in Afghanistan prompted Western powers to use Tajik airspace and land supply lines. As a result, Tajik elites were immunized against lukewarm calls for democratic reform.

Afghanistan clearly demonstrates how a bad neighborhood can jeopardize a postwar democratic transition. An explosive mix of neighborhood factors—contagion, negative demonstration effects, outside support for undemocratic oppositional groups, and scarce Western leverage and linkages—has created an environment where democracy and peace are unlikely to take root.

For most of its recent history, regional powers have sought to dominate Afghanistan, a strategic location linking the Middle East with Central Asia and the Indian subcontinent. The result has been almost perpetual violent conflict. Meaningful state building, let alone democratic state building, has been impossible. In *The Fragmentation of Afghanistan*,[23] Barnett Rubin describes how Pakistan's secret service, the Inter-Services Intelligence (ISI), funneled military aid donated by the United States and other states to various factions of the mujaheddin fighting the Soviet occupiers, paving the way for the subsequent civil war. The Taliban later emerged victorious but fell from power in 2001. The Afghanistan of President Karzai (chosen through the Bonn Agreement of 2001 to be the West's trusted partner in postwar democratization) is no less vulnerable to regional politics and spillovers than were previous Afghan regimes: Afghan Taliban fighters find sanctuary in the tribal areas of neighboring Pakistan; the ISI once again supports factions of the Afghan Taliban; the global jihad industry fuels the war with money and fighters; and Iran is exercising its influence over the Tajik of western Afghanistan. Neighborhood factors have consistently fanned the flames of civil war and political fragmentation that have crippled this country for more than three decades.

In addition, five out of Afghanistan's six neighbors—Tajikistan, Uzbekistan, Turkmenistan, Iran, and China—are among the world's most authoritarian regimes. Pakistan is rated "partly free" by Freedom House, yet few would argue that it is a staunch advocate of democracy.

Afghanistan is only weakly integrated in Western networks; hence there is no "linkage" according to Levitsky and Way's sense of the term.[24] Moreover, as we have argued previously, the considerable leverage peacebuilders could have exerted in Afghanistan was countervailed by the fact that they, due to geostrategic reasoning, prioritized stability over liberal reform and hence continued to support the decidedly undemocratic domestic elite. Consequently, linkage and leverage proved impotent against the high adoption costs for democracy, to which neighborhood factors clearly contributed. Afghanistan today remains critically fractionalized, hobbled by various regional influences that are only exacerbated by the weakness of the central state administration, the strength of the Taliban, ethnic and linguistic heterogeneity, and the entrenched local power brokers openly hostile toward Kabul.

## Mixed Environments: Macedonia, Bosnia, Kosovo

Neighborhood factors have had mixed effects on the countries of Southeast Europe. Highly contagious conflicts led to violent spillovers throughout the region and helped create a region in which often ferocious ethnonationalism prevailed against the demand for democracy. On the other hand, the lure of the EU did cause some adjacent states to moderate their politics.

In Macedonia, positive neighborhood effects clearly outweighed negative ones. In early 2001, tensions between the Macedonian majority and the Albanian minority threatened to escalate into full-scale civil war. The armed conflict was, to a large extent, a spillover from Kosovo and Southern Serbia. The

Albanian minority maintained close political ties to actors in Kosovo, with whom they were often also linked by family ties. Albanians in Macedonia had also supported Kosovo Albanians in their struggle against the Serbian regime in the 1980s and 1990s. Macedonian Albanians could therefore count on the logistical and financial support of comrades in their own struggle against the Macedonian government. In early 2001, the Albanian minority in Macedonia demanded that Albanian settlements in Macedonia and Kosovo be unified and granted territorial autonomy. These demands were quickly abandoned, however, when the international community strongly rejected any territorial change. On August 13, 2001, under massive pressure from NATO and the EU, the Ohrid Framework Agreement was signed by the Macedonian government and ethnic Albanian representatives, ending the conflict.

Under the agreement, Macedonia implemented a series of reforms to decentralize its administration, modernize its public sector, and improve relations with the Albanian minority. This process was supported by both Macedonian and ethnic Albanian political elites because it helped fulfill the Copenhagen Criteria necessary to receive full EU membership. Macedonia had already put its signature to the Stabilization and Association Agreement in April 2001, signaling its interest in EU and NATO memberships—a significant step toward closer integration.

Macedonian and Albanian elites pushed through contested reforms and maintained control of their electorates by referring to EU entry requirements. As a result, the EU granted Macedonia "candidate country" status in late 2005, a considerable accomplishment considering that Macedonia had been on the brink of large-scale civil war just four years earlier. While Macedonia today faces ongoing challenges with regard to its ethnic composition and leadership, it is addressing these concerns within what is considered a democratic and pro-EU set of institutions and processes.

Neighborhood factors thus contributed both to the onset of ethnic conflict in Macedonia and to its quick and successful resolution. The short war was to a large extent caused by spillovers and support from neighboring Kosovo, but neighborhood factors—above all EU and NATO interest in securing Europe's most volatile region—also account for the efficient reaction of international actors. Furthermore, the prospect of joining the EU and NATO clearly provided incentives for Macedonians and ethnic Albanians to accommodate demands for peace and establish a more inclusive political system. In essence, the leverage exerted by the EU, combined with the benefits domestic elites hoped to gain, created an opportunity for both parties to establish strong links with Europe.

Neighborhood factors contributed to the onset of civil war in Bosnia in 1992, determined its violent course, and shaped the policies of postwar democratic transitions. While not the only factor, the support that Serbian and Croatian governments afforded their ethnic brethren in Bosnia certainly contributed to the outbreak of hostilities. Croatia and Serbia continued this support even after the 1995 Dayton Agreement ended the violence. While Croatia and Serbia officially endorsed the peace, their policies remained predominantly driven by ethnonationalism and support for kin. This support allowed minority Serbs and Croats to dominate much of the political and economic landscape in Bosnia and to become "spoilers" in the multiethnic state-building project. They were able to take hard-line positions against any particularly intrusive efforts by the international community either to build up state institutions or to democratize them. As a result, after ten years of internationally sponsored efforts, Bosnia remained a weak and only partially democratic state.

By 2000, Croatia and Serbia had transitioned into reasonably democratic regimes. Still, they did not become positive role models for Bosnia, nor did they abandon their support for Bosnia's ethnonationalist elites. They still supported (if in a less overt and generous manner) their ethnic clients in Bosnia, who still sought to impede the multiethnic state-building project. Being "democratic" in Belgrade and Zagreb did not mean ending support for kin but rather keeping a lower profile while doing so. For example, Zagreb denounced expansionist tendencies in Bosnia after 2000, yet continued to bankroll the Bosnian Croat elite and their supporters—everything from defense to social welfare funding. In Serbia, the ousting of Slobodan Milosevic in 2000 brought the democratically elected president Vojislav Kostunica to power. Kostunica, however, maintained support for Bosnian Serbs. And even with the more pro-reform Zoran Djindjic and later Boris Tadic, there were clear limits on the reforms that Serb leaders could push domestically while balancing nationalist interests at home and in Bosnia. This support empowered the Serb ethnic elite and their politics, undermining the state-building and democratization project pursued by the international community.

One might expect that Bosnia's position in Southeast Europe would place it under heavy EU influence. Yet the history of the conflict proved to Bosnian elites that the EU was incapable of decisive action. Furthermore, among the many international actors competing for influence in Bosnia, the EU failed to obtain a dominant position. When the EU eventually strengthened its political commitment and increased its resource flows to Bosnia, domestic elites adopted democratic rhetoric but stubbornly maintained their ethnonationalist political preferences. Furthermore, peacebuilders had a limited ability to influence Bosnia's neighbors, Croatia and Serbia. They lacked the mandate to do so officially and depended on good relations with Croatia, which at the time was a military staging base for the Bosnian effort. Cordial relations with the Zagreb government—both the Tudjman and later the reform administration—underpinned the peace mission.

In sum, contagion contributed to the onset of war, and neighborhood support cemented the ethnonationalist outlook of two of the three warring parties in Bosnia, making a transition to liberal democracy virtually impossible. The strategic importance of the region and its proximity to Europe helps explain the peacebuilding intervention that followed. The interventionists' leverage was limited, however, because they were uncoordinated, lacked a regional mandate, and were forced to accommodate Croatia. Under such circumstances, the EU's ability to promote peace and democracy was radically impaired.

As in Bosnia, Kosovo's geostrategic importance to Europe explains the international community's eagerness to deploy a massive peacebuilding mission with substantial resources. To this extent, Kosovo profited from its geographic location. But neighborhood factors also played a negative role. While the war between Serbia and the Kosovo Liberation Army (KLA) originated, at least in part, in Serbia's aggressive denial of Kosovar autonomy and later independence, the war became feasible only when large numbers of small arms surfaced from the collapse of neighboring Albania in mid-1997. Earlier that year, Albania was rocked by a severe economic and political crisis in which anger over fraudulent elections, as well as the government's inability to compensate Albanians for losses suffered under a massive pyramid scheme, plunged the country into a near-civil war in which some 2,000 people were killed. Thousands of small firearms were stolen from security forces and funneled to the KLA.[25] In this respect, contagion did play a role, albeit a minor one, in the war's inception.

In June, 1999, the Kosovo War ended after more than two months of NATO air raids. During the subsequent postwar transition, neighborhood factors played only a minor role. Perhaps the most direct factor was staunch

Serbian support for Kosovo's Serbian minority, which exacerbated the conflict between the Kosovar majority and ethnic Serbians and jeopardized the international community's project of a multiethnic and democratic Kosovo. It is worth noting that Serbia's transition to democracy in 2000 did not change its position on Kosovo. Belgrade continued to oppose Kosovo's bid for independence and aggressively lobbied international institutions to take up its case. Consequently, Kosovo's Serbian minority had little incentive to accept the Kosovo state-building project, and Kosovars continued to perceive them as spoilers. As a result, Kosovo is far from realizing a multiethnic, inclusive democracy.

As in Bosnia, the pacifying and democratizing impact of the EU was limited. Given Kosovo's dependence on peacebuilders for security and on the EU for trade, aid, remittances, and political support, this is perhaps surprising. But, as we discussed in Chapter 4, peacebuilders, and especially the EU, were unable to translate potential leverage into reform. Due to the region's general volatility and strategic importance, peacebuilders prioritized stability over democracy and ultimately sacrificed much of their leverage by granting Kosovo greater autonomy and, eventually, independence. So while the massive peacebuilding intervention in Kosovo can largely be attributed to its position on the map, neighborhood factors did not in the end contribute significantly to democracy.

## Conclusion

Neighborhood factors such as the demonstration effect, linkage with and leverage by Western states, transnational support for a particular group, and violent contagion have, alone or in combination, influenced the postwar trajectories in each of our nine cases under investigation. But these factors vary in their size and effect, due partly to their relative importance and partly to the manner in which peacebuilders reacted to them. In general we find that neighborhood often affects a country's vulnerability to war but only rarely influences the process of postwar democratization.

Macedonia is the only case where we see a benign impact of neighborhood on democratic development, where the combined effect of high-level diplomacy (which is per se not a neighborhood factor), rapid NATO involvement (which backed diplomatic pressure), and the lure of EU ascension prevented the war's escalation and helped institute a democratic system.

We have also seen that the carrot of EU membership proved less enticing in Kosovo and Bosnia, where the politics of ethnic parochialism outweighs incentives for democratization. It appears that the EU was able to moderate authoritarian behavior but could not, in the end, incite democratic behavior. Whether this was a product of timing, the level of reward on offer, or due to other regional factors merits further study. The cases of Serbia and Croatia also suggest that not all democratization processes create positive demonstration effects and that not all democratic countries cease to support undemocratic elites in neighboring countries. In Bosnia and Kosovo, the ongoing support from "kin governments" created a significant obstacle to democratic development. External support for spoilers, it seems, is a highly efficient way to hinder democratic development.

In Namibia, Mozambique, and East Timor, neighborhood factors contributed to long and protracted wars. Peace was made impossible by South Africa's involvement in Namibia and Mozambique and by Indonesia's colonial regime in East Timor. Only after these regional shadows were lifted—creating a democratic opening in South Africa and Indonesia—was a meaningful peace process feasible. In this sense, neighborhood factors did contribute to postwar democratic transitions. However, neither South Africa nor Indonesia played a significant role in the subsequent democratic transitions of Namibia, Mozambique, and East Timor. These three examples show that peace and democracy may not be achievable for weak states in the immediate neighborhood of malevolent states—a lesson that Afghanistan knows all too well.

Finally, in Afghanistan, Rwanda, and Tajikistan, neighborhood factors constrained the possibility of democratic transition. Negative demonstration effects, fear of contagion, and support for undemocratic groups created an environment that was so hostile to democracy that peacebuilders tended to prioritize stability instead. Rwanda and Tajikistan are cases in point.

In general, "negative" neighborhood influence appears to be most powerful when domestic elites are competing for political dominance. Afghanistan, Bosnia, Kosovo (among the minority), and to some extent Tajikistan (early on following the peace treaty) all had contested state-building projects that amplified the potential influence of regional actors.

Table 6.2 summarizes our findings regarding the influence of neighborhood effects on peace and democracy, as well as on domestic actors' adoption costs.

At the risk of oversimplification, we conclude that neighborhood factors often provide insurmountable barriers to postwar democratic transitions but

**TABLE 6.2.** The effect of neighborhood factors on peace and democracy.

| Country | Mechanism | Environment | Effect on adoption costs and preferences for democracy |
|---------|-----------|-------------|------------------------------------|
| Macedonia | EU leverage, linkage, and support | Enabling peace and democracy | Strong |
| Namibia | Democratization of regional power | Enabling peace | Weak |
| Mozambique | Democratization of regional power | Enabling peace | Weak |
| Timor | Democratization of regional power | Enabling peace | Weak |
| Bosnia | Conflict contagion Regional linkage/support; EU leverage, linkage, and support | Mixed | Moderate |
| Kosovo | Regional linkage/support; EU leverage linkage and support | Mixed | Moderate/weak |
| Afghanistan | Conflict contagion; regional linkage, leverage, and support | Constraining peace and democracy | Strong |
| Rwanda | Conflict contagion | Constraining democracy | Moderate |
| Tajikistan | Demonstration effect, regional support | Constraining democracy | Strong |

only rarely enable such transitions. This finding is in contrast with much of the democratization literature, which tends to highlight "positive" regional effects. This bias may be explained in part by the euphoria that accompanied the post–Cold War "democratic wave," by the teleological understanding of democratic transition that accompanied this enthusiasm, or by the tendency of scholars to view the EU as a magic bullet. More attention to specifically "antidemocratic" influences at the regional level would likely cause other issues worthy of further study to surface.

Finally, given that neighborhood factors often seem to play an important but negative role in countries emerging from war, it is surprising that peacebuilding missions only rarely acknowledge or even address these factors (see Table 6.3). For example, only three of the nine cases under consideration (Bosnia, Namibia, and Kosovo) included neighboring countries as formal

**TABLE 6.3.** Elements of regional policy in UN peacebuilding mandates.

| | Afghanistan | Bosnia | Kosovo | Macedonia | Mozambique | Namibia | Rwanda | Tajikistan | Timor |
|---|---|---|---|---|---|---|---|---|---|
| Inclusion of regional powers as signatories or implementers | No | Yes | Yes | No | No | Yes | No | No | No |
| Specific reference to regional issues in UN mandate | Yes | Yes | Yes | No | No | Yes | No | No | Yes |
| Revised or follow-on mission that includes regional component | No | No | No | No | No | No | Yes | No | No |
| Adjusted to a de facto regional approach | Yes | Yes | No | No | No | No | No | Yes | No |

signatories to important treaties. Five mission mandates (Afghanistan, Bosnia, Kosovo, Namibia, and Timor) explicitly referred to regional issues but did not specify to what extent or with what resources these issues would be addressed. This gives rise to an important question: How can peacebuilders craft mandates in a way that addresses the malign effect of neighborhood factors? We believe this problem deserves further research.

# 7   Conclusion

*Explaining Postwar Democratic Transitions*

## Peacebuilding Is Interaction

Peacebuilding missions often bring peace, but rarely bring democracy. The literature has traditionally explained the limited success of postwar democratization as a function of various factors, among them a lack of administrative capacity in postwar societies to implement and maintain the complex and costly political institutions required for democratic and accountable governance; insurmountable cooperation problems among former warring parties (often exacerbated by the duration and intensity of the war and by identity cleavages); a geopolitical location vulnerable to spillovers from neighboring countries; and finally, with regard to peacebuilding missions themselves, inadequate mandates, lack of resources and personnel, and poor implementation.

These factors surely present daunting challenges to postwar democratization and capture important aspects of why postwar democratic transitions tend not to result in democracy. Indeed, democratization after war is a formidable task. This somewhat sobering finding raises, however, two important questions, neither of which is well addressed by existing scholarship. First, what causal processes explain why most postwar democratic transitions do not lead to democracy? Second, how do internationally led peacebuilding missions contribute to a democratic outcome?

As mentioned in our introduction, a careful comparison of recent peacebuilding efforts reveals that none of the factors commonly thought to account for successful or failed democratic postwar transitions—such as levels of postwar GDP, duration, intensity and type of war, modalities of postwar settlement, and footprint of the mission—is directly or consistently associated with a given outcome across all our cases. In other words, we do not detect a meaningful pattern that identifies these factors as direct causal mechanisms. As the cases from our sample show, some successful democratic peacebuilding operations were launched in poor countries lacking domestic administrative or economic capacity, whereas others failed in considerably more affluent countries with high levels of development and viable administrative structures in place. Some robust and highly intrusive operations failed, and some succeeded. This is also true of small-footprint peacebuilding operations. Moreover, some missions brought democracy even after a bloody and drawn-out war, and some did not, even if the war was relatively short. These few examples (the list goes on) underscore that we lack a consistent causal explanation of postwar democratic transition.

The existing literature does little to help us understand whether or how peacebuilding missions influence the odds for democratic success. The existing qualitative evidence is inconclusive at best, and the few available quantitative studies have failed to identify a statistically significant association between peacebuilding operations and democratization. In concluding one of these studies, Page Fortna writes that "peacebuilding has no clear or strong positive effect on democratization, relative to cases where belligerents are left to their own devices."[1] Certainly it is quite surprising that the presence of peacebuilders and their resources, which have a massive impact on the social fabric of postwar societies, leave no systematic trace in our cases with regard to democratization. As we have argued throughout this book, this "non-finding" may be an artifact of methodological and conceptual problems in the literature, which have so far not been adequately addressed by statistical approaches.

In this book, we offer an alternative conceptualization of peacebuilding. We have depicted peacebuilding as an interactive process not only between former adversaries but also between peacebuilders and the victorious elites of a postwar society. We have also demonstrated that the preferences of domestic elites are to a great extent shaped by the costs they incur in adopting democracy, as well as the leverage that peacebuilders can muster to increase the costs of nonadoption. Implicit in this understanding of peacebuilding is our assumption that the preferences of peacebuilders and domestic elites are hardly ever aligned.

Our approach thus parts with one of the most prominent yet underexamined assumptions of the peacebuilding literature (and presumably of peacebuilding practice): that the interests of domestic elites and peacebuilders coincide. As our sample cases demonstrate, this is rarely the case. Typically, domestic elites in postwar societies are keen to benefit from the resources—both material and symbolic—that peacebuilders can bring, but they are less eager to adopt democracy because they believe democratic reforms may endanger some or all of their substantive interests. Put differently, adopting democracy can be too costly a proposition for domestic elites, and the policies and resources of peacebuilders are typically unable to offset this cost.

## Adoption Costs

Theoretically, an infinite number of factors may increase the costs of adopting democracy. But a careful reading of the cases in our sample reveals that the actual number of factors that account for high or low adoption costs is relatively small.

First and foremost, adoption costs are determined by whether domestic elites perceive in democracy a threat to security. If they believe democracy will endanger security, which in volatile postwar societies is often tied to the physical safety of the ruling elite, then domestic elites are, quite understandably, reluctant to embrace democracy. Rwanda and Afghanistan exemplify this situation. In both cases, domestic elites felt that democratic openings might abet opposition groups still capable of organizing violence. Security is clearly the predominant concern in domestic elite calculations, but our case studies reveal that other factors play a role as well. In general, domestic elites also opposed democratization when they thought it could threaten their security as well as their primary objectives. Again, Rwanda and Afghanistan are obvious examples, but Serb and Croat elites in Bosnia were also reluctant to embrace democracy because they feared it might endanger the political dominance and exclusionist policies of their respective ethnic groups, as well as their own positions as the political leaders of these groups. Conversely, in countries where the political elite faced little or no political competition, such as postwar Namibia and Timor, adoption costs were low.

Perceived security threats and fears of losing political power in multi-ethnic settings clearly increase adoption costs. But domestic elites also incur costs by not adopting democracy, which also influences their calculations. As the examples from our sample show, such costs are highest for elites seeking independence. Namibia, Timor, and Kosovo all sought independence and therefore depended on the support of the peacebuilders and of the international community at large. Because the international community typically looks askance at openly undemocratic policies, the costs of not embracing democracy therefore increased. Countries seeking independence thus find it difficult to avoid a commitment to democracy. In other words, the quest for independence lowers adoption costs.

Interestingly, this reinforces another mechanism by which the quest for independence can reduce adoption costs. Independence struggles tend to build high elite coherence and considerable popular support for a country's leadership. This improves the chances for a successful democratization process because elites can safely assume a victory at the ballot box. Furthermore, when independence is acquired by secession, newly established elites in the secessionist region often encounter little political opposition because preceding elites in the ancien régime have lost power. This was the case in Namibia, Kosovo, and East Timor. Under such circumstances, new elites can afford democratic reforms without losing power.

These examples demonstrate the importance of adoption costs. Broadly speaking, perceived security threats and fears of weakened political power can increase adoption costs, but heavy dependence on external actors to achieve prime objectives can increase the costs of *not* adopting democracy. Domestic elites will base their support or disdain for democracy on an assessment of the specific contexts they face. But what factors—domestic and external—shape these contexts? What factors create circumstances in which the adoption of democracy is exceedingly risky and expensive, and what factors account for a situation in which domestic elites perceive the benefits of democracy to outweigh its costs? And can peacebuilders actually shape these situations by changing the calculus of domestic elites, for example by addressing security concerns, by granting autonomy or even sovereignty, or by coercing or bribing domestic elites to adopt reforms?

To investigate these questions, previous chapters took a close look at the legacies of the war, the footprint of the peacebuilding mission, the role of development aid, and the impact of the geopolitical location of the country. We summarize our findings in the following sections.

## The War and How It Ended

The characteristics of the war and how it ended are commonly thought to be major determinants for the prospects of future peace. A vast literature has argued that factors such as a war's intensity and the level of destruction and duration of the war, as well as whether the main warring parties defined themselves along ethnic lines, all have an impact on whether the peace will hold.[2] It is tempting to think that these same factors also determine whether the peace will be a democratic one. Yet our empirical evidence shows that the war-related variables that explain the duration of peace after war have little direct or systematic impact on the success of postwar democratization, with one important caveat: Stability is a necessary but insufficient condition for democratization. It is evident that democratization is impossible in a situation where civil war is ongoing, where parts of the state's territory are beyond the control of a legitimate government, and where citizens cannot exercise their democratic rights.

This is not to say that a war's characteristics do not have an impact on the process of postwar democratic transition. War and how it ended are important factors when explaining democratic outcomes, but the causal mechanisms are different from those that account for the occurrence or recurrence of war. As we demonstrated in Chapter 3, war characteristics influence the calculations of domestic elites with regard to the costs they face when adopting or not adopting democracy. These costs are influenced by the social and political context that has been shaped by the war and how it ended.

Evidence from our case studies revealed three causal paths. First, war can create a playing field where both players are locked in a hurting stalemate and think that their best option is to engage in cooperation, with the aim of finding a political arrangement that offers each side a potential stake in power. Among our cases, Mozambique is the only example of such a situation. Second, the costs of embracing democracy are also related to how much domestic elites depend on external actors to realize their prime objectives. In cases where wars were fought to win independence, domestic elites depended heavily on external support, which increased the costs of noncompliance with democratic standards. Put differently, the objective of the war determined the costs for democratization. Finally, and perhaps the most consequential legacy of war, is the existence of a hostile political opposition still capable of organizing violence. If domestic elites think that competitive elections or protection of civil liberties will strengthen rival groups that retain the ability to resort to violence, the adoption costs of democracy will increase.

In line with these observations, we find that in successful cases of postwar democratization (Namibia, East Timor, Macedonia, and Mozambique), domestic elites had little to fear from a democratic embrace. In each case, threats to the physical security of domestic elites were low. In Namibia and East Timor, the formerly dominant elites had lost their political power on winning independence. In Macedonia and in East Timor, all parties had a clear interest in cooperating, and peacebuilders provided credible security guarantees. In Bosnia, the war and how it ended led to a more ambiguous and volatile situation. Here, the war left three embittered ethnic groups deeply mistrustful of each other, but the massive presence of peacebuilders and the de facto partition of Bosnia and Herzegovina mitigated the security threats to these three groups. Nevertheless, for nationalist Serb and Croat politicians, the democratic peace settlement jeopardized their primary goals of maximizing ethnic autonomy, which caused adoption costs to remain high. At the same time, external actors developed effective instruments to punish politicians who resisted the peace settlement, thus lowering the balance of adoption costs. In sum, the massive footprint of the peacebuilding mission in Bosnia did offset some of the adoption costs caused by the legacy of a bitter interethnic war. The outcome was, as we know, a political regime that is neither fully democratic nor fully autocratic.

In cases where the dominant political elites feared that steps toward democratization would empower groups capable of waging war, the result was a clear reluctance to embrace democracy. Examples are Rwanda, Afghanistan, and, to a certain extent, Bosnia. In Afghanistan, the new government feared both the Taliban and the amorphous coalition of militia leaders, former warlords, and tribal leaders who were opposing the power of the central government. In Rwanda, the RFP feared that a democratic opening could trigger new ethnic violence and destabilize the fragile stability that was reached after the end of the civil war. In Bosnia, the Serbs and the Croats believed that democratization could threaten the political dominance and, in some cases, the physical safety of their respective ethnic groups within the ethnic fiefdoms created by the Dayton peace agreement. In all of these examples, domestic elites' fear of a powerful opposition group capable of organizing violence was a consequence of the war and how it ended.

War, therefore, influences postwar democratic transitions but does so by shaping perceptions of threats, which in turn are informed by an assessment of the probability that the opposition will use force and whether this group can effectively organize violence. The ability of international actors to deter such violence will also factor into the calculations of domestic elites. Such perceptions are difficult to capture by statistical analysis. Common proxies for war characteristics rely on how efficient organizers of violence were in the past (measured in terms of destruction, or the length of time groups were able to retain their capacity to organize violence) but do not measure new elites' threat perceptions or the ability or willingness of these groups to disrupt the new political process with violence.[3] Hence, it is not surprising that common measures of war characteristics (duration, intensity, type) do not predict democratization.

## The Footprint of the Mission

War and its legacies can increase the costs of adopting democracy. Peacebuilding missions are designed to offset these costs by providing security guarantees for those who favor peace and democracy, by credibly deterring those who do not, and by providing incentives for democratization. To do this, peacebuilders typically provide massive resources. As we discussed in Chapter 4, peace missions have become ever more ambitious since the end of the Cold War. Investments in personnel and resources have increased, and so has the duration of peace missions. Our sample cases averaged eighty-four months in length, had a peak strength of 24,000 military and civilian personnel, and cost US$30 billion over the first five years (this figure includes UN administration and related military expenses, but not aid money). Mission footprints have become bigger and heavier.

We demonstrated in Chapter 4 that a larger footprint does not necessarily lead to more democracy. This seems counterintuitive at first. It is tempting to assume that more intrusive and better-resourced missions give peacebuilders greater leverage to initiate democratic reform. But, as our cases show, the most intrusive missions do not typically result in democracy, suggesting that even highly intrusive missions can fail to offset all of the costs associated with democratization. There are two reasons for this.

First, even missions with a very heavy footprint are not able to offset atypically high adoption costs. As shown in Table 3.2 (p. 46), adoption costs were highest in Rwanda, Afghanistan, and Bosnia, followed by Kosovo. With the exception of Rwanda, each of these countries also hosted a highly intrusive mission; yet, due to high adoption costs, peacebuilders proved unable to coax the political regimes in a more democratic direction. The source of these costs differed across cases. In Bosnia and Kosovo the politicization of ethnic identity caused ethnic elites to oppose a more democratic regime, and in Afghanistan elites perceived democratization to threaten their elaborate system of governance by patronage and their security.

But it is not just that highly intrusive missions are unable to offset high adoption costs. A highly intrusive mission can also per se harm a democratization project. In our sample, East Timor, Kosovo, Bosnia, and Afghanistan had highly intrusive missions. In each case, an initially cooperative peacebuilding process between peacebuilders and domestic elites gradually shifted into open confrontation. This is because greater mission intrusiveness and external tutelage per se generated greater domestic resistance and stirred demands for local ownership and self-determination. A system of "benevolent autocracy" aimed at creating democracy apparently caused means to vitiate the ends. Due to this normative inconsistency, peacebuilders in highly intrusive missions risk losing their credibility, which can seriously impair their relationship with both domestic elites and local populations. When the populace starts to resist peacebuilders and their policies, as they did on various occasions in Afghanistan, Kosovo, and East Timor, peacebuilders often adjust their agendas and/or capitulate to demands for more autonomy to save face. In so doing, peacebuilders forfeit some of the leverage they acquired due to the intrusiveness of their mission to improve relationships with domestic elites. The fate of further democratization thus becomes contingent on the political will of domestic elites. Because of this, mission intrusiveness is governed by the rule of diminishing returns: As a mission footprint gets bigger, it is more likely to inspire a backlash that ultimately defeats its stated objectives.

It is useful to contrast high-cost, highly intrusive cases with low-cost, less intrusive cases. East Timor, Namibia, Mozambique, Macedonia, Kosovo, and Tajikistan are all instances where elites perceived the adoption costs to be low. With the exception of East Timor, peacebuilding missions in these countries were relatively nonintrusive. Yet, in each case, with the exception of Tajikistan, democratization was successful. By contrast, Bosnia, Afghanistan, and Rwanda all had high adoption costs and, with the exception of Rwanda, received highly intrusive missions. These observations suggest that mission intrusiveness is a less important factor than adoption costs and that high adoption costs cannot be offset by intrusive interventions. When adoption costs are low, however, minimally intrusive missions may be adequate—though this is not always the case. Low adoption costs do not always lead to democratization. In Tajikistan, domestic elites did not feel particularly threatened by a democratic transition, yet there was little public demand for democracy, peacebuilders had very little leverage, and Tajikistan felt buoyed by Russian support, which did not push for democratization. As a result, Tajikistan remains an authoritarian state.

We are aware that our simple distinction between democratization success and failure masks significant differences among those regimes that did not clear the threshold of an electoral democracy. For example, Bosnia and Kosovo are certainly less authoritarian than Rwanda or Tajikistan. It seems plausible that the democratic edge of Kosovo and Bosnia over Rwanda and Tajikistan could not have happened without the massive presence of peacebuilders. As we have previously stated, however, our argument is not that highly intrusive missions do not affect democratization efforts or that a country will be better off with no mission rather than an intrusive one. We argue instead that highly intrusive missions by themselves are unable to offset high adoption costs and that they tend to cause a backlash that ultimately reduces peacebuilder leverage. Therefore, countries with highly intrusive missions do not always clear the threshold of electoral democracies. By contrast, cases with low adoption costs are more likely to democratize, even if the mission has a light footprint.

## Aid Money to the Rescue?

As with the mission footprint, it is tempting to assume that aid should be important in promoting a liberal peace. Aid constitutes a major resource that peacebuilders bring to the postconflict situation, and it may help to change preferences or to build up capacities. However, our findings suggest that aid per se has a limited impact on democratic outcomes. However, we argue that aid relationships work on outcomes in more complex and nuanced ways, most importantly by creating the potential for donors to exercise conditionality and by facilitating the trust between domestic elites and external actors that is necessary for peacebuilder leverage. These positive effects come not from aid per se but through the relationships that donors who contribute to and participate in peacebuilding missions have established with domestic elites over long years of aid provision.

The empirical evidence in these cases suggests that the impact of aid is found first and foremost in the *relationships* that it creates between donors who fund and/or implement key aspects of peacebuilding and local actors. Thus the kinds of factors that might at first glance seem important—the amounts and types of support for democratization—are in fact secondary. Relationships create or diminish leverage.

As our cases demonstrate, aid does not effectively increase donor leverage or mitigate adoption costs when donors (1) are unable or unwilling to apply conditionality, (2) lack a clear commitment to democracy over other concerns, (3) lack the coherence necessary to act decisively and predictably, and (4) lack the local knowledge and connections necessary to exploit opportunities and gain leverage. The degree to which peacebuilders leverage the resources available to them (and indeed their ability to mobilize resources from their own governments) depends to a considerable extent on preexisting relationships between donors and domestic elites and on relationships forged or modified throughout the peacebuilding process.

## Neighborhood

Finally, we also looked at regional factors and investigated how the geostrategic location of a postwar country can influence its prospects for a democratic peace. Perhaps our most straightforward finding is that neighborhood factors very rarely have a positive effect on postwar democratization. Only in Macedonia did the prospect of EU membership provide positive incentives for domestic elites to comply with many peacebuilder demands, leading to a more inclusive political regime. In three other cases, East Timor, Namibia, and Mozambique, neighborhood factors helped create environments conducive to ending long and protracted wars. Only after the regional hegemons of South Africa and Indonesia embarked on their own democratization was peace, a precondition for democracy, possible. All three of these countries subsequently embarked on successful democratic transitions. This process was not shaped by neighborhood effects but rather by favorable domestic conditions that lowered adoption costs, as well as by an adequate international response. The lesson to be learned here is that neighborhood factors can and often do hamper a country's prospects for peace. But a good neighborhood alone is not a sufficient condition for democratization.

Examples from our cases suggest that there are two causal mechanisms by which neighborhood factors can negatively affect the chances of a postwar democratic transition. First, transnational security threats can increase the risks to domestic elites of adopting democracy, as could be observed in Afghanistan, Tajikistan, and Rwanda. In these cases, the impact of negative demonstration effects, fear of contagion, and support for undemocratically minded groups reinforced each other, and domestic elites believed that democratization would increase these risks. Peacebuilders were not typically in a position to mitigate these threats because their mandate and resources were inadequate to address regional issues. Faced with such a difficult environment, they then tended to lower expectations, prioritizing stability over pure democracy.

A second transnational effect stems from authoritarian states that back up a postwar regime, thereby shielding it from peacebuilder demands for liberal peace. The clearest example of this is Tajikistan. Russia's support for the Tajik political elite effectively counterbalanced peacebuilder pressure for democratic reform.

Our cases also suggest that the supposed positive impact of the European Union on democratization ought to be put into perspective. While the EU and its economic and security promises did provide some incentives to postwar regimes in the Balkans, these effects were to a large extent counteracted by the highly intrusive international mission in Bosnia and Kosovo, which proved not to be conducive to democratic development.

In sum, we find that negative neighborhood effects prevail, whereas positive effects seem to be the exception to the rule. With the caveat that our sample is small and that our generalizations should be treated with caution, we suggest that the emphasis of the literature on positive neighborhood effects should be revisited.

## Leverage Revisited

Our theory posits that the outcome of postwar peacebuilding depends on adoption costs incurred by domestic elites and on the leverage that peacebuilders hold over them. Among the most important potential sources of leverage is the mission "footprint"; that is, the combination of personnel, administrative resources, mandate, and aid money that peacebuilders bring. One might reasonably expect that a large footprint combined with ample aid money will offset some adoption costs and encourage domestic elites to adopt a democratic agenda. But, as we have seen, large-footprint missions are ineffective when adoption costs are high, which is the case when domestic elites perceive democratization to be a security threat. It appears that when adoption costs reach a certain threshold, increasing a mission's footprint yields no additional return. This mechanism is further enforced by the fact that greater mission intrusiveness and external tutelage per se generate greater domestic resistance to peacebuilder policies. This backlash often leads peacebuilders to abandon part of their democratization agenda and to grant more autonomy to domestic elites.

Our case studies also reveal other mechanisms that reduce leverage. One is "black knight support": Tajikistan's domestic elites were effectively shielded from what little leverage peacebuilders had by Russian support. Thus governments that enjoy the support of a nondemocratic country may be less inclined to bow to international pressure.[4]

Second, there is the paradox of weakness. Quite counterintuitively, under certain circumstances domestic elites may gain bargaining power from their position of relative weakness. Domestic elites who face strong domestic opposition may argue that any attempts to institute liberal reforms may trigger a backlash, endangering not only the government's survival but also national stability. Under such circumstances, peacebuilders may be inclined to provide ongoing support without evidence of reform because stability is considered more important. Domestic elites can thus capitalize on their weakness, receiving a maximum of support for a minimum of concessions. Most likely, a decision to support a weak regime that resists reform rests on its strategic importance. The paradox of weakness is typified by Afghanistan, where the international community continues to support President Karzai despite his open scorn for their liberal agenda. Karzai has exploited the fact that his loss is the Taliban's gain. His tenuous position thus constrains the international community's scope of action.

As this example shows, potential leverage is not always put to work because peacebuilders for various reasons refuse to use it. In fact, peacebuilders seldom bring to bear the full weight of their leverage because they have to balance their vision of a democratic outcome with other objectives. Peacebuilders typically operate under serious constraints that may temper their zeal for radical reforms: They operate under time constraints because voters at home do not support expensive peacebuilding missions that last indefinitely.[5] They will also need to avoid casualties, which dictates a cautious approach. In addition, peacebuilders are highly dependent on domestic actors because their cooperation is essential for project implementation; peacebuilders cannot reach the many milestones and benchmarks that their strategies call for without a nonconfrontational relationship with domestic elites. Because of all these constraints, peacebuilders only rarely try to force cooperation. Rather, when they encounter open, and more often passive, resistance, they will adapt the peacebuilding package and agree on a peace that is less than liberal. Within our sample, we did not find a single case where pressure was consistently applied over time. The case where peacebuilders have most often used robust prerogatives is Bosnia, but even there we do not find a consistent strategy designed to maximizing their leverage.

Our cases also suggest that peacebuilder leverage often becomes weaker over time. As peacebuilders deploy resources and become invested in a postwar country, they become hostage to the need to demonstrate success. Domestic elites are aware that a mission withdrawal would signal a failure to peacebuilder constituencies at home, a potential catastrophe for democratically accountable leaders. Domestic elites may therefore be able to resist or subvert some aspects of the peacebuilders' contract without fear that such behavior will jeopardize political and material support. Because of this, peacebuilder leverage peaks immediately before deployment. Unfortunately, no mechanism can prevent domestic elites from reneging on commitments agreed on prior to a mission start. As with so many forms of sustained social interaction, problems of compliance and moral hazard also plague peacebuilding missions and contribute to outcomes that are at times far from a liberal peace. And because longer missions are also the most intrusive (the average duration of heavy-footprint missions is 129 months, compared to forty-one months for light-footprint missions), it is these missions that are most affected by the brief shelf life of leverage.

Leverage depreciates especially rapidly when it depends on domestic elites' desire for independence, as was the case in Namibia, Timor, and Kosovo. To obtain their prime political objective, domestic elites were highly dependent on the support of the peacebuilders and the wider international community, which afforded peacebuilders substantial clout. However, once independence was won, peacebuilders lost their biggest bargaining chip.

A somewhat similar mechanism can be observed with regard to EU ascension, which was the main carrot offered to domestic elites in Macedonia. Once ascension was granted, however, peacebuilders predictably lost some leverage. There is, however, an important difference between independence and EU accession. The process of obtaining EU accession is a structured and phased process, where certain benchmarks must be fulfilled along the way. Hence leverage is spread out over time, and the hope is that, once a country has cleared all benchmarks, it has locked itself into a system of institutional constraints that will make it difficult to reverse progress in good governance. A similar mechanism for "slow release" is evidently not available when it comes to sovereignty movements and independence. Once independence is won, dependence on external actors is dramatically reduced. Hence, granting independence in exchange for a promise of democratic reform creates a moral hazard problem.

Our cases also emphasize that peacebuilder leverage cannot be guaranteed by the size and scope of a mission nor by the resources external actors bring to bear. Instead, leverage is conditioned by the interests and perceptions of domestic elites. This stands conventional wisdom on its head, suggesting that the prevailing focus on the nature and performance of external peace missions is misplaced. Our findings imply that the single most important factor determining the success or failure of a peacekeeping mission is its reception among domestic elites who will view it either as a means to achieve their goals or as a stumbling block. This in turn depends on a number of idiosyncratic factors in addition to those already mentioned. In addition to aid dependency, the degree to which domestic actors need international support to realize their objectives, as well as the presence of regional actors able to provide alternatives to compliance with international peacebuilding efforts, leverage depends on the history and relationships between domestic elites and particular international actors, as Mozambique demonstrates.

## Methodological Lessons

In this book, we have proposed a new conceptualization of peacebuilding as an interactive process between domestic elites and peacebuilders. We have mined nine empirically rich case studies to support our argument and to glean insights into the causal mechanisms that produce democratic outcomes. Now that we have completed this exercise, it is time to discuss whether our insights add up to a "theory-writ-large" of peacebuilding. That is, are we able to construct a generalized and parsimonious narrative about the causes of a democratic transition in the framework of a peacebuilding mission? Or, conversely, is each case unique, so that no patterns can be observed across cases, and hence explanations must be confined to a single case?

Seasoned practitioners of peacebuilding typically lean toward the second option. Experience tells them that the causes that lead to war are highly idiosyncratic. This includes the domestic political arena, the mandate of the peacebuilding mission, and leader personalities. Thus, they would argue that the anatomy of every major peacebuilding mission is highly particular and therefore beyond pithy generalizations.

Practitioners are not alone in this assessment. The OECD's Development Assistance Committee (DAC), a policy clearinghouse focused on fragile states and conflict zones, highlights the importance of recognizing specific circumstances when designing interventions. Their often-quoted "principles of good international engagement in fragile states" emphasize context.[6] Donors are advised to consider the "constraints of capacity, political will and legitimacy" and to take into consideration "sound political analysis to adapt international responses to country and regional context," and they are discouraged from using a "blue-print approach."[7]

At first glance our own results support the claim that peacebuilding missions (and hence the determinants of their success) are not easily generalizable. Across our nine cases, none of the variables that might be expected to determine the outcome of a peacebuilding mission—war characteristics, characteristics of war termination, levels of aid, mission footprint, or regional factors—is consistently associated with a given outcome, a finding in line with most quantitative studies.

However, we do not think that processes of postwar democratic transitions unfold in an entirely random and unpredictable way, nor do we think that peacebuilding missions have no effect whatsoever on postwar democratic transitions. Rather, we think that most existing studies have operated under a faulty conceptualization of peacebuilding, focusing unduly on structural characteristics such as GDP, intensity and duration of war, and the footprint and the formal mandate of the mission. As we have demonstrated in our analysis, these structural variables, in conjunction with other factors, are only indirectly associated with outcomes.

The outcome of peacebuilding operations is determined to a large extent by adoption costs and leverage. Both can be influenced by a wide range of determinants that make it difficult to single out a specific factor that applies across most or all cases. Furthermore, successful or failed peacebuilding clearly is a phenomenon governed by equifinality. That is, different combinations of factors can lead to similar outcomes. The task then is to discover various causal patterns instead of identical variables across all cases. Statistical inference is not good at capturing equifinality, and statistical models that try can quickly become highly complex and difficult to interpret.[8] By contrast, case studies can accommodate complex causal relations such as equifinality and multiple conjunctural causation.

For these reasons, we chose a small-$n$ comparative design that was better suited to investigate processes of postwar democratic transitions and to detect the underlying logic that is common to all cases. Atypically low or high leverage and adoption costs are a consequence of particular social constellations, rather than of particular structural variables. For example, peacebuilders' leverage over domestic elites in Mozambique was to a large extent a result of their long-standing bilateral relations, which helped to build up not only dependence but also trust and social learning. Such constellations are not easy to proxy with a set of structural variables. Likewise, the perception of security threats, so crucial to calculating adoption costs, is to a large extent based on historical experience, long-held stereotypes about "the other," or on expectations about future behavior. Such perceptions and expectations are also not easily proxied by variables that are commonly used to quantify the study of civil wars. Yet it is these social constellations that in the end account for adoption costs and thus the final outcome. A small-$n$ design can identify and describe such constellations. However, the generalizations that can be produced from such an analytical narrative will lead to middle-range theories, which are, in the classic formulation of Merton, "theories that lie between the minor but necessary working hypotheses that evolve in abundance during day-to-day research and the all-inclusive systematic efforts to develop a unified theory that will explain all the observed uniformities of social behavior, social organization and social change."[9]

A middle-range theory has limited explanatory power across a large number of cases, but when the universe of cases is small and differences between them substantial, as is the case with major peacebuilding missions, they can help us better understand them by isolating a few important explanatory factors that explain important aspects of the outcomes. While they do not pretend to explain all social phenomena, they identify causal mechanisms that are generalizable up to a point. Such "bounded generalizations"[10] may well help to devise more efficient peacebuilding.

## Toward More Effective Peacebuilding?

Over the course of our investigation of the determinants of democratic peacebuilding, we shed light on a number of causal mechanisms. Most importantly, we demonstrated that peacebuilding is an interactive process between domestic elites and peacebuilders and hence their capacities *and* preferences matter for the outcome. This is in itself perhaps a trivial observation, yet it is by no means a trivial exercise to factor in a realistic assessment of the preferences of domestic elites into a thick description of peacebuilding. Generally, the relevant literature has focused on the capacities of peacebuilders alone and has blackboxed the preferences of domestic elites. As a matter of fact, these preferences are diverse and matter greatly. A theory of peacebuilding ought to take into account factors that influence these preferences, namely adoption costs and leverage. Better understanding the sources of both is a precondition to improving peacebuilding policies.

Our research suggests that a key component of adoption costs is the degree to which the democratic settlement threatens the security of local actors. Threats to security can stem from discontented domestic groups, but, in many cases, the threats can also be transnational in character, as was the case in Afghanistan, Rwanda, and the Balkans. Because democratic peacebuilding is only efficient when it succeeds in offsetting some of the adoption costs, providing security guarantees to domestic elites is crucial. As we have seen, domestic elites tend not to bank on security promises, even when peacebuilders provide massive resources. This trust gap is partly due to the fact that Western democracies (which bear the weight of all major peacebuilding missions) often find it difficult to commit to long-term, expensive, and potentially risky missions. There is no easy fix for this, but it is clear that only a strong and credible commitment by peacebuilders provides enough incentive for domestic elites to bet on the final success of a peacebuilding operation. Peacebuilders have to ensure that domestic elites view them as valuable and trusted allies; only then will local leaders prefer a lasting alliance with peacebuilders to a pact with those segments of their society that are opposed to liberal reform.

This can create an environment in which peacebuilders and domestic elites closely cooperate toward a common objective. Peacebuilders should also learn to better address transnational sources of insecurity. As we have seen in more than half of our cases, domestic elites felt considerably threatened by transnational spillovers of violence and were therefore reluctant to embrace more liberal reforms at home. Even so, the peacebuilding mandates did not tackle regional sources of instability.

Another component to adoption costs is the degree to which democratic politics either threatens or advances the primary goals of domestic elites. Where domestic elites depend on international actors to achieve key substantive goals, they are more likely to embrace the democratization agenda urged by donors. However, much of the leverage gained from this dependence is doomed to rapid depreciation. In the political economy of peacebuilding, leverage is a highly perishable good. Once peacebuilders deploy and invest in a mission, they begin to depend on the cooperation of domestic elites, and power relations between peacebuilders and domestic elites, which initially favor the former, will change. There is a moral hazard problem in peacebuilding that is rarely addressed in the literature and, we would argue, completely ignored in practice. This is another realm where peacebuilding missions can and should become smarter.

There are different ways in which peacebuilders can mitigate the problem of fleeting leverage. One option, which has been much discussed in the peacebuilding literature, is to speak with one voice and to achieve internal unity in their priorities. All peacebuilding operations are plagued by massive coordination problems among the myriad participants. At best, a lack of coordination hampers efficient implementation and delivery of aid and development programs. At worst, an operation can be compromised when different actors pursue different strategic objectives. Increased cooperation among peacebuilders would increase their credibility and leverage over domestic elites. Whether peacebuilders would be willing to use this leverage is a different question.

Peacebuilders should also endeavor to reach a comprehensive agreement with all players as early as possible. Their leverage is greatest before deployment. Reaching an agreement with as many stakeholders as possible prior to deployment does not fully guard against moral hazard but may help to build ownership for various fractions of domestic elites, increase communication and trust among them, and potentially lead to peer pressure and social learning.

The most salient problem, and the hardest to address, is the issue of moral hazard. This problem is greatest when domestic elites require the support of peacebuilders to obtain sovereignty. In such situations peacebuilders have a high degree of leverage, only to lose it once sovereignty has been obtained. One way to address this problem is the "standards before status" approach, which was tried by the United Nations in Kosovo and ended in failure. The "standards before status" were a set of UN-endorsed benchmarks for the democratic development of Kosovo, covering various aspects of good governance, with a particular aim to protect Kosovo's non-Albanian ethnic communities. In 2003, the international community proclaimed that Kosovo's status would not be addressed until it had met these standards. When the postponement of Kosovo's final status threatened to destabilize the country, however, the international community tacitly abandoned these benchmarks, and in 2008 Kosovo was granted independence. This example underlines that peacebuilders typically prioritize stability over democratic change.

It is difficult to imagine a set of policies that could increase peacebuilders' appetite for risk. Some scholars have therefore suggested that the international community reduce the rents associated with sovereignty. If sovereignty were less desirable, then peacebuilder resources provided through cooperation would become more valuable. In short, sovereignty could be made less profitable if granted in restricted form to those states that prove either unable or unwilling to commit to good governance. It is clear that this cannot be adequately addressed within the confines of current norms that stipulate that all states should enjoy both autonomy and international recognition. Alternative institutional arrangements would need to be developed, including trusteeships and shared sovereignty arrangements that engage external actors in specific aspects of domestic governance on a quasi-permanent basis.[11] As attractive as these ideas might be in theory, it is also clear that, in order to realize them in a nonarbitrary, consistent, and predictable way, a major overhaul of global norms of governance would be necessary.

To sum up, there are ways to increasing peacebuilders' leverage. However, those that can be affordably implemented are likely to have a very limited impact, whereas others that promise a larger impact are unlikely to come to fruition so long as there is not a major overhaul of global governance. This then reinforces one of the most important insights that this research has produced—namely that the impact of external actors on postwar democratic transitions is limited at best.

The ability of peacebuilders to influence peacebuilding outcomes is severely constrained by circumstances beyond their control. This also holds true for what many observers see as a panacea: more robust missions coupled with more aid. As we have seen, more intrusive and longer missions do not lead to more democracy because the duration of the mission tends to reduce peacebuilder leverage, intrusiveness tends to create backlash, and even highly intrusive missions seem unable to completely offset high adoption costs. More resources alone are not the answer. The problem with peacebuilding is not primarily a lack of resources but the understanding and balancing and/or mitigation of the costs of embracing democracy for domestic elites. Large amounts of aid or highly intrusive missions promote successful peacebuilding only insofar as they either lower adoption costs or raise the costs of defection from a democratic settlement. As our cases show, democratic outcomes are more likely when domestic elites are highly dependent on external actors either to achieve their primary goals (for example, independence or secession) or to survive (for example, highly aid-dependent countries). Where local actors do not need external actors, or where accepting democratic politics entails too high a cost, peacebuilder leverage is dramatically reduced regardless of their resources.

This finding, in our view, suggests that peacebuilders should pursue a policy of selective intervention. The democracy package should be prescribed only for cases likely to produce wins, and democracy promoters should not invest heavily otherwise. Our framework helps to identify cases where international peacebuilding missions stand a real chance of success because domestic constellations are benign. Investing where success is possible seems a reasonable proposition. It is another question as to whether the foreign offices and development agencies of democratic states can communicate to their constituencies that they intend to support postwar democratization only in cases where a high return on investment is probable. But given that "democratic midwifery" is the best that external actors can hope for, they should carefully pick those cases where their intervention can make a difference.

Finally, peacebuilders and the wider international community should lower their expectations. This should lead to a more realistic appraisal of the good things that peacebuilding missions can and have achieved.[12] While robust peacebuilding cannot socially engineer liberal democracies, they can end violence, create conditions in which refugees can return home, provide critical emergency aid, and help rebuild state capacities. All of this makes a dramatic difference in the lives of millions of people. Given the many challenges and constraints of democratic peacebuilding, the fact that about one-third of all recent major peacebuilding missions has resulted in an electoral democracy is perhaps not such a bad track record.

REFERENCE MATTER

# Notes

## Preface

1. Putzel 2010.

2. Afghanistan (Hamish Nixon and Brendan Whitty), Bosnia (Kristie Evenson), East Timor (Henri Myrttinen), Kosovo (Jens Narten), Macedonia (Tome Sandevski), Mozambique (Carrie Manning and Monica Malbrough), Namibia (Christof Hartmann), Rwanda (Rachel Hayman), and Tajikistan (Anna Matveeva).

3. "Post-War Democratic Transitions," retrieved on August 3, 2012 from http://aix1.uottawa.ca/~czurcher/czurcher/Transitions.html.

4. The period of interest was the first five years after the start of the postconflict peacebuilding mission, and the starting date for this period ranged from 1989 to 2002.

5. *Taiwan Journal of Democracy* (5) 1 (July 2009). The case of Macedonia was not included in the journal issue.

## Chapter 1

1. Freedom House rates a country as "free" and as a "liberal" democracy, when it scores between 2.5 and 1 on a 7-point scale, whereas 7 denotes the least free regime.

2. Diamond 1999, 10.

3. Freedom House defines an electoral democracy as a country that has a competitive multiparty system; universal adult suffrage for all citizens (apart from legal restrictions that may apply to citizens convicted of certain crimes); regularly contested elections by secret ballot with "reasonable ballot security" and the absence of massive fraud that distorts results; and "significant public access" of major political parties to voters through open campaigning and the media (Freedom House 2005).

4. We use the World Bank's Database of Political Institutions to code "fully closed authoritarian" regimes and "electoral authoritarian regimes" (Beck et al. 2001). Regimes with a mean value of 1 through 4 of the variables *liec* and *eiec* were coded as "fully closed authoritarian." Regimes that measured 5 through 7 were coded as electoral authoritarian. *Liec* measures the electoral competitiveness of the legislature. The scale is 1 = no legislature; 2 = unelected legislature; 3 = elected one candidate; 4 = one party, multiple candidates; 5 = multiple parties are legal, but only one party won seats; 6 = multiple parties did win seats, but the largest party received more than 75 percent of the seats; 7 = largest party got less than 75 percent. The same coding applies for *eiec* (see Keefeer 2010). Brownlee (2009) first used the DPI to code electoral authoritarianism.

5. Kaplan 2008.

6. See Lipset 1959; also Mamdani 1996 and Niemi and Barkan 1987.

7. Gleditsch and Ward 2006 and Lake and Rothchild 1998.

8. Levitsky and Way 2010.

9. Doyle and Sambanis 2006; Hartzell, Hoddie, and Rothchild 2009; Fortna 2004; Jarstad and Sisk 2008; and Paris 2004.

10. On the concept of the "intervention society," see Bonacker et al. 2009.

11. For example, see Carothers 2002 and Paris 2004, 179.

12. Doyle and Sambanis 2006, 27–68, and Doyle and Sambanis 2000. Similar evidence is also provided by Fortna 2008a and Zuercher 2006.

13. George and Bennett 2005.

14. Ragin 1987.

15. Hayman 2009.

16. Case studies were contributed by Christof Hartmann, Rachel Hayman, Kristie Evenson, Carrie Manning and Monica Malbrough, Anna Matveeva, Henri Myrttinen, Jens Narten, Hamish Nixon, Sarah Riese, Nora Roehner, Tome Sandevski, and Brendan Whitty.

17. The template is also available on the project webpage: "Post-War Democratic Transitions," available at http://aix1.uottawa.ca/~czurcher/czurcher/Transitions.html.

18. Hartmann 2009.

19. Manning and Malbrough 2009.

20. Hayman 2009.

21. Evenson 2009.

22. Narten 2009a.

23. Myrttinen 2009, 219.

24. Matveeva 2009.

## Chapter 2

This chapter builds up on ideas first put forward by Michael Barnett, Songying Fang, and Christoph Zürcher. See Barnett and Zürcher 2008 and Barnett, Fang, and Zürcher 2008.

1. Fortna and Howard 2008, 229.
2. Andersson 2000; Ottaway 2002; and Paris 2004.
3. Chesterman 2004, 5.
4. Bueno de Mesquita and Downs 2006.
5. Wantchekon 2004 and Wantchekon and Neeman 2002.
6. Wantchekon 2004, 19.
7. Ibid., 19–23.
8. Data from Doyle and Sambanis 2000.
9. Mansfield and Snyder 2007; Paris 2004; and Collier 2009.
10. Höglund 2008, 80.
11. Snyder 2000 and Gurr 2000.
12. Statistical analysis shows that well-to-do societies become more stable with increased levels of democracy, but poorer societies are actually more vulnerable when they are democratic (Collier 2009).
13. See, for example, Berdal 2009; Elwert 2003; and Jean and Rufin 1994.
14. Kitschelt and Wilkinson 2007; Ilkhamov 2007; Eisenstadt and Roniger 1984; Reno 1999; and Bratton and van de Walle 1994.
15. Clapham 1985.
16. Bratton and van de Walle 1997.
17. Cable 09KABUL1767 2009.
18. Boege et al. 2009, 603.
19. See, for example, Joshi and Mason 2011.
20. Ibid.
21. Putnam 1988.
22. Bunce 1990, 400.
23. Rubin 2010.
24. On the importance of legitimacy in the peacebuilding process, see Narten 2006, 2008.
25. Steffek 2003, 249.
26. Ibid., 253.
27. Manning and Malbrough 2009; Myrttinen 2009; Narten 2009b; and Sandevski 2009.
28. Nixon and Whitty 2009 and Matveeva 2009.
29. Hayman 2009.
30. Ragin 1987 and Brady and Collier 2004.

## Chapter 3

1. Doyle and Sambanis 2006; Hartzell, Hoddie, and Rothchild 2001; Hartzell and Hoddie 2003; and Fortna 2004.
2. Doyle and Sambanis 2006, 127.
3. Collier, Hoeffler, and Söderbom 2004; Mason and Fett 1996; Regan 2002; Fearon 2004; and Hartzell, Hoddie, and Rothchild 2001.

4. Walter 2004.

5. Doyle and Sambanis 2000, 786.

6. Regan and Aydin 2006, 751.

7. Hartzell and Hoddie 2003, 328, and Kreutz 2010, 1.

8. Fortna 2004 and Mattes and Savun 2009.

9. Doyle and Sambanis 2000, 786.

10. Harbom, Melander, and Wallensteen 2008.

11. Fortna 2004, 286, and Kalyvas and Balcells 2010.

12. Kreutz 2010 and Licklider 1995.

13. Toft 2009.

14. Derouen, Lea, and Wallensteen 2009, 369–370.

15. Kreutz 2010.

16. Hartzell, Hoddie, and Rothchild 2001, 198, and Walter 1999.

17. Roeder and Rothchild 2005.

18. Zahar 2005; Spears 2002; Hartzell and Hoddie 2003; and Kerr 2005.

19. Seavers 2000.

20. Walter 2002 and Hartzell and Hoddie 2003.

21. Derouen, Lea, and Wallensteen 2009.

22. Roeder and Rothchild 2005.

23. Riese 2008.

24. Hartzell and Hoddie 2003, 328.

25. Hartzell and Hoddie 2003; Walter 1999; and Mattes and Savun 2009.

26. Kalyvas and Balcells 2010.

27. Reno 2011, 98–99.

28. Ibid., 105.

29. Manning and Malbrough 2009; Myrttinen 2009; Narten 2009a; and Sandev-ski 2009.

30. Whitty and Nixon 2009 and Matveeva 2009.

31. Whitty and Nixon 2009, 2.

32. Matveeva 2009, 171.

33. Ibid., 172.

34. Hayman 2009.

35. Ibid.

36. Evenson 2009.

37. Manning 2008 and Evenson 2009.

38. Doyle and Sambanis 2000.


## Chapter 4

1. On Bosnia: Barria and Roper 2007; Bose 2002; Chandler 2000, 2006; Cox 2001; Ignatieff 2003; and Solioz 2007; on Kosovo: Ignatieff 2003; King and Mason 2006; Rossbacher 2004; and Yannis 2001; on East Timor: Chopra 2000, 2002; and on Afghani-

stan: Cramer and Goodhand 2002; Ignatieff 2003; Middlebrook and Sedra 2004; Nixon 2007; and Suhrke 2009.

2. Dobbins et al. 2003, 2005; de Zeeuw 2005; and Zuercher 2006.

3. Chesterman 2004; Guttieri and Piombo 2007; and Morphet 2002.

4. Wilde 2001: 602; Caplan 2002, 2004; and Chopra 2000.

5. Total troop numbers reached 80,000, including personnel deployed to Croatia and the surrounding in support of the BiH operation.

6. Papic and Sadikovic 2006.

7. Bose 2002.

8. Rubin 2002.

9. Goodhand and Sedra 2007.

10. Ross 2007, 42.

11. Ibid., 38, 45.

12. Bhatia, Lanigan, and Wilkinson 2004; and Goodhand and Sedra 2007.

13. Goodhand and Sedra 2007.

14. Rubin 2010.

15. Raufer 2003.

16. Council of Europe 2010.

17. The violence that erupted in East Timor in April and May 2006 was not linked to the international presence but was the result of an internal crisis triggered by a conflict between different segments of the Timorese armed forces. The crisis caused the security sector to implode and led to the subsequent expansion of armed violence throughout the country.

18. Gosztonyi 2003; Chandler 2006; and Knaus and Martin 2003.

## Chapter 5

1. Boyce 2002 and Frerks 2006.

2. Interestingly, donor willingness to accept "Rwanda's departure from standard democratic models limiting political competition" is cited in an OECD report on state building as an example of good state-building practice (OECD 2010, 120).

3. Leftwich 1993.

4. U.S. National Security Strategy 2002.

5. Scott and Steele 2011.

6. Finkel, Perez-Linana, and Seligson 2007; and Scott and Steele 2011.

7. Scott and Steele 2011, 55.

8. de Zeeuw and Kumar 2006, 7.

9. Cox, Ikenberry, and Inoguchi 2000; and Schraeder 2002.

10. OECD 2010; Elhawary, Foresti, and Pantuliano 2010 ; World Bank 2011; and Booth 2011.

11. Hook 1995.

12. See Woods 2005 and Goodhand 2002. It should be noted that another strand

of the literature invokes the moral aspects of assisting the poor *despite* the absence of significant security or other national interest in these countries by donors, which reflects the poverty paradigm that has held sway amongst many major donors since the mid-1990s (Riddell 1987, 2007; Lancaster 2007; and Brown 2005).

13. de Zeeuw and Kumar 2006 and Crawford 2001.

14. Brown 2005.

15. Uvin 1998.

16. Collier 2009, 5.

17. Ottaway and Chung 1999.

18. Carothers 1999.

19. Burnell 2000 and Youngs 2002.

20. Bratton and Logan 2009; François and Sud 2006; de Zeeuw and Kumar 2006; Brown 2005; and OECD 2010.

21. Wright 2009.

22. See Stokke 1995; Killick 1998; Uvin 2004; Brown 2005; and Crawford 1997, 2001.

23. Brown 2005.

24. Carothers 2002, 2007.

25. Uvin 2004; Carothers 1999; Crawford 2001; François and Sud 2006; Bratton and Logan 2009; Goodhand 2002; Glennie 2008; and Whitfield 2009.

26. Brown 2001; Goldsmith 2001; Hanlon 2004; and Brautigam and Knack 2004.

27. Jarstad and Sisk 2008; de Zeeuw and Kumar 2006; Carothers 1999; and OECD 2010.

28. Elhawary, Foresti, and Pantuliano 2010; Wimpelmann 2006; World Bank 2011; and OECD 2010.

29. World Bank 2011.

30. OECD 2010, 11.

31. Elhawary, Foresti, and Pantuliano 2010 3.

32. Ibid., 18.

33. OECD 2010, 10–11.

34. Ibid., 40.

35. Booth 2011, 9.

36. Ibid., 15.

37. OECD 2010, 40.

38. Ibid., 153.

39. Ibid., 40.

40. Elhawary, Foresti, and Pantuliano 2010, 16.

41. Matveeva 2008.

42. Myrttinen 2008.

43. Ibid., 30–32.

44. Namibia and Mozambique are excluded from this figure as DAC data prior to 1995 were not available. Neither were disaggregated data in-country. For Kosovo, project data were included.

45. Myrttinen 2009.

46. Evenson 2008, 60.

47. Note that there was a strong focus on elections in Namibia also, but there is no evidence of aid for democracy from major donors. Financing of this fell within the mandate of the peacekeeping mission, so the details are not captured in aid statistics.

48. Whitty and Nixon 2009, 74.

49. For a full discussion of these effects in the Mozambique case, see Manning and Malbrough 2010.

50. Hayman 2009.

51. Manning and Malbrough 2010; Jett 1999; and Ball and Barnes 2000.

52. Evenson 2009, 122.

53. This is not to say that conditions have not been applied in other areas, especially the economy and administrative governance.

54. Beyond our case studies, there are examples where conditionality has worked in relation to democracy. For example, donors withheld aid to Kenya in 1992 and by doing so helped to bring about multiparty elections (see Glennie 2008, 51).

55. The authors of both the Tajikistan and East Timor studies noted that China's increasing engagement in these countries was being treated with wariness by other international actors, offering another avenue of support from a country that traditionally does not apply governance conditionality to its aid.

56. Hayman 2009.

57. Pressure on donor agencies to spend money also militates against the application of conditionality. This appears to have been important in Afghanistan, but it is a phenomenon that goes across the board in development aid. Moreover, donors appear increasingly reluctant to say they are imposing conditions on aid. Under the rhetoric of aid effectiveness (see Fraser and Whitfield 2009), donors are eager to stress that they are rather working with governments to help them achieve their own stated objectives.

58. Matveeva 2008, 91.

59. Hartmann 2009, 48.

60. Whitty and Nixon 2009.

## Chapter 6

1. Gleditsch and Ward 2006; Gleditsch and Buhaug 2008; and Levitsky and Way 2005, 2006.

2. Lake and Rothchild 1998.

3. Ibid., 3.

4. Brubaker 1995, 1996.

5. Lake and Rothchild 1998.

6. Beissinger 2002 and Zürcher 2007.

7. Fearon 1998.

8. Ibid., 112.

9. Gleditsch 2007; Gleditsch and Buhaug 2008.

10. Starr 1991; Starr and Lindborg 2003.

11. Gleditsch and Ward 2006; Cederman and Gleditsch 2004.

12. Beissinger 2002 and Wheatley and Zuercher 2008.

13. Gleditch and Ward 2006.

14. Mainwaring and Perez-Linan 2007.

15. Keck and Sikkink 1998 and Schmitz 2004, 408.

16. Levitsky and Way 2005, 2006.

17. Levitsky and Way 2010, 372.

18. Emerson and Noutcheva 2005.

19. Vachudova 2005.

20. Schimmelfennig, Engert, and Knobel 2003.

21. Matveeva 2009, 182–183.

22. Data from World Bank Development Indicators (WDI), retrieved on August 3, 2012, from http://data.worldbank.org/data-catalog/world-development-indicators.

23. Rubin 2002.

24. Levitsky and Way 2010.

25. Judah 2000.


## Chapter 7

1. Fortna 2008a, 74.

2. Doyle and Sambanis 2006; Hartzell et al. 2001; Fortna 2004; Collier, Hoeffler, and Söderbom 2004; and Kreutz 2010.

3. It is not necessarily safe to assume that a group that was highly effective at organizing violence during wartime will be equally effective after a peace agreement. Reaching a peace agreement often requires compromise or causes shifts in the balance of power within these groups. Moreover, the costs and benefits of using violence to disrupt a peace settlement may be different from the costs and benefits of using violence during the war.

4. Levitsky and Way 2010, 91.

5. Bueno de Mesquita and Downs 2006.

6. OECD 2007.

7. Ibid., 1.

8. George and Bennet 2005, 22.

9. Merton 1968, 39; see also Hedström and Udehn 2009.

10. Bunce 2000.

11. Krasner 2004; Fearon and Laitin 2004.

12. For a thorough and balanced elaboration of this argument, see Paris 2010.

# Bibliography

Andersson, A. 2000. "Democracies and UN Peacekeeping Operations, 1990–1996." *International Peacekeeping* 7: 1–22.

Ball, N., and S. Barnes. 2000. "Mozambique." In *Good Intentions: Pledges of Aid for Postconflict Recovery*, edited by Shepard Forman and Stewart Patrick, 159–203. Boulder, CO: Lynne Rienner Publishers.

Barnett, Michael, Songying Fang, and Christoph Zürcher. 2008. "The Peacebuilders Contract: A Game Theoretical Approach." Paper prepared for the annual meeting of the American Political Science Association, Boston, Massachusetts, August 28–31.

Barnett, Michael, and Christoph Zürcher. 2008. "The Peace-Builder's Contract: How External Statebuilding Reinforces Weak Statehood." In *The Dilemmas of Statebuilding: Confronting the Contradictions of Postwar Peace Operations*, edited by Roland Paris and Timothy D. Sisk, 23–52. London: Routledge.

Barria, Lilian A., and Steven D. Roper. 2007. "Judicial Capacity Building in Bosnia and Herzegovina: Understanding Legal Reform beyond the Completion Strategy of the ICTY." *Human Rights Review* 9: 317–330.

Beck, Thorsten, George Clarke, Alberto Groff, Philip Keefer, and Patrick Walsh. 2001. "New Tools in Comparative Political Economy: The Database of Political Institutions." *World Bank Economic Review* 15: 165–176.

Beissinger, Mark R. 2002. *Nationalist Mobilization and the Collapse of the Soviet State*. Cambridge, UK: Cambridge University Press.

Berdal, Mats. 2009. *Building Peace after War*. London: Routledge.

Bhatia, M., K. Lanigan, and P. Wilkinson. June 2004. "Minimal Investments, Minimal Results: The Failure of Security Policy in Afghanistan." Briefing paper, Afghanistan Research and Evaluation Unit.

Boege, Volker, Anne Brown, Kevin Clements, and Anna Nolan. 2009. "Building Peace and Political Community in Hybrid Political Orders." *International Peacekeeping* 16: 599–615.

Bonacker, Thorsten et al., eds. 2009. *Interventionskultur. Zur Soziologie Von Interventionsgesellschaften.* Wiesbaden: VS Verlag.

Booth, David. 2011. "Aid, Institutions and Governance: What Have We Learned?" *Development Policy Review* 29, Supplement s5–s26.

Bose, Sumantra. 2002. *Bosnia after Dayton: Nationalist Partition and International Intervention.* London: Hurst & Co.

Boyce, J. K. 2002. "Aid Conditionality as a Tool for Peacebuilding: Opportunities and Constraints." *Development and Change* 33: 1025–1048.

Brady, Henry E., and David Collier. 2004. *Rethinking Social Inquiry: Diverse Tools, Shared Standards.* Oxford: Rowman & Littlefield.

Bratton, Michael, and Carolyn Logan. 2009. "Voters but Not Yet Citizens: Democratization and Development Aid." In *Smart Aid for African Development*, edited by Richard Joseph and Alexandra Gillies, 181–206. Boulder, CO: Lynne Rienner Publishers.

Bratton, Michael, and Nicolas van de Walle. 1997. *Democratic Experiments in Africa: Regime Transitions in Comparative Perspective.* Cambridge, UK: Cambridge University Press.

Brautigam, Deborah A., and Stephen Knack. 2004. "Foreign Aid, Institutions, and Governance in Sub-Saharan Africa." *Economic Development and Cultural Change* 52: 255–285.

Brown, Stephen. 2001. "Authoritarian Leaders and Multiparty Elections in Africa: How Foreign Donors Help to Keep Kenya's Daniel Arap Moi in Power." *Third World Quarterly* 22: 725–739.

———. 2005. "Foreign Aid and Democracy Promotion: Lessons from Africa," *The European Journal of Development Research* 17: 179–198.

Brownlee, Jason. 2009. "Potents of Pluralism: How Hybrid Regimes Affect Democratic Transitions." *American Journal of Political Science* 53: 515–532.

Brubaker, Rogers. 1995. "National Minorities, Nationalizing States, and External National Homelands in the New Europe." *Daedalus* 124: 107–132.

———. 1996. *Nationalism Reframed: Nationhood and the National Question in the New Europe.* Cambridge, UK: Cambridge University Press.

Bueno de Mesquita, Bruce, and George W. Downs. 2006. "Intervention and Democracy." *International Organization* 60: 627–49.

Bunce, Valerie. 1990. "The Struggle for Liberal Democracy in Eastern Europe," *World Policy Journal,* 7: 395–430.

———. "Comparative Democratization: Big and Bounded Generalizations." *Comparative Political Studies* 33: 703–734.

Burnell, Peter. 2000. *Democracy Assistance: International Cooperation for Democratization.* London: Frank Cass.

Cable 09KABUL1767. 2009. *Karzai on the state of US–Afghan relations*, created July 7 and released by Wikileaks on December 2, 2010; retrieved on March 5, 2011, from http://213.251.145.96/cable/2009/07/09KABUL1767.html.

Caplan, Richard. 2002. *A New Trusteeship? The International Administration of Wartorn Territories.* Oxford, UK: Oxford University Press.

———. 2004. "Partner or Patron? International Civil Administration and Local Capacity-Building." *International Peacekeeping* 11: 229–247.

Carothers, Thomas. 1999. *Aiding Democracy Abroad: The Learning Curve.* Washington, DC: Carnegie Endowment for International Peace.

———. 2002. "The End of the Transition Paradigm." *Journal of Democracy* 13: 5–21.

———. 2007. "A Quarter Century Promoting Democracy." *Journal of Democracy* 181: 112–118.

Cederman, Lars-Erik, and Kristian Skrede Gleditsch. 2004. "Conquest and Regime Change: An Evolutionary Model of the Spread of Democracy and Peace." *International Studies Quarterly* 48: 603–629.

Chandler, David. 2000. *Bosnia: Faking Democracy after Dayton.* London: Pluto Press.

———. 2006. *Empire in Denial: the Politics of State-Building.* London: Pluto Press.

Chesterman, Simon. 2004. *You, the People: The United Nations, Transitional Administration and State-Building.* New York: Oxford University Press.

Chopra, Jarat. 2000. "The UN's Kingdom of East Timor." *Survival* 42: 27–39.

———. 2002. "Building State Failure in East Timor." *Development and Change* 33: 979–1000.

Clapham, Christopher. 1985. *Third World Politics: An Introduction.* Madison: University of Wisconsin Press.

Collier, David, and Henry E. Brady. 2004. *Rethinking Social Inquiry: Diverse Tools, Shared Standards.* Oxford: Rowman & Littlefield.

Collier, Paul. 2009. *Wars, Guns and Votes.* New York: Harper.

Collier, Paul, Anke Hoeffler, and Måns Söderbom. 2004. "On the Duration of Civil War." *Journal of Peace Research* 41: 253–73.

Council of Europe. 2010. *Inhuman Treatment of People and Illicit Trafficking in Human Organs in Kosovo.* Report (provisional version, December 12, 2010), Committee on Legal Affairs and Human Rights. Retrieved on June 24, 2012, from http://assembly.coe.int/asp/apfeaturesmanager/defaultartsiteview.asp?ID=964.

Cox, Marcus. 2001. *State Building and Post-Conflict Reconstruction: Lessons from Bosnia.* Geneva: Centre for Applied Studies in International Negotiations.

Cox, Michael, G. John Ikenberry, and Takashi Inoguchi, eds. 2000. *American Democracy Promotion: Impulses, Strategies, and Impacts.* London: Oxford University Press.

Cramer, Christopher, and Jonathan Goodhand. 2002. "Try Again, Fail Again, Fail Better? War, the State, and the 'Post-Conflict' Challenge in Afghanistan." *Development and Change* 33: 885–909.

Crawford, Gordon. 1997. "Foreign Aid and Political Conditionality: Issues of Effectiveness and Consistency." *Democratization* 4: 69–108.

———. 2001. *Foreign Aid and Political Reform. A Comparative Analysis of Democracy Assistance and Political Conditionality.* Basingstoke, UK: Palgrave.

Derouen, Karl R. Jr,, Jenna Lea, and Peter Wallensteen. 2009. "The Duration of Civil War Peace Agreements." *Conflict Management and Peace Science* 26: 367–387.

de Zeeuw, Jeroen. 2005. "Projects Do Not Create Institutions: The Record of Democracy Assistance in Post-Conflict Societies." *Democratization* 12: 481–504.

de Zeeuw, Jeroen, and Krishna Kumar, eds. 2006. *Promoting Democracy in Postconflict Societies.* Boulder, CO: Lynne Rienner Publishers.

Diamond, Larry. 1999. *Developing Democracy: Toward Consolidation.* Baltimore: Johns Hopkins University Press

Dobbins, James, John G. McGinn, Keith Crane, Seth Jones, and Rollie Lal. 2003. *America's Role in Nation-Building: From Germany to Iraq.* Santa Monica, CA: Rand.

Doyle, Michael, and Nicholas Sambanis. 2000. "International Peacebuilding: A Theoretical and Quantitative Analysis." *American Political Science Review* 94: 779–801.

———., eds. 2006. *Making War and Building Peace: United Nations Peace Operations.* Princeton, NJ: Princeton University Press.

Eck, Kristine, and Lisa Hultman. 2007. "Violence against Civilians in Civil Wars." *Journal of Peace Research* 44 (2).

Eck, Kristine, Joakim Kreutz, and Ralph Sundberg. 2010. *Introducing the UCDP Non-State Dataset.* Uppsala: Uppsala University.

Eisenstadt, S. N., and L. Roniger. 1984. *Patrons, Clients and Friends: Interpersonal Relations and the Structure of Trust in Society.* Cambridge, UK: Cambridge University Press.

Elhawary, Samir, Marta Foresti, and Sara Pantuliano. 2010. "Development, Security and Transitions in Fragile States." Meeting Series Report. London: Overseas Development Institute.

Elwert, Georg. 2003. "Intervention in Markets of Violence." In *Potentials of (Dis)Order. Explaining Violence in the Caucasus and in the Former Yugoslavia*, edited by Jan Koehler and Christoph Zürcher, 219–243. Manchester, UK: Manchester University Press.

Emerson, Michael, and Gergana Noutcheva. 2005. "Europeanisation as a Gravity Model of Democratization." *Herald of Europe* 2: 1–33.

Evenson, Kristie. 2008. *External Democracy Promotion in Post-Conflict Zones: Evidence from Case Studies: Bosnia.* Berlin: Freie Universität Berlin.

———. 2009. "Bosnia and Herzegovina Statebuilding and Democratization in the Time of Ethnic-Politics and International Oversight." *Taiwan Journal of Democracy* 5: 93–125.

Fearon, James D. 1998. "Commitment Problems and the Spread of Ethnic Conflict." In *The International Spread of Ethnic Conflict: Fear Diffusion, and Escalation*, edited by David Lake and Donald Rothchild, 107–127. Princeton, NJ: Princeton University Press.

———. 2004. "Why Do Some Civil Wars Last So Much Longer Than Others?" *Journal of Peace Research* 41: 275–301.

Fearon, James D., and David Laitin. 2004. "Neotrusteeship and the Problem of Weak States." *International Security* 28: 5–43.

Finkel, Steven, Anibal Perez-Linan, and Mitchell A. Seligson. 2007. "The Effects of U.S. Foreign Assistance on Democracy-Building, 1990–2003." *World Politics* 59: 404–439.

Fortna, Virginia Page. 2004. "Does Peacekeeping Keep Peace? International Intervention and the Duration of Peace after Civil War." *International Studies Quarterly* 48: 269–292.

———. 2008a. "Peacekeeping and Democratization." In *From War to Democracy: Dilemmas of Peacebuilding*, edited by Anna Jarstad and Timothy D. Sisk, 39–79. Cambridge, UK: Cambridge University Press.

———. 2008b. *Does Peacekeeping Work? Shaping Belligerents' Choices after Civil War.* Princeton, NJ: Princeton University Press.

Fortna, Virginia Page, and Lise Morjé Howard. 2008. "Pitfalls and Prospects in the Peacekeeping Literature." *Annual Review of Political Science* 11: 283–301.

François, Monika, and Inder Sud. 2006. "Promoting Stability and Development in Fragile and Failed States." *Development Policy Review* 24: 141–160.

Fraser, Alistair, and Lindsay Whitfield. 2009. "Understanding Contemporary Aid Relationships." In Lindsay Whitfield, ed., *The Politics of Aid: African Strategies for Dealing with Donors.* Oxford, UK: Oxford University Press.

Freedom House. 2005. "Methodology." Retrieved on July 20, 2011, from www.freedomhouse.org/template.cfm?page=35&year=2005.

Frerks, G. 2006. *The Use of Peace Conditionality in Conflict and Post-Conflict Settings: A Conceptual Framework and a Checklist.* The Hague: Netherlands Institute of International Relations.

George, Alexander L., and Andrew Bennett, eds. 2005. *Case Studies and Theory Development in the Social Sciences.* Cambridge, MA: MIT Press.

Gleditsch, Kristian Skrede. 2007. "Transnational Dimensions of Civil War." *Journal of Peace Research* 44: 293–309.

Gleditsch, Kristian Skrede, and Halvard Buhaug. 2008. "Contagion or Confusion? Why Conflicts Cluster in Space." *International Studies Quarterly* 52: 215–234.

Gleditsch, Kristian Skrede, and Michael D. Ward. 2006. "Diffusion and the International Context of Democratization." *International Organization* 60: 911–933.

Gleditsch, Nils Peter, Peter Wallensteen, Mikael Eriksson, Margareta Sollenberg, and Havard Strand. 2002. "Armed Conflict 1946–2001: A New Dataset." *Journal of Peace Research* 39 (5).

Glennie, J. 2008. *The Trouble with Aid: Why Less Could Mean More for Africa.* London and New York: Zed Books.

Goldsmith, A. A. 2001. "Donors, Dictators and Democrats in Africa." *Journal of Modern African Studies* 39: 411–436.

Goodhand, Jonathan. 2002. "Aiding Violence or Building Peace? The Role of International Aid in Afghanistan." *Third World Quarterly* 23: 837–859.

Goodhand, Jonathan, and Sedra, Mark. 2007. "Bribes or Bargains? Peace Conditionalities and 'Post Conflict' Reconstruction in Afghanistan." *International Peacekeeping* 14: 41–61.

Gosztonyi, Kristof. 2003. "Non-Existent States with Strange Institutions." In *Potentials of Disorder: Explaining Violence in the Caucasus and in the Former Yugoslavia*, edited by Jan Koehler and Christoph Zuercher, 46–61. Manchester, UK:
Manchester University Press.

Gurr, Ted Robert. 2000. *Peoples Versus States: Minorities at Risk in the New Century*.
Washington, DC: United States Institute of Peace.

Guttieri, Karen and Jessica Piombo. 2007. *Interim Governments: Institutional Bridges
to Peace and Democracy?* Washington DC: United States Institute of Peace Press.

Hanlon, J. 2004. "Do Donors Promote Corruption? The Case of Mozambique." *Third
World Quarterly* 25: 747–763.

Harbom, Lotta, Erik Melander, and Peter Wallensteen. 2008. "Dyadic Dimensions of
Armed Conflict, 1946–2007." *Journal of Peace Research* 45: 697–710.

Hartmann, Christof. 2009. "Democracy as a Fortuitous By-Product of Independence:
UN Intervention and Democratization in Namibia." *Taiwan Journal of Democracy*
5: 27–50.

Hartzell, Caroline, and Matthew Hoddie. 2003. "Institutionalizing Peace: Power Sharing and Post-Civil War Conflict Management." *American Journal of Political Science* 47: 318–322.

Hartzell, Caroline, Matthew Hoddie, and Donald Rothchild. 2001. "Stabilizing the
Peace after Civil War: An Investigation of Some Key Variables." *International Organization* 55: 183–208.

Hayman, Rachel. 2009. "Going in the 'Right' Direction? Promotion of Democracy in
Rwanda Since 1990." *Taiwan Journal of Democracy* 5: 51–75.

Hedström, Peter, and Lars Udehn. 2009. "Analytical Sociology and Theories of the
Middle Range." In *The Oxford Handbook of Analytical Sociology*, edited by Peter
Headström and Peter Bearman, 25–50. Oxford, UK: Oxford University Press.

Höglund, Kristine. 2008. "Violence in War-to-Democracy Transitions." In *From War
to Democracy: Dilemmas of Peacebuilding*, edited by Anna K. Jarstadt and Timothy Sisk, 80–103. Cambridge, UK: Cambridge University Press.

Hook, Steven. 1995. *National Interest and Foreign Aid*. Boulder, CO: Lynne Rienner
Publishers.

Ignatieff, Michael. 2003. *Empire Lite: Nation building in Bosnia, Kosovo, Afghanistan*.
London: Vintage.

Ilkhamov, Alisher. 2007. "Neopatrimonialism, Interest Groups and Patronage Networks: The Impasses of the Governance System in Uzbekistan." *Central Asian
Survey* 26: 65–84.

Jarstad, Anna K., and Timothy Sisk, eds. 2008. *From War to Democracy: Dilemmas of
Peacebuilding*. Cambridge, UK: Cambridge University Press.

Jean, François, and Jean-Christophe Rufin, eds. 1994. *Economie des guerres civiles*.
Paris: Hachette.

Jett, D. C. 1999. *Why Peacekeeping Fails*. New York: Palgrave.

Joshi, Madha, and David T. Mason. 2011. "Peasants, Patrons, and Parties: The Tension between Clientelism and Democracy in Nepal." *International Studies Quarterly* 55: 151–175.

Judah, Tim. 2000. *Kosovo: War and Revenge*. New Haven, CT, and London: Yale University Press.

Kalyvas, Stathis N., and Laia Balcells. 2010. "International System and Technologies of Rebellion: How the End of the Cold War Shaped Internal Conflict." *American Political Science Review* 104: 415–429.

Kaplan, Seth D. 2008. *Fixing Fragile States: A New Paradigm for Development*. Westport, CT: Greenwood Publishing Group.

Keck, Margaret E., and Kathryn Sikkink. 1998. *Activists beyond Borders: Advocacy Networks in International Politics*. Ithaca, NY, and London: Cornell University Press.

Keefeer, Philip. 2010. "Database of Political Institutions: Changes and Variable Definitions." The World Bank. Retrieved on October 18, 2011, from http://siteresources .worldbank.org/INTRES/Resources/469232-1107449512766/DPI2010_Codebook2 .pdf.

Kerr, Michael. 2005. *Imposing Power-Sharing*. Dublin: Irish Academic Press.

Killick, T. 1998. *Aid and the Political Economy of Policy Change*. London and New York: Routledge.

King, Iain, and Whit Mason. 2006. *Peace at Any Price: How the World Failed Kosovo*. London: C. Hurst & Co.

Kitschelt, Herbert, and Steven Wilkinson. 2007. *Patrons, Clients, and Policies: Patterns of Democratic Accountability and Political Competition*. Cambridge, UK: Cambridge University Press.

Knauss, Gerald, and Felix Martin. 2003. "Travails of the European Raj." *Journal of Democracy* 14: 60–74.

Krasner, Stephen D. 2004. "Sharing Sovereignty: New Institutions for Collapsed and Failing States." *International Security* 29: 85–120.

Kreutz, Joakim. 2010. "How and When Armed Conflicts End: Introducing the UCDP Conflict Termination Dataset." *Journal of Peace Research* 47: 243–250.

Lake, David A., and Donald S. Rothchild, eds. 1998. *The International Spread of Ethnic Conflict: Fear, Diffusion, and Escalation*. Princeton, NJ: Princeton University Press.

Lancaster, C. 2007. *Foreign Aid. Diplomacy, Development, Domestic Politics*. Chicago: The University of Chicago Press.

Leftwich, A. 1993. "Governance, Democracy and Development in the Third World." *Third World Quarterly* 14: 605–624.

Levitsky, Steven, and Lucan Way. 2005. "International Linkage and Democratization." *Journal of Democracy* 16: 20–34.

———. 2006. "Linkage versus Leverage, Rethinking the International Dimension of Regime Change." *Comparative Politics* 38: 379–400.

———. 2010. *Competitive Authoritarianism: Hybrid Regimes after the Cold War*. New York: Cambridge University Press.

Licklider, Roy. 1995. "The Consequences of Negotiated Settlements in Civil Wars, 1945–1993." *American Political Science Review* 89: 681–690.

Lipset, Seymour Martin. 1959. "Some Social Requisites of Democracy: Economic Development and Political Legitimacy." *American Political Science Review* 53: 69–105.

Mainwaring, Scott, and Anibal Perez-Linan. 2007. "Why Regions of the World Are Important: Regional Specificities and Region-Wide Diffusion of Democracy." In *Regimes and Democracy in Latin America: Theories and Methods*, edited by Gerardo L. Munck, 199–229. Oxford, UK: Oxford University Press.

Mamdani, Mahmood. 1996. *Citizen and Subject: Contemporary Africa and the Legacy of Late Colonialism*. Princeton, NJ: Princeton University Press.

Manning, Carrie. 2008. *The Making of Democrats: Elections and Party Development in Postwar Bosnia, El Salvador, and Mozambique*. New York: Palgrave MacMillan.

Manning, Carrie, and Monica Malbrough. 2009. "Learning the Right Lessons from Mozambique's Transition to Peace." *Taiwan Journal of Democracy* 5: 77–91.

———. 2010. "Bilateral Donors and Aid Conditionality in Post-Conflict Peacebuilding: The Case of Mozambique." *Journal of Modern African Studies* 48: 143–169.

Mansfield, Edward D., and Jack Snyder. 2007. *Electing to Fight: Why Emerging Democracies Go to War*. Cambridge, MA: MIT Press.

Mason, T. David, and Patrick J. Fett. 1996. "How Civil Wars End: A Rational Choice Approach." *Journal of Conflict Resolution* 40: 546–568.

Mattes, Michaela, and Burcu Savun. 2009. "Fostering Peace after Civil War: Commitment Problems and Agreement Design." *International Studies Quarterly* 53: 737–759.

Matveeva, Anna. 2008. *External Democracy Promotion in Post-Conflict Zones: Evidence from Case Studies: Tajikistan*. Berlin: Freie Universität Berlin.

———. 2009. "Tajikistan. Stability First." *Taiwan Journal of Democracy* 5: 163–186.

Merton, R. K. 1968. *Social Theory and Social Structure*. New York: Free Press.

Middlebrook, Peter, and Mark Sedra. 2004. "Afghanistan's Problematic Path to Peace: Lessons in State Building in the Post-September 11 Era." *Foreign Policy in Focus* March 24.

Morphet, Sally. 2002. "Current International Civil Administration: The Need for Political Legitimacy." *International Peacekeeping* 9: 140–162.

Myrttinen, Henri. 2008. *External Democracy Promotion in Post-Conflict Zones: Evidence from Case Studies: East Timor*. Berlin: Freie Universität Berlin.

———. 2009. "Timor-Leste: A Relapsing 'Success' Story." *Taiwan Journal of Democracy* 5: 219–239.

Narten, Jens. 2006. "Building Local Institutions and Parliamentarianism in Post-War Kosovo: a Review of Joint Efforts by the UN and OSCE from 1999–2006," *Helsinki Monitor* 17: 144–159.

——. 2008. "Post-Conflict Peacebuilding and Local Ownership: Dynamics of External-Local Interaction in Kosovo under United Nations Administration." *Journal of Intervention and Statebuilding* 2: 369–390.

——. 2009a. "Assessing Kosovo's Postwar Democratization between External Imposition and Local Self-Government." *Taiwan Journal of Democracy* 5: 127–162.

——. 2009b. "Dilemmas of Promoting 'Local Ownership': The Case of Postwar Kosovo." In *The Dilemmas of Statebuilding: Confronting the Contradictions of Postwar Peace Operations*, edited by Roland Paris and Timothy D. Sisk, 252–284. London: Routledge.

*National Security Strategy of the United States of America*, 2002. Retrieved on June 15, 2012, from http://merln.ndu.edu/whitepapers/USnss2002.pdf.

Niemi, Richard G., and Joel D. Barkan. 1987. "Age and Turnout in New Electorates and Peasant Societies." *American Political Science Review* 81: 583–588.

Nixon, Hamish. 2007. *Aiding the State? International Assistance and the Statebuilding Paradox in Afghanistan*. Afghanistan: Afghanistan Research and Evaluation Unit.

Organisation for Economic Co-operation and Development (OECD). 2007. "Principles for Good International Engagement in Fragile States and Situations." Retrieved on December 22, 2011, from www.oecd.org/dataoecd/28/5/43463433.pdf.

——. 2010. *Do No Harm. International Support for Statebuilding*. OECD Conflict and Fragility Series. Paris: OECD.

Ottaway, Marina. 2002. "Rebuilding State Institutions in Collapsed States." *Development and Change* 33: 1001–1023.

Ottaway, Marina, and Therese Chung, 1999. "Debating Democracy Assistance: Toward a New Paradigm." *Journal of Democracy* 10: 99–113.

Papic, Zarko, and Lada Sadikovic. 2006. "International Dimensions of Democracy." in *Democracy Assessment of Bosnia and Herzegovina*. Bosnia and Herzegovina: Open Society Institute. Retrieved on February 26, 2008, from www.soros.org.ba/!en/novost.asp?id=61.

Paris, Roland. 2004. *At War's End: Building Peace after Civil Conflict*. Cambridge, UK: Cambridge University Press.

——. 2010. "Saving Liberal Peacebuilding." *Review of International Studies* 36: 337–365.

Putnam, Robert D. 1988. "Diplomacy and Domestic Politics: The Logic of Two-Level Games." *International Organization* 42: 427–460.

Putzel James 2010. "Do No Harm: International Support for Statebuilding." Paris: OECD DAC Fragile State Group.

Ragin, Charles. 1987. *The Comparative Method: Moving beyond Qualitative and Quantitative Strategies*. Berkeley: University of California Press.

Raufer, Xavier. 2003. "A Neglected Dimension of Conflict: The Albanian Mafia." In *Potentials of Disorder: Explaining Violence in the Caucasus and in the Former Yugoslavia*, edited by Jan Koehler and Christoph Zuercher, 62–74. Manchester, UK: Manchester University Press.

Regan, Patrick M. 2002. "Third-Party Interventions and the Duration of Intrastate Conflicts." *Journal of Conflict Resolution* 46: 55–73.

Regan, Patrick M., and Aysegul Aydin. 2006. "Diplomacy and Other Forms of Intervention in Civil Wars." *Journal of Conflict Resolution* 50: 736–756.

Reno, William. 1999. *Warlord Politics and African States*. Boulder, CO: Lynne Rienner Publishers.

———. 2011. *Warfare in Independent Africa*. Cambridge, UK: Cambridge University Press.

Riese, Sarah. 2008. "Power-Sharing after Conflict: A 'Qualitative Comparative Analysis' of the Conditions for Success.'" Berlin: Free University. Unpublished ms.

Riddell, Roger. 1987. *Foreign Aid Reconsidered*. London: James Currey Ltd and Overseas Development Institute.

———. 2007. *Does Foreign Aid Really Work?* Oxford, UK: Oxford University Press.

Roeder, Philip G., and Donald Rothchild. 2005. *Sustainable Peace: Power and Democracy after Civil Wars*. Ithaca, NY: Cornell University Press.

Ross, Carne. 2007. *Independent Diplomat: Dispatches from an Unaccountable Elite*. Ithaca, NY: Cornell University Press.

Rossbacher, Dina. 2004. *Friedenssicherung – Am Beispiel der Interimsverwaltung der Vereinten Nationen im Kosovo (UNMIK) – Die Zivilverwaltung als neue Form der Friedenssicherung*. Hamburg: Verlag Dr. Kovac.

Rubin, Alissa. 2010. "Afghan President Rebukes West and U.N." *New York Times*, April 1.

Rubin, Barnett R. 2002. *The Fragmentation of Afghanistan*. New Haven, CT: Yale University Press.

Sandevski, Tome. 2009. *External Democracy Promotion in Post-Conflict Zones— Evidence from Case Studies: Macedonia*. Berlin: Freie Universität Berlin.

Schimmelfennig, Frank, Stefan Engert, and Heiko Knobel. 2003. "Costs, Commitment and Compliance: The Impact of EU Democratic Conditionality on Latvia, Slovakia and Turkey." *Journal of Common Market Studies* 41: 495–518.

Schmitz, H.P. 2004. "Domestic and Transnational Perspectives on Democratization." *International Studies Review* 6: 403–426.

Schraeder, Peter J., ed. 2002. *Exporting Democracy: Rhetoric vs. Reality*. Boulder, CO: Lynne Rienner Publishers.

Scott, James M., and Carie A. Steele. 2011. "Sponsoring Democracy: The United States and Democracy Aid to the Developing World: 1988–2001." *International Studies Quarterly* 55: 47–69.

Seavers, Brenda M. 2000. "The Regional Sources of Power-Sharing Failure: The Case of Lebanon." *Political Science Quarterly* 115: 247–271.

Skrede, Kristian Gleditsch, and Michael D. Ward. 2006. "Diffusion and the International Context of Democratization." *International Organization* 60: 911–933.

Snyder, Jack, 2000. *From Voting to Violence: Democratization and Nationalist Conflict*. New York: W. W. Norton.

Solioz, Christophe. 2007. *Turning Points in Post-War Bosnia: Ownership Process and European Integration.* Baden-Baden: Nomos.

Spears, Ian S. 2002. "Africa: The Limits of Power-Sharing." *Journal of Democracy* 13: 123–136.

Starr, Harvey. 1991. "Democratic Dominoes: Diffusion Approaches to the Spread of Democracy in the International System." *Journal of Conflict Resolution* 35: 356–381.

Starr, Harvey, and Christina Lindborg. 2003. "Democratic Dominoes Revisited: The Hazards of Governmental Transitions, 1974–1996." *The Journal of Conflict Resolution* 47: 490–519.

Steffek, Jens. 2003. "The Legitimation of International Governance: A Discourse Approach." *European Journal of Internatonal Relations* 9: 249–275.

Stokke, Olav. 1995. "Aid and Political Conditionality: Core Issues and State of the Art." In *Aid and Political Conditionality*, edited by Olav Stokke, 2–67. London: Frank Cass.

Suhrke, Astri. 2009. "The Dangers of a Tight Embrace: Externally Assisted Statebuilding in Afghanistan." In *The Dilemmas of Statebuilding: Confronting the Contradictions of Postwar Peace Operations*, edited by Roland Paris and Timothy D. Sisk, 227–221. London: Routledge.

Toft, Monica Duffy. 2009. *Securing the Peace: The Durable Settlement of Civil Wars.* Princeton, NJ: Princeton University Press.

Uvin, Peter. 1998. *Aiding Violence. The Development Enterprise in Rwanda.* West Hartford, CT: Kumarian Press.

———. 2004. *Human Rights and Development.* West Hartford, CT: Kumarian Press.

Vachudova, Milada Anna. 2005. *Europe Undivided. Democracy, Leverage, and Integration after Communism.* Oxford, UK: Oxford University Press.

Walter, Barbara F. 1999. "Designing Transitions from Civil War: Demobilization, Democratization, and Commitments to Peace." *International Security* 24: 127–155.

———. 2002. *Committing to Peace: The Successful Settlement of Civil Wars.* Princeton, NJ: Princeton University Press.

———. 2004. "Does Conflict Beget Conflict? Explaining Recurrent Civil War." *Journal of Peace Research* 41: 371–388.

Wantchekon, Leonard. 2004. "The Paradox of 'Warlord' Democracy: A Theoretical Investigation." *American Political Science Review* 98: 17–33.

Wantchekon, Leonard, and Zvika Neeman. 2002. "A Theory of Post-Civil War Democratization." *Journal of Theoretical Politics* 14: 439–64.

Wheatley, Jonathan, and Christoph Zuercher. 2008. "On the Origin and Consolidation of Hybrid Regimes: The State of Democracy in the Caucasus." *Taiwan Journal of Democracy* 4: 1–31.

Whitfield, Lindsay, ed. 2009. *The Politics of Aid: African Strategies for Dealing with Donors.* Oxford, UK: Oxford University Press

Whitty, Brendan, and Hamish Nixon. 2009. "The Impact of Counter-Terrorism Objectives on Democratization and Statebuilding in Afghanistan." *Taiwan Journal of Democracy* 5: 187–218.

Wilde, Ralph. 2001. "From Danzig to East Timor and Beyond: The Role of International Territorial Administration." *American Journal of International Law* 95: 583–606.

Wimpelmann, Torunn. 2006. "The Aid Agencies and the Fragile State Agenda." CMI Working Paper 21. Retrieved on June 29, 2012, from http://bora.cmi.no/dspace/bitstream/10202/71/1/Working%20paper%20WP%202006-21.pdf

Woods, Ngaire. 2005. "The Shifting Politics of Foreign Aid." *International Affairs* 81: 393–409.

World Bank. 2011. "Conflict, Security and Development." World Development Report 2011. Retrieved on June 29, 2012, from http://wdr2011.worldbank.org/fulltext/.

Wright, Joseph. 2009. "How Foreign Aid Can Foster Democracy in Authoritarian Regimes." *American Journal of Political Science* 53(3): 552–571.

Yannis, Alexandros. 2001. Kosovo under International Administration. *Survival* 43: 31–48.

Youngs, Richard. 2002. *The European Union and the Promotion of Democracy: Europe's Mediterranean and Asian Policies.* London: Oxford University Press.

Zahar, Marie-Joelle. 2005. "Power Sharing in Lebanon: Foreign Protectors, Domestic Peace, and Democratic Failure." In *Sustainable Peace: Power and Democracy after Civil Wars*, edited by Philip G. Roeder and Donald Rothchild, 219–240. Ithaca, NY: Cornell University Press.

Zuercher, Christoph. 2006. "Is More Better? Evaluating External-Led State Building after 1989." In *CDDRL Working Papers*, Stanford: Center on Democracy, Development, and the Rule of Law, Stanford Institute on International Studies.

Zürcher, Christoph. 2007. *The Post-Soviet Wars: Rebellion, Ethnic Conflict and Nationhood in the Caucasus.* New York: New York University Press.

# The Authors

**Christoph Zürcher** is Professor of Political Science at the Graduate School of Public and International Affairs at the University of Ottawa. He is the author of *The Post-Soviet Wars: Rebellion, Ethnic Conflict and Nationhood in the Caucasus* (2007), as well as other publications in German and Russian.

**Carrie Manning** is Professor and Chair of Political Science at Georgia State University in Atlanta, Georgia. She is the author of *The Making of Democrats: Elections and Party Development in Postwar Bosnia, El Salvador, and Mozambique* (2008) and *The Politics of Peace in Mozambique: Post-Conflict Democratization* (2002).

**Kristie D. Evenson** is an independent researcher engaged with donors to evaluate and develop effective democratization and civil society related programming. She resides in Split, Croatia, and is a PhD candidate at the University of Bristol, School for Policy Studies, UK.

**Rachel Hayman**, PhD, is Head of Research at the International NGO Training and Research Centre (INTRAC) in Oxford, UK, and an Associate of the Centre of African Studies at the University of Edinburgh, UK.

**Sarah Riese** is a PhD candidate at Free University Berlin. She studies interaction processes between interveners and intervened in Bosnia and Herzegovina.

**Nora Roehner, PhD**, currently serves as advisor for the government of Afghanistan in Kabul, specializing in municipal governance and administration.

# Index

adoption costs: in Afghanistan, 33, 34, 46, 49, 50–51, 54, 67, 69, 72–74, 78, 80, 103, 119, 122, 128, 133, 138–39, 141; in Bosnia, 33, 46, 51–53, 54, 67, 69, 70–72, 78, 80, 128, 136, 138–39; defined, 29; in East Timor, 32, 33, 34, 46, 47–48, 49, 54, 67–68, 69, 77, 79, 102, 128, 133, 136, 138, 141; in Kosovo, 32, 33, 43, 46, 47–49, 67, 80, 102, 128, 136, 138–39; in Macedonia, 32, 33, 46, 47–48, 54, 67, 68, 69, 79, 102, 128, 136, 138; in Mozambique, 32, 33, 46, 47, 48–49, 54, 67, 68, 69, 79, 102, 104, 119, 128, 136, 138, 141; in Namibia, 32, 33, 34, 46, 47–49, 54, 67, 68, 79, 102, 118, 119, 128, 133, 136, 138, 141; regarding primary objectives of domestic elites, 26, 29, 30, 31, 32, 33, 34, 47, 48–49, 50, 52, 53, 54, 56, 68, 70, 75–78, 79, 80, 88, 91, 102–3, 115, 123–24, 133, 134, 135, 140, 144, 148, 150; relationship to aid, 84, 91, 97, 101, 103, 110, 111, 140; relationship to democratic transition outcomes, 28, 29–30, 34, 36, 49–51, 53–54, 55–56, 58, 67–74, 78, 79–80, 81, 82, 84, 91, 102–4, 110, 111, 112, 116–17, 132–36, 138–39, 141–42, 146, 150; relationship to war characteristics, 7–8, 34, 47–48, 49–50, 53–56; relationship to war settlement characteristics, 7, 47–48, 49–50, 51–54; in Rwanda, 33, 34, 46, 49–50, 54, 67, 68, 78, 79–80, 103, 119, 128, 133, 138, 139, 141; regarding security of domestic elites, 23, 24–25, 26, 29, 30, 31, 32, 33, 34, 39, 40, 44, 46, 47–48, 49, 50, 51, 52, 53–54, 56, 67–68, 70, 78, 91, 102, 103, 104, 109–10, 115, 133–34, 136–37, 138, 141, 142, 146, 147–48; in Tajikistan, 33, 46, 49, 50–51, 67, 68, 79, 103, 119, 128, 138, 139, 141

Afghanistan: adoption costs in, 33, 34, 46, 49, 50–51, 54, 67, 69, 72–74, 78, 80, 103, 119, 122, 128, 133, 138–39, 141; aid to, 12, 16, 73, 74, 83, 93, 94, 95, 96, 97, 98, 99, 100, 107, 108, 109, 111, 119, 121, 161n57; Al Qaeda in, 19; clientelism in, 24–25, 29, 33, 72, 73, 74, 138; constitution shaping in, 63; cost of peacebuilding mission, 65;

Afghanistan *(continued)*
  democratic transition outcome in,
    1, 2, 5, 11, 12, 16, 19, 34, 42, 57, 66,
    67, 69, 75, 78, 93, 95, 97, 100, 109,
    119, 121, 122, 127, 128, 138–39;
    domestic political actors in, 24–25,
    30, 32, 33, 34, 46, 49, 50, 51, 54,
    72–74, 78–79, 80, 81, 103, 119, 122,
    127, 128, 133, 136–37, 138, 141, 142,
    147; economic conditions in, 12,
    61, 63; ethnic groups in, 39, 78, 122;
    as failure, 5, 11, 16, 19, 34, 69, 100,
    109, 122, 127, 138–39; footprint of
    peacebuilding mission, 1, 4, 57,
    60, 61, 62, 64, 66, 67, 69, 78–79,
    80, 138–39; Freedom in the World
    score, 12, 93; GDP per capita, 12;
    judicial powers in, 63; Karzai, 24–25,
    30, 33, 72, 73–74, 81, 121–22, 142;
    legislative powers in, 62; mandate
    of peacebuilding mission, 129, 130;
    neighborhood factors for, 19, 54,
    113, 117, 119, 121–22, 127, 129, 130,
    141; Polity IV score, 12, 93; postwar
    stability in, 12, 41, 42, 69, 89, 98,
    100, 136–37; relations with Pakistan,
    19, 81, 121, 122; Soviet occupation,
    121; Taliban opposition, 19, 121,
    122, 136, 142; US intervention in,
    85; war characteristics in, 19, 35,
    41, 42, 50, 120–21; war settlement
    characteristics in, 19, 39, 41, 42, 50,
    72
aid: to Afghanistan, 12, 16, 73, 74, 83,
    93, 94, 95, 96, 97, 98, 99, 100, 107,
    108, 109, 111, 119, 121, 161n57; aid
    conditionality, 48, 49, 50, 51, 63, 73,
    82, 83, 87, 88, 101–2, 105–8, 110–11,
    139–40, 161nn54,55,57; aid donors, 9,
    15, 17, 30, 33, 49, 50, 54, 63, 71, 73–74,
    82–84, 86, 87, 88–91, 92, 93, 95, 97,
    98, 99, 100, 101, 103–4, 105–10, 119,
    139–40, 145, 159n12, 161nn47,57;

aid per capita, 10, 12, 16, 92, 93, 94,
    95–96, 97, 98, 99, 100, 103; bilateral
    aid, 30, 84, 101, 102, 104; to Bosnia,
    12, 13, 16, 70, 71, 92, 94, 95–96, 97,
    98, 99, 105, 106, 108, 109, 111, 124,
    125; as democracy aid, 9, 15, 84,
    85–93, 94, 97–101, 103; dependency
    on, 17, 30–31, 33, 48–49, 51, 54, 63,
    69, 102, 105, 109, 120, 144, 150;
    donor coherence absent, 83, 106,
    107, 110, 140; to East Timor, 12, 49,
    92, 93, 94, 95–96, 97, 98, 99, 103,
    108, 161n55; as general aid, 9, 84, 91,
    92–97, 99; to Kosovo, 13, 16, 48–49,
    75, 76–77, 93, 94, 95–96, 97, 98, 99,
    100, 103, 105, 106, 107, 108, 111, 126;
    to Macedonia, 92, 94, 96, 98, 102–3,
    106, 108, 111; to Mozambique, 12,
    16, 17, 33, 48–49, 83, 92, 94, 95, 97,
    98, 100, 102–3, 104, 106, 108, 111;
    to Namibia, 12, 17, 33, 92, 94, 95,
    98–99, 109, 161n47; relationship
    to adoption costs, 84, 97, 101,
    103, 110, 111, 140; relationship to
    democratization, 4, 7, 9, 10, 11, 15,
    30–31, 33, 34, 47, 48–49, 54, 55, 63,
    69, 82, 83, 84, 85–111, 131, 134–35,
    139–40, 142, 145, 150; relationship
    to peacebuilder leverage, 9, 30–31,
    51, 69, 83, 84, 87, 101–10, 120, 140; to
    Rwanda, 13, 16, 17, 51, 69, 83, 93, 94,
    95, 96, 98, 99, 103, 105–6, 107, 108,
    109, 111, 119, 120; sectoral patterns
    of distribution, 94, 96–97, 98–99,
    100; to Tajikistan, 13, 16, 93, 94, 95,
    96, 98, 99, 103, 105, 106, 108–9, 111,
    119, 121, 161n55; temporal patterns
    of distribution, 94–97, 98, 100
Albania, 125
Angola: aid to, 13; democratic transition
    outcome in, 2, 13, 66; economic
    conditions in, 13, 61, 63; Freedom in
    the World score, 13; GDP per capita,

13; peacebuilding mission in, 2, 13, 60, 61, 63, 64, 65, 66; Polity IV score, 13; postwar stability in, 13; war settlement in, 17

Arab Spring, 114

Armed Conflict Dataset, 12, 13

Australia, 95, 118

authoritarian regime, electoral, 2, 12, 14, 16; defined, 3, 156n4

authoritarian regime, fully closed, 2, 3, 14, 16; defined, 156n4

Aydin, Aysegul, 37

Bahrain, 114

Beck, Thorsten, 2, 12

Belgium, 107

Bonn Agreement of 2001, 33, 69, 71, 72, 74, 121–22

Bosnia: adoption costs in, 33, 46, 51–53, 54, 67, 69, 70–72, 78, 80, 128, 136, 138–39; aid to, 12, 13, 16, 70, 71, 92, 94, 95–96, 97, 98, 99, 105, 106, 108, 109, 111, 124, 125; clientelism in, 52; constitution shaping in, 63; cost of peacebuilding mission, 65; Dayton Peace Agreement, 18, 33, 52–53, 70–72, 106, 124, 136; democratic transition outcome in, 1, 2, 5, 9, 11, 12, 13, 16, 18, 36, 42, 45, 57, 66, 67, 69, 71–72, 92, 97, 99, 105, 124, 125, 126, 127, 128, 136, 138–39; domestic political actors in, 29, 32, 46, 52–53, 54, 70–72, 78, 79, 109, 124–25, 127, 128, 133, 136–37, 138, 143, 147; economic conditions in, 5, 12, 13, 61, 63; ethnic groups in, 29, 32, 39, 46, 51, 52–53, 70–72, 78, 80, 124–25, 127, 133, 136, 138; executive powers in, 62; as failure, 5, 11, 16, 18, 69, 136, 138–39; footprint of peacebuilding mission, 1, 4, 9, 57, 60, 61, 64, 66, 67, 69, 70, 78, 80, 138–39, 141, 159n5; Freedom in the World

score, 12, 13, 92; GDP per capita, 12, 13, 57; judicial powers in, 63; legislative powers in, 62; mandate of peacebuilding mission, 70, 71, 129, 130; neighborhood factors for, 54, 95, 113, 117, 124–25, 126, 127, 128, 129, 130; Office of the High Representative (OHR), 52, 70, 71, 79, 105; Polity IV score, 12, 13, 92; postwar stability in, 12, 13, 36, 41, 42, 45, 69, 81, 136–37; relations with Croatia, 124, 125, 127; relations with Serbia, 124, 125, 126, 127; war characteristics in, 18, 23, 35, 41, 42, 51–52, 124–25, 136; war settlement characteristics in, 18, 33, 39, 41, 42, 45, 52–53, 70–72, 106, 124, 136

Bratton, Michael, 24

Brown, Stephen, 87

Brownlee, Jason, 156n4

Brubaker, Rogers, 113

Buhaug, Halvard, 114

Bunce, Valerie: on democracy, 29

Burnell, Peter, 87

Burundi: aid to, 12; democratic transition outcome in, 2, 12, 66; economic conditions in, 12, 61; Freedom in the World score, 12; GDP per capita, 12; peacebuilding mission in, 2, 12, 39, 60, 61, 63, 64, 65, 66; Polity IV score, 12; postwar stability in, 12; war characteristics in, 119

Bush, George W., 85

Cambodia: aid to, 13; democratic transition outcome in, 2, 13, 66; economic conditions in, 13, 61, 63; Freedom in the World score, 13; GDP per capita, 13; peacebuilding mission in, 2, 13, 60, 61, 62, 63, 64, 66; Polity IV score, 13; postwar stability in, 13

Canada, 107

Carothers, Thomas, 87
case studies, 14–19, 35, 156n16; and
    process tracing, 10–11
causal mechanisms, 36, 43, 67, 97, 117,
    131, 132, 144–45, 146–47; and case
    studies, 10–11, 15–16; involving aid,
    100–101; involving high adoption
    costs, 58, 78, 135–36, 141; involving
    intrusive mission footprint, 58, 75,
    78–79, 139; involving neighborhood
    factors, 117, 119, 141; multiple,
    conjunctural causation, 34, 55–56;
    and process tracing, 10–11
Central African Republic: aid to, 13;
    democratic transition outcome in, 2,
    13, 66; economic conditions in, 13,
    61; Freedom in the World score, 13;
    GDP per capita, 13; peacebuilding
    mission in, 2, 13, 60, 61, 64, 65, 66;
    Polity IV score, 13; postwar stability
    in, 13
China, 93, 115, 122, 161n55
Clapham, Christopher: on clientelism,
    24
clientelism/patronage, 6, 26, 51, 52, 82,
    90; in Afghanistan, 24–25, 29, 33, 72,
    73, 74, 138; in Bosnia, 52; in Rwanda,
    51; in Tajikistan, 33
Cold War, end of, 85, 94–95, 128, 137
Collier, Paul, 157n12
constitution shaping, 61, 62–63
contagion: defined, 113; fear of, 120–21,
    127, 141, 148; relationship to
    democratic transition outcomes,
    114, 116–17, 120–21, 125, 126, 127,
    128, 131, 141, 148
Cote d'Ivoire: aid to, 13; democratic
    transition outcome in, 2, 13, 66;
    economic conditions in, 13, 61;
    Freedom in the World score, 13;
    GDP per capita, 13; peacebuilding
    mission in, 2, 13, 60, 61, 63, 64, 65,

66; Polity IV score, 13; postwar
    stability in, 13
Croatia: aid to, 12; democratic transition
    outcome in, 2, 12, 66, 127; economic
    conditions in, 12, 61; Freedom in the
    World score, 12; GDP per capita, 13;
    peacebuilding mission in, 2, 12, 60,
    61, 62, 63, 64, 66; Polity IV score,
    12; postwar stability in, 12; relations
    with Bosnia, 124, 125, 127

definition of peacebuilding mission,
    10, 20
Democratic Republic of the Congo, 34,
    50, 51, 119; aid to, 13; democratic
    transition outcome in, 2, 13, 66;
    economic conditions in, 13, 61;
    Freedom in the World score, 13;
    GDP per capita, 13; peacebuilding
    mission in, 2, 13, 60, 61, 63, 64, 65,
    66; Polity IV score, 13; postwar
    stability in, 13
demonstration effects, 113–15, 116, 117,
    120, 121, 126, 127
Derouen, Karl R., Jr., 39
de Zeeuw, Jeroen, 86
diffusion, 113, 114, 117. See also
    contagion
Djindjic, Zoran, 124
domestic political actors: in
    Afghanistan, 24–25, 30, 32, 33, 34,
    46, 49, 50, 51, 54, 72–74, 78–79,
    80, 81, 103, 119, 122, 127, 128, 133,
    136–37, 138, 141, 142, 147; attitudes
    regarding democracy, 5–6, 7–8, 9,
    21–26, 27–28, 29–30, 32, 34, 36, 39,
    43–44, 46, 47–49, 50–51, 52, 53–54,
    55–56, 57, 67–68, 69, 70–74, 75,
    77, 79, 87, 89, 90, 97, 102, 116, 120,
    128, 133–37, 138, 140, 141, 142, 143,
    147–48, 150; attitudes regarding
    good governance, 23, 24, 81, 89;

attitudes regarding political power,
23–25, 26, 33, 34, 54, 102, 103, 104,
127, 133–34; in Bosnia, 29, 32, 46,
52–53, 54, 70–72, 78, 79, 109, 124–25,
127, 128, 133, 136–37, 138, 143, 147;
in East Timor, 32, 33, 34, 46, 47–48,
49, 67–68, 77–79, 96, 102, 118, 128,
133, 134, 136, 138, 143–44; in Kosovo,
32, 33, 46, 47–49, 54, 74–76, 77,
78–79, 102, 106, 126, 127, 128, 134,
136, 138, 143–44, 147; in Macedonia,
32, 33, 46, 47–48, 49, 54, 68, 79,
102–3, 123–24, 128, 136, 138, 144; in
Mozambique, 32, 33, 46, 47, 48–49,
54, 68, 79, 102–3, 104, 111, 128, 136,
138, 146; in Namibia, 23, 29, 32, 33,
34, 46, 47–49, 54, 68, 70, 102, 118,
119, 133, 134, 136, 143–44; primary
objectives of, 7–8, 26, 29, 30, 31, 32,
33, 34, 47, 48–49, 50, 52, 53, 54, 56,
68, 70, 75–78, 79, 80, 88, 91, 102–3,
115, 123–24, 133, 134, 135, 140, 144,
148, 150; in Rwanda, 32, 34, 46,
49–50, 54, 69, 103, 105–6, 109–10,
119, 120, 128, 133, 136–37, 141, 147;
secondary elites, 27–28, 73–74, 78,
80, 122, 136; security of, 5, 7–8, 9,
23, 24–25, 26, 29, 30, 31, 32, 33, 34,
39, 40, 44, 46, 47–48, 49, 50, 51,
52, 53–54, 56, 67–68, 70, 78, 89, 91,
102, 103, 104, 109–10, 115, 133–34,
136–37, 138, 141, 142, 146, 147–48; in
Tajikistan, 32, 33, 34, 46, 49, 50–51,
54, 68, 103, 119, 121, 127, 128, 138,
139, 141, 142. *See also* adoption
costs; clientelism; interaction
between peacebuilders and domestic
political actors
Doyle, Michael, 8, 37–38, 42

East Timor: adoption costs in, 32, 33,
34, 46, 47–48, 49, 54, 67–68, 69, 77,
79, 102, 128, 133, 136, 138, 141; aid
to, 12, 49, 92, 93, 94, 95–96, 97, 98,
99, 103, 108, 161n55; constitution
shaping in, 63; cost of peacebuilding
mission, 65; democratic transition
outcome in, 1, 2, 5, 11, 12, 16, 18,
34, 41, 42, 43, 44, 45, 47, 49, 54, 57,
66, 67–68, 78, 79, 92, 94, 97, 99, 100,
117, 127, 136, 138, 140–41; domestic
political actors in, 30, 32, 33, 34, 46,
47–48, 49, 67–68, 77–79, 96, 102,
118, 128, 133, 134, 136, 138, 143–44;
economic conditions in, 5, 12, 61, 63;
executive powers in, 62; footprint of
peacebuilding mission, 1, 4, 57–58,
60, 61, 62, 64, 66, 67, 69, 77, 78–79,
80, 138; Freedom in the World score,
12, 92; FRETILIN, 32, 46; judicial
powers in, 63; legislative powers in,
62; local consultative organs in, 31;
mandate of peacebuilding mission,
129, 130; neighborhood factors in,
117, 118, 119, 127, 128, 129, 130,
140–41; Polity IV score, 12, 92;
postwar stability in, 12, 42, 43, 45,
77–78, 81, 96, 159n17; as success, 5,
11, 16, 18, 34, 43, 100, 117, 136, 138,
140–41; war characteristics in, 33,
35, 41, 42, 43, 44, 45, 47–48, 127; war
settlement characteristics in, 41, 42,
43, 45, 47
Eck, Kristine, 12
economic conditions, 22, 23, 90, 132; in
Afghanistan, 12, 61, 63; in Bosnia,
5, 12, 13, 61, 63; in East Timor,
5, 12, 61, 63; in Kosovo, 3, 13, 61,
63; in Macedonia, 12, 61, 103; in
Mozambique, 5, 12, 17, 61, 63, 103; in
Namibia, 12, 61; in Rwanda, 13, 61,
63; in Tajikistan, 13
Egypt, 114
Eikenberry, Karl W., 24–25

electoral democracy, 13, 16; Freedom
House definition, 1, 2, 3, 11, 12,
42, 92, 94, 155n3; as threshold of
success, 1–2, 5, 11, 14, 36, 43–44, 67,
139, 151
Estonia, 114
ethnic groups, 7, 17, 25, 37, 38, 40, 90,
113–14, 124–26, 135; in Afghanistan,
39, 78, 122; in Bosnia, 29, 32, 39, 46,
51, 52–53, 70–72, 78, 80, 124–25, 127,
133, 136, 138; in Kosovo, 75, 76, 77,
125–26, 127, 138, 149; in Macedonia,
49, 123; in Rwanda, 41, 69, 78, 119,
136
European Union, 95, 108, 116;
democracy promotion by, 9, 18, 48,
71, 87, 108, 111, 116, 124–25, 126,
128, 141; European Commission,
107; membership in, 48, 54, 68, 71,
103, 111, 122, 123, 126–27, 140, 144

Fearon, James D., 114
footprint of mission: in Afghanistan,
1, 4, 57, 60, 61, 62, 64, 66, 67, 69,
78–79, 80, 138–39; in Bosnia, 1, 4, 9,
57, 60, 61, 64, 66, 67, 69, 70, 78, 80,
138–39, 141, 159n5; defined, 63–64;
duration of mission, 11, 15, 57, 58,
59, 60, 64–65, 66, 81, 137, 143, 150;
in East Timor, 1, 4, 57–58, 60, 61, 62,
64, 66, 67, 69, 77, 78–79, 80, 138; in
Kosovo, 1, 4, 9, 18, 48, 58, 60, 61, 62,
64, 66, 67, 77, 78–79, 80, 138–39, 141;
large vs. small footprints, 1, 4, 5, 8,
64, 65, 67, 69, 78–79, 80–81, 94–95,
96, 132, 138–39, 141, 142, 143, 150;
in Macedonia, 9–10, 48, 60, 61, 64,
66, 67, 69, 79, 138; management and
operation costs, 11, 57, 58, 59, 60, 64,
65, 67, 137; in Mozambique, 60, 61,
64, 66, 67, 69, 79, 138; in Namibia,
60, 61, 64, 66, 67, 79, 138; number of

personnel, 11, 12, 13, 15, 57, 58, 59,
60, 75; relationship to democratic
transition outcomes, 1, 5, 7, 8–10, 11,
15, 16, 55, 57–58, 65, 66, 67, 78–81,
131, 132, 134–35, 136, 137–39, 141,
145, 150; in Rwanda, 60, 61, 64, 66,
67, 69, 138, 139; scale of mission, 11,
12, 13, 15, 57–58, 59, 60, 63–68; scope
of mission, 11, 58, 59, 61, 62–68; in
Tajikistan, 60, 61, 63, 64, 66, 67, 68,
69, 138. See also aid; mandate
Fortna, Page: on democratization, 20,
132; on identity wars, 37; on military
victory, 38
France, 107
Freedom House, 69, 75, 120, 122;
definition of electoral democracy,
1, 2, 3, 11, 12, 42, 92, 94, 155n3;
definition of liberal democracy, 1, 2,
12, 16, 155n1
Freedom in the World scores, 12, 13, 66,
92, 93

Georgia, 114, 115
geostrategic position, 3, 7, 9–10, 47,
122, 125, 126, 135, 140. See also
neighborhood factors
Germany, 99, 107
Gleditsch, Kristian Skrede, 12, 114
good governance, 84, 85, 88–89, 90, 149
gross domestic product (GDP), 10, 12,
13, 15, 22, 57, 132, 145

Habibie, B. J., 118
Habyarimana, Juvénal, 69
Haiti: aid to, 13; democratic transition
outcome in, 2, 13, 66; economic
conditions in, 13, 61; Freedom in the
World score, 13; GDP per capita, 13;
peacebuilding mission in, 2, 13, 60,
61, 63, 64, 65, 66; Polity IV score, 13;
postwar stability in, 13

Hartzell, Caroline, 37, 39, 40
Hoddie, Matthew, 39, 40
Hultman, Lisa, 12
human rights, 15, 20, 26, 62, 91, 108

Indonesia, 118, 127, 140
in-kind support, 93
interaction between former adversaries,
    3–4, 5, 22, 33, 48, 51, 78, 131, 132,
    136–37, 142; power sharing, 7, 26, 35,
    36, 37, 38, 39–40, 39–41, 44, 45, 47,
    52, 53. *See also* stability, postwar
interaction between peacebuilders
    and domestic political actors: as
    bargaining process, 6, 7, 15, 21,
    26–28, 34, 55, 70–71, 76–77, 80–81,
    142; impact of mission intrusiveness
    on, 58, 78–79, 80, 124, 138, 139, 142,
    150; moral hazard in, 143, 144, 148,
    149; role in outcome of postwar
    democratic transitions, 5–7, 9, 10–11,
    15, 16, 21, 22–23, 24–28, 26–28, 29,
    30–31, 48–49, 50–51, 52, 55, 56, 57,
    59, 68–69, 70–74, 75–77, 78–81, 82,
    101–11, 112, 117, 121, 132–35, 140,
    144–46, 147–49; as two-level game,
    27–28. *See also* leverage exerted by
    peacebuilders
Iran, 122
Iraq: US intervention in, 85

Kagame, Paul, 120
Karzai, Hamid, 24–25, 30, 33, 72, 73–74,
    81, 121–22, 142
Kazakhstan, 120
Kenya, 161n54
Kosovo: adoption costs in, 32, 33, 43, 46,
    47–49, 67, 80, 102, 128, 136, 138–39;
    aid to, 13, 16, 48–49, 75, 76–77, 93,
    94, 95–96, 97, 98, 99, 100, 103, 105,
    106, 107, 108, 111, 126; constitution
    shaping in, 63; cost of peacebuilding

mission, 65; democratic transition
    outcome in, 1, 2, 5, 9, 11, 13, 16, 18,
    36, 41, 42, 43, 45, 47, 49, 57, 66, 67,
    75, 77, 78, 93, 95, 97, 99, 100, 105,
    126, 127, 136, 138–39, 149; domestic
    political actors in, 30, 32, 33, 46,
    47–49, 54, 74–76, 77, 78–79, 102,
    106, 126, 127, 128, 134, 136, 138,
    143–44, 147; economic conditions
    in, 3, 13, 61, 63; ethnic groups in,
    57–58, 75, 76, 77, 125–26, 127, 138,
    149; executive powers in, 62; as
    failure, 5, 11, 16, 100, 126, 138–39,
    149; footprint of peacebuilding
    mission, 1, 4, 9, 18, 48, 58, 60, 61,
    62, 64, 66, 67, 77, 78–79, 80, 138–39,
    141; Freedom in the World score,
    13, 93; GDP per capita, 13; judicial
    powers in, 63; legislative powers in,
    62; local consultative organs in, 31;
    mandate of peacebuilding mission,
    75, 129, 130; neighborhood factors
    for, 54, 95, 117, 125–26, 127, 128, 129,
    130; as outlier case, 67, 74–78; Polity
    IV score, 13, 93; postwar stability
    in, 13, 18, 36, 42, 43, 45, 76, 81, 126;
    war characteristics in, 18, 33, 35,
    41, 42, 43, 47, 122–23, 123, 125; war
    settlement characteristics in, 18, 41,
    42, 43, 45, 47, 125
Kostunica, Vojislav, 124
Kreutz, Joakim, 12, 37
Kumar, Krishna, 86
Kyrgyzstan, 114, 115

Lake, David A., 113
Latvia, 114
law enforcement, 59, 61, 63
Lebanon, 39
leverage exerted by peacebuilders, 32, 34,
    47, 55, 82, 84, 116, 117, 119, 121, 122,
    124, 125, 132–33, 138, 139, 146, 147;

leverage exerted by peacebuilders
(continued)
as decreasing over time, 33, 52,
81, 143–44, 148–50; impact of
independence on, 32, 46, 77–78,
143–44; relationship to aid, 9, 30–31,
36, 48–49, 51, 69, 71, 83, 84, 87, 91,
97, 101–11, 120, 137, 140; relationship
to democratic transition outcomes,
28, 48–49, 51, 56, 57, 59, 68, 69,
79–80, 97, 112, 126, 141–43
Levitsky, Steve, 115–16, 122
liberal democracy, 3, 4, 11, 13, 20, 25;
Freedom House definition, 1, 2, 12,
16, 155n1
Liberia: aid to, 12; democratic transition
outcome in, 2, 12, 66; economic
conditions, 12, 61; Freedom in the
World score, 12; GDP per capita, 12;
peacebuilding mission in, 2, 12, 60,
61, 64, 65, 66; Polity IV score, 12;
postwar stability in, 12
Libya, 114
Lipset, Seymour Martin: on
democratization, 3
Lithuania, 114

Macedonia: adoption costs in, 32, 33, 46,
47–48, 54, 67, 68, 69, 79, 102, 128,
136, 138; aid to, 92, 94, 96, 98, 102–3,
106, 108, 111; constitution shaping
in, 63; cost of peacebuilding mission,
65; democratic transition outcome
in, 2, 9–10, 11, 12, 16, 18, 41, 42, 44,
47, 49, 66, 67, 79, 92, 94, 100, 123–24,
126, 128, 136, 138; domestic political
actors in, 32, 33, 46, 47–48, 49, 54,
68, 79, 102–3, 123–24, 128, 136, 138,
144; economic conditions in, 12,
61, 103; ethnic groups in, 49, 123;
footprint of peacebuilding mission,
9–10, 48, 60, 61, 64, 66, 67, 69, 79,
138; Freedom in the World score,

12, 92; GDP per capita, 12; mandate
of peacebuilding mission, 68, 129;
neighborhood factors for, 117,
122–24, 126, 128, 129, 140; Ohrid
Framework Agreement, 99, 123;
Polity IV score, 12, 41, 92; postwar
stability in, 12, 41, 42; Stabilization
and Association Agreement, 108,
123; as success, 11, 16, 18, 100,
123–24, 136, 138; war characteristics
in, 18, 35, 41, 42, 44, 45, 47, 122–23;
war settlement characteristics in, 41,
42, 47, 99
mandate, 31, 55, 145; in Afghanistan,
129, 130; in Bosnia, 70, 71, 129, 130;
Chapter VII UN mandate, 21, 59,
68; definitions, 2, 10; in East Timor,
129, 130; in Kosovo, 75, 129, 130; in
Macedonia, 68, 129; in Mozambique,
17, 119, 129; in Namibia, 68, 129, 130,
161n47; and regional issues, 9, 119,
128, 129, 130, 141, 148; in Rwanda,
129; scope of, 4, 10, 11, 17, 21, 58, 59,
60, 62, 64, 68, 70, 71, 125, 131, 142; in
Tajikistan, 129
market economy, 20, 62, 63
Mattes, Michaela, 37
Matveeva, Anna, 50–51, 120
Merton, R. K., 146
middle-range theories, 146–47
Milosevic, Slobodan, 124
moral hazard, 143, 144, 148, 149
Mozambique: adoption costs in, 32,
33, 46, 47, 48–49, 54, 67, 68, 69, 79,
102, 104, 119, 128, 136, 138, 141;
aid to, 12, 16, 17, 33, 48–49, 54, 83,
92, 94, 95, 97, 98, 100, 102–3, 104,
106, 108, 111; cost of peacebuilding
mission, 65; Democracy Assistance
Group/Electoral Process Monitoring
Group, 104; democratic transition
outcome in, 2, 5, 11, 12, 16, 17, 41, 42,
43, 44, 47–48, 49, 66, 67, 79, 92, 94,

97, 100, 117, 118, 119, 127, 128, 136, 140–41; domestic political actors, 32, 33, 46, 47, 48–49, 54, 68, 79, 102–3, 104, 111, 128, 136, 138, 144, 146; economic conditions in, 5, 12, 17, 61, 63, 103; footprint of peacebuilding mission, 60, 61, 64, 66, 67, 69, 79, 138; Freedom in the World score, 12, 92; GDP per capita, 12; mandate of peacebuilding mission, 17, 119, 129; neighborhood factors for, 115, 117, 118, 119, 127, 128, 129, 140–41; Polity IV score, 12, 92; postwar stability in, 12, 42, 43; as success, 5, 11, 16, 17, 43, 100, 117, 136, 138, 140–41; war characteristics in, 17, 33, 35, 41, 42, 43, 44, 45, 47, 127, 135; war settlement characteristics in, 41, 42, 47

Namibia: adoption costs in, 32, 33, 34, 46, 47–49, 54, 67, 68, 79, 102, 118, 119, 128, 133, 136, 138, 141; aid to, 12, 17, 33, 92, 94, 95, 98–99, 109, 161n47; constitution shaping in, 63; cost of peacebuilding mission, 65; democratic transition outcome in, 2, 5, 11, 12, 16–17, 29, 34, 41, 42, 43, 44, 45, 47, 49, 54, 66, 67, 78, 79, 92, 94, 100, 117, 118, 127, 128, 136, 138, 140–41; domestic political actors in, 23, 29, 30, 32, 33, 34, 46, 47–49, 54, 68, 70, 102, 118, 119, 133, 134, 136, 143–44; economic conditions in, 12, 61; footprint of peacebuilding mission, 60, 61, 64, 66, 67, 79, 138; Freedom in the World score, 12, 92; GDP per capita, 12; mandate of peacebuilding mission, 68, 129, 130, 161n47; neighborhood factors for, 17, 115, 117, 119, 127, 128, 129, 130, 140–41; Polity IV score, 12, 92; postwar stability in, 12, 42, 43, 45; as

success, 11, 16–17, 34, 43, 100, 117, 136, 138, 140–41; SWAPO, 16–17, 32, 46, 48; war characteristics in, 16–17, 33, 35, 41, 42, 43, 44, 45, 47–48, 127; war settlement characteristics in, 41, 42, 43, 45, 47

Narten, Jens, 18

NATO, 18, 75, 123, 125, 126

neighborhood factors, 11, 15; for Afghanistan, 19, 54, 113, 117, 119, 121–22, 127, 129, 130, 141; for Bosnia, 54, 95, 113, 117, 124–25, 126, 127, 128, 129, 130; demonstration effects, 113–15, 116, 117, 120, 121, 126, 127; for East Timor, 117, 118, 119, 127, 128, 129, 130, 140–41; external support, 113, 115, 116, 117, 118, 120, 121, 122, 123, 124, 125, 126, 127, 128, 141, 142; for Kosovo, 54, 95, 117, 125–26, 127, 128, 129, 130; for Macedonia, 117, 122–24, 126, 128, 129, 140; for Mozambique, 115, 117, 118, 119, 127, 128, 129, 140–41; for Namibia, 17, 115, 117, 119, 127, 128, 129, 130, 140–41; news coverage, 114–15; relationship to democratic transition outcomes, 3, 9, 17, 51, 54, 112–13, 114–17, 118–19, 126–30, 135, 140–44, 145; relationship to peace, 112–13, 117, 118, 127, 128; for Rwanda, 34, 50, 51, 54, 113, 117, 119, 128, 129, 141; spillovers of violence/contagion, 113–14, 116, 119, 120–21, 122–23, 125, 126, 127, 128, 131, 141, 148; for Tajikistan, 68, 113, 117, 119, 120–21, 128, 129, 141; Western leverage, 116, 117, 122, 126, 128; Western linkage, 115–16, 117, 121, 122, 126, 128. See also geostrategic position

Netherlands, 107

Nixon, Hamish, 50

Non–State Conflict Dataset, 12

OECD: Principles for Good Engagement
in Fragile States and Situations, 83;
on state-building in Rwanda, 159n2
OECD Development Assistance
Committee (DAC), 145, 160n44;
Creditor Reporting System (CRS),
91, 92, 93–94, 95; Fragile States
Group, 89, 90, 91
One-Sided Violence Dataset, 12
OSCE (Organization for Security and
Co-operation in Europe), 18

Pakistan: Inter-Services Intelligence
(ISI), 121, 122; relations with
Afghanistan, 19, 121, 122
paradox of weakness, 28, 142
Paris Declaration on Aid Effectiveness, 83
patronage. *See* clientelism/patronage
peacebuilders: attitudes regarding
state building, 25, 70, 84, 88, 90–91,
99, 105; constraints on, 21, 143;
economic policies shaped by, 61,
63; executive policing by, 59, 61;
with executive powers, 61, 62,
79; with judicial powers, 61, 63;
with legislative powers, 61, 62, 79;
legitimacy of, 31; new constitution
shaped by, 61, 62–63; peace
enforcement by, 59, 61; Security
Sector Reform (SSR) by, 61, 62;
standards-before-status approach
by, 76, 77, 149. *See also* interaction
between peacebuilders and domestic
political actors
Political Terror Scale (PTS), 12, 13
Polity IV scores, 12, 13, 14, 41, 92, 93
power sharing, 7, 19, 26; relationship to
democratic transition outcome, 35,
36, 39–40, 44, 45, 47, 52; relationship
to duration of peace, 37, 38, 39–41;
as territorial autonomy, 39, 41, 42,
43, 45, 47, 48, 53
Prio Battle Deaths data, 42

qualitative comparative case analysis:
and process tracing, 10–11; vs.
quantitative analysis, 59, 132, 146;
small-*n* comparative design, 59,
146–47
quantitative studies, 35–38, 41, 43,
80, 85–86, 137, 145, 157n12; vs.
comparative analysis, 59, 132, 146

Regan, Patrick M., 37
Reno, William, 48
rent seeking, 6, 34
Rhodesia, 17
Riese, Sarah, 40
Rothschild, Donald S., 113
Rubin, Barnett: *The Fragmentation of
Afghanistan*, 121
rule of law, 20, 91
Russia: as authoritarian, 115; relations
with Tajikistan, 51, 54, 68, 78, 79, 93,
106, 109, 120, 139, 141, 142
Rwanda: adoption costs in, 33, 34, 46,
49–50, 54, 67, 68, 78, 79–80, 103, 119,
128, 133, 138, 139, 141; aid to, 13, 16,
17, 51, 69, 83, 93, 94, 95, 96, 98, 99,
103, 105–6, 107, 108, 109–10, 111,
119, 120, 159n2; clientelism in, 51;
cost of peacebuilding mission, 65;
democratic transition outcome in, 2,
5, 11, 13, 14, 16, 17, 34, 42, 66, 67, 69,
75, 79–80, 93, 95, 105, 109–10, 119–20,
127, 139; domestic political actors in,
32, 34, 46, 49–50, 54, 69, 103, 105–6,
109–10, 119, 120, 128, 133, 136–37,
141, 147; economic conditions in,
13, 61, 63; ethnic groups in, 41, 69,
78, 119, 136; as failure, 5, 11, 16,
17, 34, 109–10, 127, 139; footprint
of peacebuilding mission, 60, 61,
64, 66, 67, 69, 138, 139; Freedom in
the World score, 13, 93; GDP per
capita, 13; mandate of peacebuilding
mission, 129; neighborhood factors

for, 34, 50, 51, 54, 113, 117, 119, 128, 129, 141; Polity IV score, 13, 93; postwar stability in, 13, 41, 42, 50, 51, 54, 89, 103, 109–10, 119–20, 127, 136–37; Rwandan Patriotic Front (RPF), 17, 32, 34, 49–50, 51, 65, 103, 119, 136; war characteristics in, 17, 23, 34, 35, 41, 42, 43, 45, 50; war settlement characteristics, 41, 42

Sambanis, Nicholas, 8, 37–38, 42
Sandevski, Tome, 42
Savun, Burcu, 37
Scott, James M., 86
Second Congo War, 119
September 11th attacks, 85, 121
Serbia, 124, 125, 126, 127
Sierra Leone: aid to, 12; democratic transition outcome in, 2, 12, 66; economic conditions in, 12, 61; Freedom in the World score, 12; GDP per capita, 12; peacebuilding mission in, 2, 12, 60, 61, 64, 66; Polity IV score, 12; postwar stability in, 12
SIPRI Multilateral Peace Missions, 60
South Africa, 17, 48, 118–19, 127, 140
Soviet Union: collapse of, 85, 114
stability, postwar, 11, 14–15, 21, 23, 26, 28, 35–36, 81, 135, 141, 149; in Afghanistan, 12, 41, 42, 69, 89, 98, 100, 136–37; in Bosnia, 12, 13, 36, 41, 42, 45, 69, 136–37; in East Timor, 12, 42, 43, 45, 77–78, 96, 159n17; in Kosovo, 13, 18, 36, 42, 43, 45, 76, 126; in Macedonia, 12, 41, 42; in Mozambique, 12, 42, 43; in Namibia, 12, 42, 43, 45; in Rwanda, 13, 41, 42, 50, 51, 54, 89, 103, 119–20, 127, 136–37; in Tajikistan, 13, 19, 36, 41, 42, 50–51, 127. See also contagion
standards-before-status approach, 76, 77, 149

state building, 20–21, 25, 70, 84, 88, 90–91, 99, 105, 151; new constitution shaping, 61, 62–63
Steele, Carie A., 86
success/failure of postwar democratic transitions, 3–5, 7, 15, 35, 131–32, 144–51; Afghanistan as failure, 5, 11, 16, 19, 34, 69, 100, 109, 122, 127, 138–39; Bosnia as failure, 5, 11, 16, 18, 69, 136, 138–39; defined, 1, 3, 11, 14; East Timor as success, 5, 11, 16, 18, 34, 43, 100, 117, 136, 138, 140–41; electoral democracy as threshold of success, 1–2, 5, 11, 14, 36, 43–44, 67, 139, 151; and equifinality, 146; Kosovo as failure, 5, 11, 16, 100, 126, 138–39, 149; Macedonia as success, 11, 16, 18, 100, 123–24, 136, 138; Mozambique as success, 11, 16, 17, 43, 100, 117, 136, 138, 140–41; Namibia as success, 11, 16–17, 34, 43, 100, 117, 136, 138, 140–41; vs. peace, 35–36, 43–44, 131, 150–51; Rwanda as failure, 11, 16, 17, 34, 109–10, 127, 139; Tajikistan as failure, 11, 16, 19, 34, 109, 120, 127, 138; Wantchekon on, 21–22
Sundberg, Ralph, 12
Sweden, 107

Tadic, Boris, 124
Tajikistan: adoption costs in, 33, 46, 49, 50–51, 67, 68, 79, 103, 119, 128, 138, 139, 141; aid to, 13, 16, 93, 94, 95, 96, 98, 99, 103, 105, 106, 108–9, 111, 119, 121, 161n55; clientelism in, 33; cost of peacebuilding mission, 65; democratic transition outcome in, 2, 5, 11, 13, 16, 19, 34, 36, 42, 66, 67, 68, 75, 79, 93, 95, 105, 109, 119, 120, 121, 122, 127, 128, 138, 139; domestic political actors, 32, 33, 34, 46, 49, 50–51, 54, 68, 103, 119, 121, 127,

Tajikistan *(continued)*
128, 138, 139, 141, 142; economic
conditions in, 13; as failure, 5, 11, 16,
19, 34, 109, 120, 127, 138; footprint
of peacebuilding mission, 60, 61,
63, 64, 66, 67, 68, 69, 138; Freedom
in the World score, 13, 93; GDP per
capita, 13; mandate of peacebuilding
mission, 129; neighborhood factors
for, 68, 113, 117, 119, 120–21, 128,
129, 141; Polity IV score, 13, 93;
postwar stability in, 13, 19, 36,
41, 42, 50–51, 127; relations with
Russia, 51, 54, 68, 78, 79, 93, 106,
109, 120, 139, 141, 142; UTO, 32; war
characteristics in, 19, 23, 35, 41, 42,
50, 68; war settlement characteristics
in, 19, 41, 42, 50–51
Thaci, Hashim, 77
Toft, Monica Duffy, 38
Tudjman, Franjo, 125
Tunisia, 114, 115
Turkmenistan, 122

Uganda, 119
Ukraine, 114, 115
United Kingdom, 107
United Nations, 2, 8, 10, 12, 22, 31, 59,
60, 84, 101, 102, 129, 137; Assistance
Mission in Rwanda (UNAMIR),
17; Chapter VII mandates, 21,
59, 68; democracy promotion
by, 18, 48, 58, 76, 77, 118, 149;
Interim Administration in Kosovo
(UNMIK), 75–76, 106; Operation
in Mozambique (UNOMOZ), 17;
Resolution 435, 118; Resolution
1244, 106; standards-before-
status approach by, 76, 77, 149;
Transitional Administration in East
Timor (UNTAET), 18, 68, 77–78,
93; Transition Assistance Group
(UNTAG), 17

United States, 107, 108–9, 116, 121;
democracy promotion by, 86–87;
war on terror, 85, 95
UN World Population Prospects, 60
Uppsala Conflict Data Program
(UCDP), 12, 13, 38
Uppsala Conflict Data Project War
Termination Dataset, 42
USAID (U.S. Agency for International
Development), 85–86
Uzbekistan, 120, 122

van de Walle, Nicolas, 24

Walter, Barbara F., 39, 40
Wantchekon, Leonard: on democratic
transitions, 21–22
war characteristics, 11, 15, 16–18, 22, 29,
162n3; in Afghanistan, 19, 35, 41, 42,
50, 120–21; in Bosnia, 18, 23, 35, 41,
42, 51–52, 124–25, 136; defined, 37;
duration, 3–4, 7, 35, 37, 42, 44–45, 47,
50, 51, 55, 56, 127, 131, 132, 135, 137,
145; in East Timor, 33, 35, 41, 42, 43,
44, 45, 47–48, 127; identity cleavages,
3–4, 7, 37, 38, 42, 43, 44, 47, 50, 55,
56, 131, 135; independence struggles,
16–17, 18, 29, 30, 32, 46, 47–49, 54,
67–68, 75, 76, 77–78, 79, 102, 118,
125–26, 134, 135–36, 143–44, 149,
150; intensity, 7, 35, 37, 38, 42, 43,
44, 45, 47, 50, 51–52, 55, 56, 131, 132,
135, 137, 145; in Kosovo, 18, 33, 35,
41, 42, 43, 47, 122–23, 123, 125; in
Macedonia, 18, 35, 41, 42, 44, 45,
47, 122–23; in Mozambique, 17, 33,
35, 41, 42, 43, 44, 45, 47, 127, 135; in
Namibia, 16–17, 33, 35, 41, 42, 43, 44,
45, 47–48, 127; number of factions,
7, 35, 37–38, 42, 44, 45, 47, 48, 49, 50,
52, 55, 56; relationship to adoption
costs, 7–8, 34, 47–48, 49–50, 53–56;
relationship to democratic transition

outcomes, 7–8, 35–36, 43–45, 46, 47, 53–56, 131, 132, 135–37, 145; relationship to duration of peace, 35, 36–41, 55, 135; in Tajikistan, 19, 23, 35, 41, 42, 50, 68; territorial vs. government control, 39, 41, 42, 43, 47–48

war settlement characteristics, 16, 33, 162n3; in Afghanistan, 19, 39, 41, 42, 50, 72; in Bosnia, 18, 39, 41, 42, 45, 52, 70–72, 136; defined, 37; in East Timor, 41, 42, 43, 45, 47; external guarantors, 6, 29, 39, 40–41, 44, 48–49, 50, 51, 52, 54, 55, 56, 57, 82, 104, 110; in Kosovo, 41, 42, 43, 45, 47, 125; in Macedonia, 41, 42, 47, 99; military victory, 7, 17, 23–24, 34, 35, 37, 38–39, 40, 41, 42, 43, 44, 45, 47–48, 51, 53, 103, 118; in Mozambique, 41, 42, 47; in Namibia, 41, 42, 43, 45, 47; negotiated settlement, 7, 17, 36, 37, 38–39, 40, 41, 42, 45, 48, 71, 85, 118; power sharing provisions, 7, 19, 26, 35, 36, 37, 38, 39–41, 42, 43, 44, 45, 47,

48, 52, 53; relationship to adoption costs, 7, 47–48, 49–50, 51–54; relationship to democratic transition outcomes, 7, 35–36, 44, 47, 50–51, 53–54, 132, 135–37, 145; relationship to duration of peace, 36–37, 38–41, 42, 43, 135; in Tajikistan, 19, 41, 42, 50–51; territorial autonomy, 39, 41, 42, 43, 45, 47, 48, 53

Way, Luca, 115–16, 122

Western leverage, 116, 117, 122, 126, 128

Western linkage, 115–16, 117, 121, 122, 126, 128

Whitty, Brendan, 50

World Bank: Database of Political Institutions, 2, 12, 156n4; World Development Indicators (WDI), 12

World Development Report (2011), 88–89

Wright, Joseph, 87

Youngs, Richard, 87

Zaire: *See* Democratic Republic of Congo